T0168022

HIKING THE WASATCH

Third Edition

Hiking the Wasatch

JOHN VERANTH

THE UNIVERSITY OF UTAH PRESS | SALT LAKE CITY

© 1988 by The Wasatch Mountain Club, Inc. Revised 1989, 1991, 1993
Revised second edition 1994
Revised third edition © 2014
All rights reserved

The Defiance House Man colophon is a registered trademark of
the University of Utah Press. It is based on a four-foot-tall Ancient
Puebloan pictograph (late PIII) near Glen Canyon, Utah.

Library of Congress Cataloging-in-Publication Data

Veranth, John.
Hiking the Wasatch/John Veranth.—Third edition.
pages   cm
ISBN 978-1-60781-325-5 (pbk. : alk. paper)—ISBN 978-1-60781-326-2 (ebook)
1. Hiking—Wasatch Range (Utah and Idaho)—Guidebooks.
2. Wasatch Range (Utah and Idaho)—Guidebooks.
I. Title.
GV199.42.W16V47 2014
796.510979—dc23   2014007965

Photo credits: John Veranth
Map credits: Dan Welton
Cover photo: Howie Garber

Printed and bound by Sheridan Books, Inc., Ann Arbor, Michigan.

CONTENTS

List of Maps   vii

List of Summit Panorama Sketches   vii

Preface   ix

Acknowledgments   xi

Glossary: Common Hiking and Mountaineering Terms   xiii

  1. Introduction to Hiking in the Wasatch   1

  2. Natural History of the Wasatch   17

  3. History and Environmental Protection   31

  4. Trailhead Directions and Trail Recommendations   41

  5. Foothills and the Wasatch Front   69

  6. Millcreek Canyon   103

  7. Big Cottonwood Canyon   126

  8. Little Cottonwood Canyon   176

  9. North and East Areas   205

10. Dry Creek and American Fork Canyon (Utah County)   223

11. Ridge Hikes and Mountaineering Scrambles   236

Mammal Checklist for the Central Wasatch Mountains   255

Suggestions for Further Reading   259

Hike Master List   263

MAPS

1. Topographic map index   7
2. Snow cover by month   64
3. Foothills and Northeast area   70
4. Tricanyon overview   106
5. Raymond Ridge–Thaynes Canyon to Butler Fork   112
6. Upper Millcreek, Dog Lake, and Reynolds Park Area   124
7. Big Cottonwood, Wasatch Boulevard, to Mineral Fork   128
8. Big Cottonwood, Cardiff Fork, to Brighton   162
9. Brighton area detail   167
10. Little Cottonwood trails   190
11. Albion Basin area detail   198
12. Great Western Trail north of Parleys Canyon   209
13. Lone Peak Wilderness to American Fork   226

SUMMIT PANORAMA SKETCHES

Mount Aire Summit   116
Reynolds Peak Summit   148
Flagstaff Summit   192
Sunset Peak Summit   202

PREFACE

The Wasatch Mountains, east of Salt Lake City, are a mountain treasure land with three wilderness areas and miles of trails. These mountains are within an hour's drive of nearly a million people, but the steep, rugged terrain can seem intimidating to new hikers and many parts of the Wasatch are relatively unknown and seldom visited.

Hiking the Wasatch was first published in 1988 and built on the original *Wasatch Trails,* published by the Wasatch Mountain Club in 1973. The result was a comprehensive guidebook covering hikes, off-trail routes, and alpine scrambles in Salt Lake County and in the Lone Peak Wilderness. There have been numerous changes to the local trails since the first two editions, mostly gains but also a few losses. The greatest changes have been along the foothill urban interface. This third edition is completely revised and updated based on the author's field checking, comments from Wasatch Mountain Club members, and information from the management agencies.

The descriptions range from nearly level walks requiring less than an hour to ascents that challenge experienced mountaineers. To help select an appropriate hike, there are lists of hikes according to the best season, the time required, the objective, and the desired level of difficulty. Detailed driving directions to trailheads are consolidated to save repetition. The easy trails have the most detailed descriptions to aid beginners, while expert trails have sparse descriptions to preserve the adventure.

Understanding the mountain environment enhances hiking enjoyment. The geology, the flora and fauna, and the human history are discussed for the curious amateur. Getting people onto the trails where they can listen to the birds, smell the flowers, and marvel at the forces that carved the land is a key step in building support for preservation of the Wasatch and other precious natural areas.

ACKNOWLEDGMENTS

My thanks go to the countless hiking leaders who introduced me to various trails over the years and to all the companions who have walked with me. Special thanks are given to the Governing Board of the Wasatch Mountain Club for supporting this project and to Dale Green for serving as an invaluable reference on trails and place-names and who meticulously mapped the Wasatch trails. Mel Davis and Alexis Kelner provided invaluable advice regarding the mechanics of publishing a book. Individuals who reviewed the first and second editions for accuracy include Charles Keller, Trudy Healy, Mike Treshow, Dave Wallace, Chris Biltoft, Mary Fleming, Oscar Robinson, Earl Cook, John Kennington, Gail Cordy, Karin Caldwell, George Nickas of the Utah Wilderness Association, Mark Wilson of Solitude, Rick May of Snowbird, and the Salt Lake City Water Department. The cooperation of the Forest Service staff, including Richard Klein (Salt Lake district ranger), Ollie Jones, Al Soucie, Kevin Plettenberg, Jeff Larson, John Hougland, Neil Hunsacker, Frank Grover, and Dale Gerry, is also appreciated. The maps in the first edition were drawn by Dan Welton, book design was by Julie Easton, and editing was performed by Dan Felsen, Alison Hottes, and Martha Veranth.

The extensive revision and updating found in this third edition were made possible through the extensive backcountry knowledge of Wasatch Mountain Club members Will McCarville, Julie Kilgore, Jack Earnhart, Brett Smith, Daniel Smith, Charles Keller, Brad Yates, and Zig Sondelski. Forest Service information was provided by Polly Popola, Steve Schide, Larry Valardi, Cheryl Butler, and Matt Lane. Pat Nelson of the Salt Lake City Water Department provided information on the management of the area north of I-80. Local government staff who contributed include Angelo Calinsino of Salt Lake County, Paul Allred of Holladay, Dan Medina of Sandy, Brian Jensen of Draper, and Lee Barnes of Lehi. Carl Fisher of Save Our Canyons provided reminders of recent and current environmental issues, and Darrin Jensen of WaterPro explained the watershed issues for the streams draining from Lone Peak. Valuable information was also gained from many of the hikers I met on the trail during field checking. Thanks to Howie Garber, Julie Kilgore, and John Regehr for generously offering photos for the revision. My wife, Martha, deserves very special thanks for tolerating the endless hours this revision project consumed.

GLOSSARY

Common Hiking and Mountaineering Terms

BOULDER-HOP: Travel across large relatively stable rocks. This is very exhausting and slow, since the hiker is constantly stepping up and jumping down.

BUSHWHACK: Off-trail travel through brush where no cleared path exists and hikers have to force their way through the branches.

CAIRN: A small pile of stones used as a trail marker.

CIRQUE: The steep-walled bowl carved by glacial action at the head of a side canyon.

COULOIR: A steep, relatively narrow groove in a rock wall. Typically, couloirs are wider than "cracks" and smaller than "gullies" and are important as routes up the mountainside.

CRAMPONS: A set of metal spikes that are strapped to the boots to provide secure footing on steep ice or consolidated snow.

KNIFE-EDGE: A very narrow ridge crest. In spots, the crest of a knife-edge is too angular to walk on, and travel requires scrambling over and around pinnacles, along ledges on the side of the ridge, or even straddling the ridge.

MASSIF: A compact mountain group consisting of several summits.

SCREE: Loose rock, typically fist size or smaller, that accumulates at the base of a rock wall. See also *Talus*.

SIDE CANYONS: In decreasing order of size, local usage is canyon, fork, gulch.

SWITCHBACK: A sharp turn, typically constructed on trails climbing steep slopes, to allow ascending in a series of more gradual segments.

TALUS: The loose rock of all sizes that falls from a cliff and accumulates at the base. The distinction between scree and talus is generally that talus is large enough not to move underfoot.

TECHNICAL CLIMBING: Mountain climbing requiring use of ropes and fixed belay anchors on either rock or ice. Also includes any sustained climbing where the arms are used to pull upward rather than being used solely for balance.

TRAVERSE: Horizontal travel across a mountainside or over a ridge. An ascending or descending traverse refers to a gradual elevation change while traveling across a much-steeper slope.

Hiking is healthful recreation for anyone, young or old. Head up a canyon and discover the trails of every description that lie beyond the roads.

1

Introduction to Hiking in the Wasatch

The Wasatch is a hiker's paradise only a few minutes' drive from the cities of the Wasatch Front. This guidebook covers all the trails and major off-trail routes in the central portion of the Wasatch Range from the south end of Davis County through Salt Lake County to American Fork Canyon in Utah County, a 15-by-30-mile area. The hike descriptions include more than 350 miles of hikes that span the full range from excellent trails to scrambles defined only by terrain features. Some hikes follow ski-area service roads or old mining, logging, and dam-access roads. Due to watershed impacts, motor vehicles are restricted on most of these primitive roads, which make well-graded, easy-to-follow walking paths. Other hikes are along official Forest Service trails that are well constructed and maintained, creating a distinct footpath for easy walking. Some well-used and popular trails are not part of the official Forest Service "system." Travel on these secondary trails is not difficult, but you have to contend with climbing over occasional logs and with picking your way through brush, across mud, and over rocks.

Extending beyond the official trails are numerous routes along foot tracks or game trails that often disappear, especially in grassy areas and boulder fields, requiring detours and searching for the route. Finally, all trails end, and you reach the brush thickets, rock ridges, and snowfields where the only choice is cross-country travel, picking your way from landmark to landmark and looking for the least difficult line.

USING THIS GUIDEBOOK

This is a comprehensive guidebook describing commonly hiked routes in a heavily used area. The goal was to be informative, but to keep the book to manageable size so it will fit in a backpack. In contrast to "best hikes" guidebooks, this book has no standard trail write-up format, because it is impractical to force the network of interconnecting routes and alternative options that exist on the ground into a strict trailhead-to-destination structure.

This book emphasizes "places to hike," not strictly defined trips to a single destination. Any hike can be modified to be easier by turning around sooner or made harder by pushing cross-country to connect with another trail or landmark. Likewise, this book does not repeat information in each trail description, as multiple constructed trails often start from a single trailhead. Readers of this book already want to hike, so I have not provided extensive prose extolling the wonders of each trail. Instead, I have included unique features that may be of use in selecting a trail. Likewise, conditions are similar over large portions of each canyon, so I have not padded the text with lists of plants and animals you will typically see along a given trail. Where appropriate, I mention the general vegetation communities and type of terrain that the trail passes through.

The amount of detail in the descriptions varies with the type of trail and the difficulty. The greatest level of detail is provided for the beginner hikes. However, on a maintained trail, little description is actually needed to follow the obvious path. Descriptions of maintained trails emphasize locating the trailhead and pointing out the highlights that add interest to the hike. Because vandalism of trail signs is a problem, descriptions of maintained trails also include hiking times, distances, and physical landmarks. To preserve the challenge and adventure, far less detail is provided on the harder routes that are traveled only by experienced hikers. On unmaintained routes, the entire description comes from landmarks and compass bearings. This book should be sufficient for hiking the popular, maintained trails. Anyone exploring the unmaintained trails, cross-country routes, and scrambling summits needs to carry a topographic map and know how to use it.

The chapters are arranged by the starting location (foothills, Millcreek Canyon, and so on), and the individual hikes are in a west-to-east or north-to-south order. The hike numbers (M-01, WF-7, and the like) cross-reference the descriptions to the locator maps used in this book. A number of trails have been added in this third edition, forcing occasional use of trail-number suffixes. The index is arranged alphabetically by hike name, with cross-reference to map identification number and description page number.

KEY POINTS

1. For general information common to all trails, read chapter 1.
2. To find how to get to a trailhead, read the directions in chapter 4.
3. To get recommendations on hikes for different interests, seasons, and abilities, see chapter 4.
4. To understand how the current recreational opportunities have come about, read chapter 3.

5. To cross-reference trail names, trailheads, and map identification numbers, see the "Hike Master List."
6. Use common sense, and remember that on-the-ground conditions are the ultimate source of information.
7. Have fun enjoying the mountains.

ROUTE DIFFICULTY

A few of the hikes in this book are ADA accessible, many are suitable for families with small children, most are a good workout for active adults, and the trail routes in chapter 11 will provide a challenge for experienced mountaineers. This section explains the route descriptions, so a hiker can understand the length and difficulty involved in reaching a particular destination. Difficulty depends on distance, elevation change, trail condition, and required route finding. Adjectives used to describe trail difficulty are defined as follows:

ADA Accessible	A hard-surface path or boardwalk with ramps.
Beginner	A well-maintained trail with a good walking surface and no unsafe terrain. The route is well defined and has adequate signs.
Easy	Hikes with less than four miles round-trip and with less than two thousand feet in elevation gain. Round-trip hiking time is forty-five minutes to three hours, but inexperienced hikers may take longer.
Intermediate	Longer hikes with more elevation gain that may involve sections where the trail is in poor condition. Round-trip hiking time is typically three to seven hours.
Advanced	Long routes requiring five to ten hours round-trip and routes with difficult terrain involving extensive route finding.
Exposure	Routes where there is little danger of falling—but if you fall, there is risk of serious injury. Crossing ledges or ridge crests with a precipitous drop below causes a feeling of being exposed to danger.
Scrambling	Routes that are intermediate between steep hiking and technical mountaineering. Scrambling involves using your hands for balance when moving across rock but does not include using your arm strength to pull yourself up, except possibly for single short climbing moves. Scrambles also include routes on hard spring snow where an ice ax is required. Reasonably athletic persons can

	handle the scrambling on the hiking routes in this book if they are accompanied by someone experienced enough to coach them through the hard spots.
Mountaineering	Any route involving dangerous terrain where technical skill and experience are required. The routes described as mountaineering scrambles should be attempted only by persons who have had some previous training such as a basic-mountaineering or rock-climbing course.
Technical Climbing	Routes that require roped belays and fixed anchors. There are no technical climbs described in this book.

The photographs illustrate the contrast between an easy walk up a graded road in White Pine Canyon and an exposed scramble on the summit ridge of Devils Castle.

TRAIL INFORMATION

Throughout the descriptions, certain words are used to describe the type and condition of the walking surface. "Roads" are paved or graded surfaces maintained for vehicles and include roads open to the public and limited-access roads blocked by gates. "Jeep roads" or "4WD roads" are unmaintained routes used by off-road vehicles, including now-closed historic vehicle routes that still appear as two-track scars or constructed grades on the ground.

"Trails" are maintained or constructed footpaths. For a path to be called a trail, at least the brush has been cleared in recent years. "Tracks," "game trails," and "user-created trails" are footpaths where the soil and the vegetation show evidence of repeated travel. "Routes" describe a general direction of cross-country travel with no defined footpath. A "bushwhack" is a route where hikers must force their way through sections of brush. Short pants are not recommended for bushwhacks. "Improvised bridges" are logs thrown across a stream. Routes that cross major streams on improvised bridges may be dangerous or impassable during the peak of the spring runoff.

PRIMARY INFORMATION SOURCES

Trail locations, distances, and elevation changes were determined from a combination of field checking with sketch pad, compass, altimeter, and, for the third edition, a global positioning system (GPS). The most recent US Geological Survey (USGS) topographic maps, ski-area maps, Forest Service maps, and commercial hiking maps were used as references. All trails in this book have been hiked by the author at some time, and most descriptions were originally field checked during 1986 and 1987. Dale Green walked and mapped the major trails in 1992 and 1993. Author's notes on changes to the trails were accumulated over the years, and final updates for this third edition were

"EASY-BEGINNER" AND "ADVANCED-SCRAMBLING" HIKES. *Left:* White Pine Canyon (L-05), a wide, well-graded dam-access road leading to an overlook. *Right:* Devils Castle (L-13.3), a ridge-crest route to a summit.

field checked in 2010 and 2011. There has been considerable expansion of the local trail system since the first edition, especially along the foothills and around the ski areas. Because the author could not get everywhere in a season, the information was also reviewed by knowledgeable hikers in the Wasatch Mountain Club. Trail management and resource-protection issues were verified with the responsible agencies.

Regardless of the checking, conditions change rapidly—avalanches and rockfall can obliterate a trail that was in excellent condition a year earlier. Brush is periodically cleared, and sections of trails are occasionally relocated. Neither the text nor the sketch maps attempt to accurately describe every bend in the trail. Use the information with a degree of skepticism and common sense.

MAPS

The maps published in this book are intended to help the reader follow the text descriptions. These maps may be sufficient for the well-maintained trails, but it is impractical to print detailed maps in a guidebook. Either the scale is too small for navigation, or the longer trails will take more than one page. Hikers will find that additional maps are useful supplements to this book.

Highly recommended is "Hiking the Wasatch: The Official Wasatch Mountain Club Trail Map for the Tri-Canyon Area—Mill Creek, Big Cottonwood, and Little Cottonwood," published by the Wasatch Mountain Club and the University of Utah Press. This map covers the hikes in the central area of this book, accurately shows trail locations, and is on the same scale as the USGS 7½-minute series maps. It was compiled by Wasatch Mountain Club member Dale Green.

The full-color "Wasatch Hiking Trails" map by Daniel Smith is excellent for providing an overview of the trails from Weber County into Utah County. The landownership and trail-mileage information was compiled using geographic information system (GIS) technology. Because the map covers a large area, the scale is too small to be useful for navigation. Serious hikers will eventually accumulate a set of the 7½-minute series USGS topographic maps. Drawn at 1:24,000 scale (approximately 2½ inches per mile), these are the most accurate maps available for topographic features, but the trail information is out of date. The USGS maps covering this area were originally issued between 1948 and 1963, but fortunately most of the local maps have now been reissued in 1998 editions. Hike descriptions in this book point out the map errors when they are significant, but don't be surprised if the USGS map shows a trail on the wrong side of a stream.

Lack of official names for many geographic features is a problem. Unnamed peaks can often be identified by the summit elevations found on topographic maps. Many names used in the route descriptions are unofficial names used by local hikers for peaks and drainages. The geologic maps and the 1903 USGS "Cottonwood Map" were additional sources of names. Other names were derived from a related feature (for example, Reynolds Peak is the summit, Peak 9422, at the head of Reynolds Gulch).

DISTANCES AND DIRECTIONS

Short distances along trails are generally stated in yards or feet. Longer distances are rounded off to the nearest quarter mile. Highway mileages given in decimal fractions were determined from odometer readings.

The best method to judge distances in a trail description is to convert the distance into hiking time. A quick mental conversion is that a quarter mile requires six minutes on level trail and up to fourteen minutes on a very steep trail. In the descriptions, "immediately" means very short distances, typically within sight, or less than one minute's walk.

The words "right" and "left" are for travel in the direction of the route description. Most descriptions are written for travel in the uphill direction, so referring to the "left side of the stream" is the reverse of the usual geographic convention.

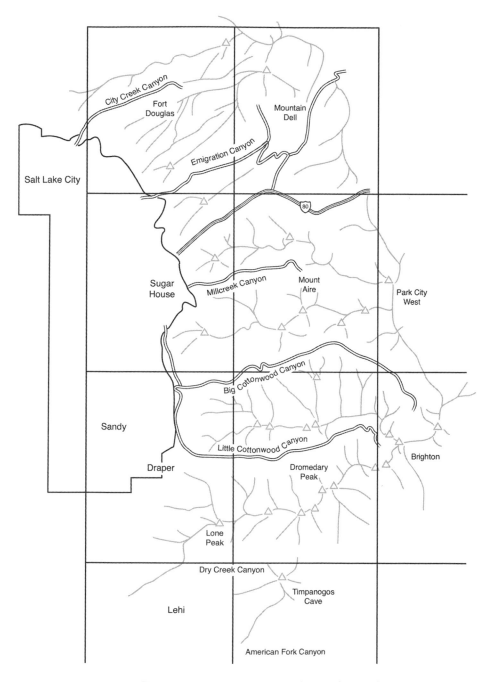

City Creek Canyon

Fort Douglas

Mountain Dell

Salt Lake City

Emigration Canyon

80

Sugar House

Millcreek Canyon

Mount Aire

Park City West

Big Cottonwood Canyon

Sandy

Little Cottonwood Canyon

Brighton

Draper

Dromedary Peak

Lone Peak

Dry Creek Canyon

Timpanogos Cave

Lehi

American Fork Canyon

USGS TOPOGRAPHIC MAPS. Ten maps at 1:24,000 scale cover the area discussed in this book.

HIKING TIMES

Hiking times are based on a typical pace for experienced hikers who are in reasonable physical condition. The durations are walking time only and do not include long rest breaks or sightseeing. A strong hiker can easily beat these times, while a family with children will take much longer. These times are consistent; if you require three hours to do a hike that has a book time of two hours, you will require six hours to do a hike with a four-hour book time. Once you have done a few hikes, you will learn how to adjust these times for your own pace.

My basic formula is as follows: two miles per hour on normal trail, plus a half hour for every thousand feet of ascent. Adjustments are made for trail conditions, intermediate summits, and high altitude. The route descriptions list a one-way time to the destination. For most trails, the return will require about three-quarters of the time required for the uphill portion, but very flat and very steep trails with rough terrain require about equal time in either direction.

How much faster than these calculated hiking times can someone go? Physically fit people who hike regularly can do the trails in 80–90 percent of the indicated times and get some aerobic conditioning in the process. The extreme comparison is between average hikers and superbly conditioned mountain runners. To be an official finisher in the Wasatch 100 ultramarathon requires going from Kaysville to Midway along the Great Western Trail (GWT) in about 55 percent of the hiking times in this book. The fastest runners each year typically cover the one hundred miles and five major ridge crossings in about twenty hours, compared to my estimate of sixty-five hours!

HIKING PACE

The proper pace, not extraordinary strength, is the key to hiking without becoming overtired. On longer hikes, take a slower pace or stop and rest often, and you will be more likely to reach your objective. Avoid becoming out of breath or developing a racing heartbeat.

The "rest step" is a proven method to conserve your leg strength by allowing a short period when the muscles are relaxed on each step. The idea is to take a step uphill, setting your foot down but not putting any weight on it while simultaneously locking the knee of your back leg. With practice, this can be accomplished while maintaining a steady pace. Take small steps on steep uphill sections. An upward movement of four to seven inches per step puts much less strain on your thighs than do ten- or twelve-inch steps.

DATA TABLE ACCURACY

The data tables included for individual hikes show the distance, elevation gain, highest elevation, and hiking time to one or more destinations. Usually, the destinations will be a series along a trail starting with a short hike and continuing farther and higher. At other times, the destinations will be alternative branches that fork from a single trailhead. This will be evident from the text description or the map. If the measurements are from a point other than the trailhead, this is noted at the bottom of the table.

If the hike is described as a one-way route, the table reflects the more common direction of travel. If the route crosses significant intermediate summits, an additional line gives the total ascent, rather than the difference from the trailhead to the destination.

There are several published tables of local trail mileages and elevation change that differ slightly from the data tables in this book. People who love geographical precision may differ with the information here. In practice, the differences are insignificant, as the true measure of a trail is the muscular effort and time required. A season-to-season change in trail conditions such as mud or numerous fallen branches can make more difference in time and effort than a 10 percent error in mileage. Rough terrain such as boulder fields and detours around wet spots makes more difference than a few contour lines of error in net elevation change. The data in the hike descriptions are sufficiently accurate to allow hike planning to avoid running out of water or daylight.

HIKER RESPONSIBILITY

The freedom of traveling in a natural environment requires judgment and responsibility from each hiker. Each hiker is personally responsible for being physically fit for the intended trip; for having proper equipment, clothing, water, and food; for evaluating the route conditions and weather; and for protecting the environment and the rights of others.

NEIGHBORHOOD PARKING

Many of the foothill trails start from city streets or small city-managed parks. Being considerate of nearby home owners is important to prevent future parking restrictions at current access points and to facilitate negotiations for future urban-interface trailheads. Minimize the number of cars in the neighborhood by carpooling, be sure not to block driveways, and avoid excessive noise. Some cities have also been aggressive in ticketing illegally parked cars near trailheads. Note regulatory signs; some of these urban trailheads are restricted after dark.

PRIVATE PROPERTY

Many trails, especially along the Wasatch Front, cross private land. This complex issue is discussed in chapter 3. Where no official right-of-way exists, access is by the permission of the owner and may be revoked at any time.

Respect all private property and avoid behavior that would cause owners to object to hikers crossing their land. Stay on the trail until you are on Forest Service land, and don't litter or cause excessive noise. Observe any signs or fences that would indicate a change in the owner's policy to hikers.

If challenged on the trail and told that you are trespassing, act respectfully and leave. The Wasatch Mountain Club has a strong interest in trail access. If you are told that hikers are not welcome on a trail, the club would like to hear about the problem. Call or write to the club's hiking director or the author.

The trails included in this book are routes that have been used by the public for many years with few landowner conflicts; however, occasional trail closures are likely as the foothills and canyons become more developed.

Protection of traditional access routes to the mountains requires the cooperation of landowners, public agencies, and citizen groups. Elected officials are becoming more involved in trail access, and planning departments are considering trail access when approving new subdivisions.

WATERSHED PROTECTION

The national forests were created for watershed protection, and water quality remains an issue today. Watershed concerns necessitate restricting traffic in City Creek Canyon and prohibiting swimming in the lakes. Dogs and horses are forbidden on the watershed, including City Creek, Big Cottonwood, and Little Cottonwood Canyons as well as the canyons draining the west side of Lone Peak, from Bells Canyon to Draper. Animals have been allowed in Millcreek Canyon, as the water is used only for irrigation, but stricter restrictions have been proposed.

Hikers and wilderness lovers must learn to enjoy an area without damaging it. Toilet facilities have been placed at popular trailheads—use them. With a little planning, you can reduce the need to "go behind a bush" especially on short day hikes, but if nature calls, be sure you go away from the trail and at least two hundred feet from streams. When defecating, dig a hole six inches deep in organic soil and cover it thoroughly when done. Lightly compact the soil and cover the excavation with loose twigs and rocks to reduce both the erosion potential and the visual impact.

Litter is both a health problem and an aesthetic issue. Do your part and carry out what you carry in on your hike. Better still, carry out some of the garbage left by less considerate hikers.

Dogs
Dogs are a major issue for hiker access to watershed areas, and this has impeded negotiations with water companies regarding new trail construction. Irresponsible owners who take their dogs into closed areas have caused one water company to consider

Many popular hiking destinations are at lakes and reservoirs. Avoid leaving anything in the water that you would not want to drink.

closure of the trails across their property to all users, which would be a major loss of hiking access. Dogs are especially an issue in the Sandy and Draper area.

What is the problem? Don't wild animals "do it" in the woods too? One issue is that dogs live around people, frequently eat human food, and therefore are more likely than wildlife to carry human diseases in their feces. Another issue is that dogs like to play in the water, whereas most wildlife are well dispersed across the habitat. Dogs playing in the water cause stream-bank erosion and sedimentation, in addition to fecal contamination. Chlorination can minimize pathogens, but treating water for sediment, taste, and odor problems is more difficult.

Dogs are specifically prohibited in the areas that provide drinking water. Note that there are many passes and ridges where one side is open to dogs and the other is watershed and closed to dogs. Observe the boundaries. Areas closed to dogs include City Creek, above the treatment plant; Parleys, Dell, and Lambs Canyons; Big Cottonwood Canyon; Little Cottonwood Canyon; and Bells Canyon south to Bear Canyon.

Salt Lake City publishes a brochure called *Dogs and the Wasatch Front Watershed* that lists places open to dogs, and that information is summarized in the trail recommendations in chapter 4. When you go to dog-legal areas, please clean up—and take the bag with you.

Invasive Plants

Invasive plants are typically nonnatives that seed readily, grow rapidly, and out-compete the historical flora of the area. This is an increasing problem worldwide, as humans are an efficient carrier of foreign seeds. In fact, some of the worst invasive plants are species that were deliberately introduced and then went wild. Hikers should clean the mud off their boots and brush attached seeds from their clothes to avoid carrying seeds to new areas.

Camping on the Watershed

For many years, prohibition of camping on the watershed severely limited the opportunity to spend more than a few hours in some of the more remote parts of the Wasatch. Except for the City Creek and Red Butte drainages, camping is now allowed, and the opportunity should not be abused.

Obviously, this means staying the required distance (two hundred feet) from lakes and streams; not fouling the water with human waste, soap suds, or food scraps; and packing out all garbage. Locate your camp to minimize visual impact by getting off the trail and utilizing natural topographic and vegetative screening. Don't chop down trees or build new fire rings for a massive bonfire. Use of a camping stove is highly recommended. Also, the Wasatch has a high forest-fire risk. For resource protection, campfires are now prohibited in most of the popular lake basins. The Wasatch is not particularly suitable for camping; backpackers should consider alternative destinations.

FIRES

There is a year-round fire closure for the Lake Blanch, Red Pine, Maybird, and American Fork Silver Lake drainages. There is also typically a forest-wide fire closure during late summer when the woods are tinder dry. Fireworks are prohibited on both national forest and the city-controlled foothills.

WILDERNESS GROUP SIZE

The group size limit in the Mount Olympus, Twin Peaks, and Lone Peak Wilderness Areas is ten people. This rule may be inconvenient, but it is the law. Large groups can be very intrusive and affect the experience of other hikers. This is especially true when a huge group shows up at an already popular destination in a fragile area.

The Forest Service manages the upper canyons for "developed recreation," and these areas are more appropriate for large hiking groups.

TRAIL ETIQUETTE

The Wasatch is a heavily used and fragile area. Hikers must strive to minimize their impact. Shortcutting switchbacks on the trails damages vegetation and causes serious erosion. Much trail maintenance labor goes into restoring areas damaged by short-cutting. Hikers who prefer steeper trails can avoid the switchbacks by choosing an alternative trail or a totally off-trail route.

Conflicts between hikers and mountain bikes are a continuing problem. Being overtaken by an aggressive downhill rider is unpleasant and may be dangerous. The nationwide rule is that bikes yield to both hikers and horses. Both hikers and bikers need to yield to horses, as they are easily spooked. Users need to follow these rules on shared trails. However, if you can easily get out of the way of the bikes, then be courteous. Communication between the first hiker and first bike rider about how many are behind them helps too.

BEING PREPARED

Each hiker must take responsibility for being physically prepared and adequately equipped for the intended trip. Good physical condition is not a prerequisite for hiking, and regular hiking is an enjoyable way to exercise; however, hikers must select routes that match their health and strength.

Equipment

Hiking does not require a large investment in equipment, but for a safe trip there are a few essentials, including:

- good comfortable boots with adequate tread
- extra clothing appropriate to the season
- a FULL water bottle
- sunglasses and sunscreen
- a small pack to carry everything

As hikes become longer and more serious, you will also need the following:

- a map or trail guide
- food, including some extra for emergencies
- raingear or other clothing for a change in the weather
- a small first-aid kit
- insect repellent in July and August
- a flashlight if there is any chance of a twilight return

Wasatch Weather

Normal atmospheric conditions result in a decrease in temperature with altitude, and mountains generate their own weather. Air passing over a mountain range is forced upward and cools as it rises and expands. Colder air holds less water vapor, so moisture condenses, forming clouds, rain, and snow. The ridges and canyons also redirect the surface winds and affect the local climate.

The climatic difference between the valley at forty-three hundred feet and the Brighton parking lot at eighty-seven hundred feet is roughly comparable to the change experienced when going north from Salt Lake City to central Canada or parts of Alaska. In mid-June when the city is hot and dry, Alta and Brighton are still buried in snow.

At high elevation, the midday sun is intense. The air directly above a mountain becomes warmer than the surrounding air at the same altitude and begins to rise. This rising air forms the towering cumulus clouds that are often seen above the Wasatch on an otherwise clear summer afternoon. They can produce anything from an overcast sky to an incredibly violent thunderstorm mixed with hail. Lightning is a special danger to hikers on summits and ridges.

The physics are simple, but the magnitude of the effects resulting from the great vertical relief must be experienced firsthand before it is fully appreciated. I have started hiking on a bright, hot summer afternoon and returned home drenched with rain, only to discover that not a drop fell in the valley. I have sat on top of Mount Olympus feeling chilled while wearing a pile jacket and mountain parka, yet knowing there was shirtsleeve weather down in the city. Taking proper clothing along is important at any time of year.

Drinking Water

You are unlikely to find drinking water on foothill hikes or on trails that follow ridges or minor drainages. Small streams, such as the one on the Mount Olympus Trail, usually dry up by midsummer, and only major drainages and lakes are reliable water sources. Water quality at higher elevations in the Wasatch is generally good, but treating lake and stream water is always recommended and prudent.

There are diverse opinions about which treatment method is best. Personally, I have used Halazone tablets, iodine tablets, iodine crystals, a dropper bottle of chlorine bleach, a high-efficiency filter, battery-powered ultraviolet lamps, and boiling. Filtering and boiling are the most certain but are too much hassle for a day hike. All chemical treatments require fifteen to twenty minutes, are less efficient in cold water, and leave a residual taste. For occasional day hikes, the iodine-treatment tablets are economical and convenient, have a good shelf life, and are readily available in outdoor stores.

For short day hikes, carrying enough water for the full trip is easiest. A quart bottle and maybe a canned beverage to enjoy with lunch are enough in cool weather. For a long hike such as Twin Peaks or Olympus in July and August, carry two or even three quarts plus treatment chemicals.

Judgment

Reaching the objective is glorious, but knowing when to turn around is prudent. Gauge your progress and allow yourself enough time and energy to return to the trailhead safely. Many avoidable accidents have occurred when an exhausted hiker was hurrying down a trail in twilight. When traveling beyond the maintained trails, be sure you are capable of handling the terrain. This is especially true with any route described as exposed scrambling or mountaineering.

OTHER WAYS OF ENJOYING THE WASATCH TRAILS

Mountain running is a demanding sport that combines alpine hiking with distance running. The distances and terrain that runners cover seem truly astounding to hikers. Runners travel very light compared to hikers and depend on strength, speed, and knowledge of the route to avoid bad weather and to get themselves to a road or aid location. Meeting a runner wearing shorts and running shoes and carrying only a water bottle is a humbling experience when you are panting uphill with a full pack. Many of the longer trails and ridge routes, especially the rolling terrain north of Parleys and along the Wasatch Crest, are popular with runners. The Wasatch Mountains are the site of races that attract runners nationwide.

Mountain bicycles are controversial on the trails. Conflicts between ascending hikers and descending bicycles on a narrow trail and erosion damage caused by the continuous wheel track are major concerns. Bicycles are vehicles and are officially prohibited in wilderness areas even though they are muscle powered. Bicyclists should keep to established routes and avoid fragile meadows and alpine areas. They should also evaluate trail conditions and avoid riding steep hiking trails, especially when trails are wet and easily eroded.

Routes suitable for bicycles include the Big Water Trail, the Millcreek to Brighton ridge route, the ski-area roads, and the old mining roads. Some ski areas, such as Solitude, are actively developing summer bike trails. The Park City area in Summit County is especially welcoming to mountain bikes and is developing an extensive network of trails.

Horses are prohibited in the watershed canyons but are occasionally seen on the foothill trails above Draper. Avoid frightening horses by stepping off the trail on the downhill side and talking with the rider as the horse passes.

ORGANIZATIONS AND INSTRUCTION

The best way to learn about the mountains and routes and about wilderness ethics is to hike with knowledgeable companions. The Wasatch Mountain Club has introduced thousands of people to the local mountains since it was founded in the 1920s. There are currently more than eleven hundred members ranging in age from college age to

The Wasatch has many seldom-visited places that can be reached by unmaintained trails or by moderate off-trail hiking. This area is a short way from the Mill B North Fork Trail.

octogenarians. The outing schedule includes four to seven hikes per weekend during the April through September season. Most hikes are open to nonmembers and are an excellent way to meet people and see the mountains. The Salt Lake and Ogden chapters of the Sierra Club also schedule hikes that are open to nonmembers.

The University of Utah outdoor recreation program conducts a number of courses ranging from hiking to technical climbing. The schedule and fees are listed in the catalog published by the Division of Continuing Education.

2

Natural History of the Wasatch

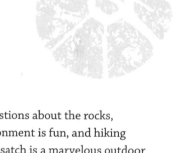

This chapter addresses some of the frequently asked questions about the rocks, trees, and wildflowers. Understanding the natural environment is fun, and hiking allows plenty of time for observing and learning. The Wasatch is a marvelous outdoor classroom—the complex geology and the numerous life zones provide unusual diversity in a small area. An extensive bibliography is included, as there is insufficient space to provide all the geological and biological detail that can be found in more technical works.

THE LAND

The Wasatch Mountains form part of the Middle Rocky Mountain geographic province, an area characterized by recent uplift, complex folding of the rock strata, and rapid erosion into peaks and valleys. The Wasatch Range extends about 160 miles, from near the Idaho border south to Mount Nebo, where the Rocky Mountain Province, the Colorado Plateau Province, and the Basin and Range Province meet. The Provo and Weber River valleys separate the Wasatch from the Uinta Mountains, which continue the Rocky Mountain Province eastward into Wyoming and Colorado.

The Rocky Mountain Province ends abruptly at the Wasatch Fault. The Salt Lake Valley and all the land west to the Sierra Nevada are in the Basin and Range Province. This province results from widespread uplifting and stretching of a thin area of the earth's crust and is characterized by isolated mountain ranges about 20 miles apart, separated by flat, sediment-filled valleys. The Wasatch Mountains were carved from an uplifted block that has been incised into peaks and canyons. The result is a spectacular west face with high summits overlooking the valley. Wasatch Front hikes, such as Lone

Peak or Mount Olympus, are long and steep. Hikers soon notice that the rugged alpine ridges and summits around Little Cottonwood Canyon change to rolling, moderate-elevation terrain north of Parleys Canyon. This is a result of an overall folding of the rock layers that form the uplifted block.

The rocks in the south part of Salt Lake County are folded upward in an arch, and the Traverse Mountains south of Draper and the Alpine Ridge are actually an extension of the broad uplift that forms the crest of the Uintas. This upward fold-ing has been magnified by the injection of molten rock from below that pushed up the older layers. This molten rock solidified deep below the surface and formed the granite found between the mouth of Little Cottonwood Canyon and Lone Peak. In the northern part of Salt Lake County, the layers are folded downward, with the low point of the fold following Emigration Canyon. The downward folding slowed the erosion, and the surface here is formed by relatively soft, younger sedimentary rocks that were completely removed from the highlands to the south.

Noted geologist Max Crittenden wrote, "The wealth and variety of geological fea-tures to be found in Salt Lake County are, for an area of its size, probably unexcelled anywhere in the world." How did all this form? What forces produced the bewildering array of steep cliffs, rounded ridges, tilted layers, igneous rocks, and loose gravel that we hike over? How did the rich mineral deposits and alpine basins form?

A BILLION YEARS ON MOUNT OLYMPUS

Let us imagine the summit of Mount Olympus, appropriately named for the home of the gods, as a stationary vantage point where we can sit and observe a billion-year drama. The modern geographical names and directions will serve as our landmarks as the continents drift, twist, sink, rise, and are eroded away again.

Our mountain spirit awakens on a vantage point high above a barren and lifeless land near the edge of a shallow sea containing algae and tiny soft-bodied creatures. The earth is already old, and the violent convulsions that formed the oldest rocks in the area are lost in the dimness of time. To the north, near Farmington Canyon, and south, near Deaf Smith–Little Willow Canyon, are rocks already a half-billion years old. These ancient sediments have already been injected with igneous intrusions, buried, heated, recrystallized, folded, and exposed again.

For millions of years, we watch sand and clay wash into shallow bays beneath us. The seabed gradually sinks until sixteen thousand feet of material has accumulated. This will become the rusty quartzites and red, greenish, and purple shales of the massive Big Cottonwood Formation, which lies between Tolcat Canyon and the crest of the Cottonwood Ridge. The process is interrupted by an extensive ice age, which carves smooth-bottomed basins deep into the Big Cottonwood series of sediments and deposits moraines of boulders, cobbles, pebbles, sand, and silt that will become the rusty-weathering Mineral Fork Tillite found between Snowbird and Hidden Falls.

The Cambrian period begins with an explosion of marine life. Within a few million years, creatures with hard body parts appear and the seas teem with trilobites. The land continues to subside, as sand and limey muds are deposited in shallow water and become the Tintic Quartzite, Ophir Shale, and Maxfield Limestone that form the north flanks of Mount Olympus and the walls of Mill B North below Mount Raymond. At times the coastline is in Nevada, and at other times the sea covers all of Utah. Most of the deposition is taking place in western Utah, while the area to the east is part of a large, relatively stable continent. The equator extends northward through our skewed vantage point. The warm climate, the low-lying land, and the shallow seas are a preview of Florida and the Bahamas.

This pattern continues as vascular plants invade the land and as cephalopods (ancestors of snails and squids) reach a peak and then are replaced by fish as the dominant large marine animals. The deposition continues to the west and north, but only occasional outcrops record this period in the central Wasatch.

Our overlook is now above shallow seas that flood the edge of the single world continent of Pangaea. Winged insects and small reptiles appear on land, as limestone, occasionally mixed with sand, is being deposited in these shallow seas. These Carboniferous Age and Permian Age limestone layers will form colorful cliffs around Alta and much of Mount Raymond, Gobblers Knob, and lower Mill D Fork.

The Triassic period begins with reptiles dominating the land while early mammals appear. Pangaea begins to separate, and an arc of islands rises to the west, separating the sea between the Wasatch and central Nevada from the open ocean. Periods of continental and marine deposition continue below us. These deposits will become the shales and limestones found between Millcreek and Parleys Canyons.

For four hundred million years, a continent to the east has been eroding and depositing sand and mud into a shallow sea to the west. Now this pattern ends as the earth hinges along the approximate location of the Wasatch. New highlands rise to the west, forming a three-thousand-mile mountain chain extending from southern Nevada to Alaska. The Wasatch is near the coast as the sea floods into eastern Utah and the massive sandstones of the redrock country begin to accumulate.

Great dinosaurs and early birds inhabit the coastal sand dunes and swamps during Utah's Jurassic period. The dunes that will form the Navajo sandstone cliffs of Capitol Reef, Zion National Park, and the Escalante drainage in southern Utah are contemporaneous with the Nugget Sandstone found in the Wasatch around Parleys Canyon and Red Butte Canyon.

Flowering plants appear as the last dinosaurs vanish from the coastal plain below us. Conifers are abundant, and deciduous trees such as maple and cottonwood are now present. High land resulting from a mountain building period (the Sevier Orogeny) lies west of the Wasatch, while in Summit County alluvial fans of sand and gravel are washing eastward into a shallow sea. This sea spreads across the flooded continental shelf and reaches all the way to Texas. Organic debris, the precursor of Utah's

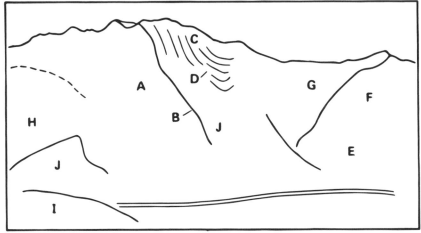

THE GEOLOGY OF MOUNT SUPERIOR VIEWED FROM THE PERUVIAN GULCH TRAIL.

Key

A. Big Cottonwood Formation—Precambrian Age.

B. Unconformal contact—a period of erosion occurred between deposition of the two formations.

C. Mineral Fork Tillite—Precambrian Age.

D. Folding and tilting of originally horizontal sediments.

E. Ophir Shale and Maxfield Limestone—Cambrian Age.

F. Fitchville Formation, Gardison and Deseret Limestone—Mississippian Age.

G. At least five major faults are in this small area.

H. Quartz monzonite, commonly called granite. Molten rock was forced below the older formations during the Tertiary period.

I. Geologically recent glacial deposits.

J. Talus deposits that are still accumulating.

Cretaceous coal seams, is accumulating in coastal swamps from Coalville in Summit County south to the Kaiparowits Plateau.

The land to the west is slowly moving eastward in a series of great thrusts that will eventually narrow Utah by forty miles. Around Mount Timpanogos, this leaves older (Carboniferous Age) rocks from the Oquirrhs on top of younger (Jurassic) rocks. These uplifted areas erode rapidly, and, in Salt Lake County, the overthrust material is washed into the eastern sea.

The Tertiary period opens with mammals taking over the land and a new series of tectonic forces shaping the continent. The Rocky Mountains begin to rise to the east, ending marine deposition in Utah. A north-to-south compression grips Utah; the Emigration Canyon area folds downward, and the area to the south rises in a series of folds that extend east along the Uinta Mountains.

This period of violent movement causes igneous activity throughout the area. A series of hot spots forms under Clayton Peak, under the Alta-Brighton area, under lower Little Cottonwood Canyon, and across the valley at Bingham Canyon. Molten magma is forced below the ancient rocks, pushing them upward. The silica-rich magma cools far below the surface, forming the light-colored, large-crystallized rock commonly called granite. Geologists will call it quartz monzonite to distinguish it from other varieties of granite, based on grain size and composition. Volcanoes in Wyoming fill the valleys of Summit County with ash and surround the Uintas with a broad piedmont. We are overlooking a spectacular place much like Yellowstone, the Hawaiian volcanoes, and Mount St. Helens on a statewide scale.

The intense heating and the effects of hot pressurized water result in local concentrations of various minerals. Where the molten rock directly contacts limestone, carbon dioxide is released and minerals such as iron and copper sulfides are deposited. Different rates of crystallization result in concentration of certain minerals near the apex of the underground chamber. Hot water migrates through recently solidified rock, dissolving and redepositing quartz, forming veins of large crystals. At times this hot water passes through areas of partially concentrated minerals and becomes mineralized. Then this solution follows fissures into the Maxfield Limestone and the Ophir Shale Formation, where the alkaline lime neutralizes the water, precipitating lead, zinc, copper, and silver. The result is a scattering of rich ore bodies ranging from narrow veins to massive deposits.

During all this time our vantage has been far above the low ridges, coastal swamps, and shallow seas. Only twenty-five million years before our story ends, the Wasatch begins to rise. The whole of western North America is uplifted nearly a mile, and the Great Basin and Rocky Mountain provinces begin to take shape. In the Great Basin, the mountains rise, while the stretching causes the intervening blocks to drop. The Salt Lake Valley and other newly formed valleys fill with thousands of feet of sediment washing from the rising mountains.

The vertical movement on the Wasatch Fault averages only six one-thousandths of an inch per year, but a ten- to fifteen-thousand-foot movement accumulates before

Geologic Period or Epoch	Million Years before Present	Wasatch Geological Features	Local Conditions Events	Evolutionary, Global, and Regional Events
Early Precambrian	?? to 1400	Farmington Canyon Complex	Multiple episodes of igneous activity and mountain building.	
Late Precambrian	1100 to 700	Big Cottonwood Formation, Mutual Formation, and Mineral Fork Tillite. Covers most of area between north face of Mt. Olympus and the Twin Peaks—Mt. Superior ridge.	Continent to the southeast. Deposition of shallow water marine and glacial sediments which were later metamorphized and folded.	Barren land. Bacteria and algae in the seas.
Cambrian	600 to 500	Tintic Quartzite, Maxfield Limestone, and Ophir Foundation. Found in narrow strip between Neffs Canyon and Canyon and Cardiff Fork.	Beginning of long period of shallow water marine deposition in a slowly sinking basin to the west.	Explosion of marine life. Sponges, jellyfish and trilobites dominate.
Ordovician	500 to 300	Deposits from this period are well represented near Logan and in West Desert but are largely removed from the Wasatch.	Salt Lake Area is a peninsula of uplifted land with sea to north and south.	Cephalopods.
Silurian				First vascular land plants
Devonian				Fish dominate sea. Early amphibians and giant ferns on land.
Carboniferous	360 to 280			Warm climate, lush forests which later form coal in Eastern states.
Mississippian		Colorful limestone outcrops near Cardiff Fork, Alta and in American Fork Canyon. Includes the black and white cliff north of Snowbird.	Shallow seas cover all of Utah.	Winged insects and first reptiles appear.
Pennsylvanian		Weber Quartzite; covers much of south side of Millcreek, Mt. Raymond and Gobblers Knob.		Uplift begins in Colorado and spreads into eastern Utah.
Permian	280 to 240	Park City Formation found low in Millcreek Canyon from Rattlesnake Gulch to Big Water Gulch. Also in Butler Fork and Mill A.	Earth hinges along the Wasatch line. Continent to east sinks and land rises in west.	Conifers spread, trilobites disappear. All land joined in continent of Pangaea.
Triassic	240 to 200	Woodside, Thayne and Ankareh Formations. Shales and limestones found along the north side of Millcreek.	Marine deposition ends in Wasatch.	Reptiles dominate land. First mammals appear. Pangaea splits.
Jurassic	190 to 140	Nugget Sandstone, Twin Creek Limestone— Continental deposits found between Millcreek and Emigration Canyons	Dune fields on a coastal plain with sea to north.	Great dinosaurs and early birds. Widening of Atlantic Ocean. Massive sandstones being deposited in shallow seas in southeast Utah.

Geologic Period or Epoch	Million Years before Present	Wasatch Geological Features	Local Conditions Events	Evolutionary, Global, and Regional Events
Cretaceous	136 to 66	Older rocks (Oquirrh Formation) above younger strata on Mt. Timpanogos. Overthrust material eroded from Salt Lake County area.	East-West compression thrusting rocks from the west on top of the Wasatch.	Dinosaurs vanish. Birds spread. Flowering plants appear.
		Conglomerate sediments found in Summit County.	Coastal plain at foot of the Sevier Mountains.	Formation of a mountainous highland to the west and shallow sea to the east. Sevier Orogeny.
Tertiary	65 to 1.8			Rocky Mountains begin to form. Mammals spread. North America and Europe separate.
Paleocene	65 to 58	Eastward trending folds lowering Emigration and Parleys area and raising land to the south near Little Cottonwood.	Compression in North-South direction. Uplift of Uinta Mountains.	
Eocene	58 to 37			
Oligocene	37 to 24	Clayton Peak, Alta, Little Cottonwood, and Bingham stocks.	Intrusion of molten rock which cooled beneath the surface, forming granite.	Similar intrusions forming LaSal, Henry, and Abajo Mountains.
Miocene	24 to 5	Wasatch Mountains, Basin, and Range terrain to the west.	Uplift begins along Wasatch Fault.	Great Basin begins to stretch resulting in block faulting. Basin and range pattern forms.
Pliocene	5 to 1.8			Valleys fill with sediments.
Quaternary	1.6 to present			Climate change brings ice ages.
Pleistocene	1.6 to 0.01	The familiar canyons, cirques, and foothill benches form.	Glaciers in upper canyons. Lake Bonneville fills the valley.	Humans migrate from central Africa and reach Europe and Asia.
Holocene	Last 10,000 years	Forests reclaim the cirques, scoured canyons, and glacial moraines. Earthquakes slice through recent deposits.	Humans arrive in the Wasatch.	
	Last 100 years	Roads, mines, ski lifts, and deforestation.	Civilization arrives.	

Note: This chart is highly simplified and utility for an amateur was favored over technical accuracy. Readers wishing a more complete presentation are encouraged to consult the references found in the bibliography.

humans arrive. Meanwhile, the Great Basin is stretching by a quarter inch per year, eventually adding thirty to sixty miles to the distance between the Wasatch and California.

At the beginning of the Quaternary period, *Homo habilis* is already walking upright and using tools in Africa, but the familiar peaks, ridges, and canyons of the Wasatch are still in their infancy. As the climate turns colder and wetter, glaciers begin to scour the land, shaping the cirques and canyons. For seven hundred thousand years, glaciers advance and retreat as continental ice ages pass. In the final ninety thousand years, the fourth major ice age sculpts the Wasatch into recognizable form.

At the peak of this ice age, thirty-three glaciers are found in Salt Lake County, ranging from the short glaciers in Deaf Smith and Ferguson Canyons to the ice field that connects the Brighton and Albion Basin cirques across Catherine Pass. A fourteen-mile glacier winds down Little Cottonwood Canyon with six tributary glaciers joining from the south. Lower Little Cottonwood Canyon is carved into a characteristic U-shaped glacial valley with steep-walled cirques, steep sidewalls, and a fairly wide low-angled floor. Moraines are being deposited along the sides and ends of glaciers. As reinvigorated glaciers override older moraines, at least seven minor periods of advance and retreat leave evidence during this last ice age alone. At the mouth of Little Cottonwood Canyon, a huge tongue of ice reaches out from between the granite walls and crosses the gravel beach to end on the shore of Lake Bonneville. Silty-gray water pours from streams under the glacier and washes into the lake, giving it a distinct green tint.

Glaciers occupy the heads of all the north-facing side canyons of Big Cottonwood. Five major tributary glaciers from Brighton to Days Fork feed into the main valley glacier, which ends just below Cardiff Fork. A multibranch glacier is scouring out the Lake Blanche basin and descends Mill B Fork but does not continue down the main canyon. Because glaciers do not reach the canyon mouth, lower Big Cottonwood Canyon retains a narrow stream-cut V shape.

Short glaciers on the north flanks of Lone Peak, in Bells Canyon, and in Neffs Canyon are visible from the lakeshore. From Mount Olympus, we cannot see the far shores of Lake Bonneville, which reaches from Idaho on the north to Nevada on the west and south nearly to Cedar City.

Volcanic activity in Idaho diverts the Bear River from the Snake River drainage into the Bonneville Basin, causing the lake level to rise. As the lake tops Red Rock Pass in southern Idaho, it carves an outlet to the Pacific, causing one of the greatest floods in the earth's history. The torrent pouring from Lake Bonneville cuts a gorge 300 feet deep and fills the Snake River Canyon at Twin Falls to overflowing. This is the lake's climax. The lake drops from the 5,135-foot Bonneville level to the 4,800-foot Provo level in only a few years, just as the climate changes and a warmer and drier period begins. The lake rises and falls several more times, but never again reaches its past glory.

Now, a new creature appears on the lakeshore: a hunter and gatherer seeking the herds of mammoth, musk ox, deer, and mountain sheep. These great herbivores will disappear from the mountains, unable to withstand the climatic change combined with hunting pressure from this new predator. In a geological instant, this creature will fill the earth, altering the landscape with its works and interrupting processes that have been going on for billions of years. Yet this new species brings a unique and precious trait, for it has the curiosity to inquire, the language to record, and the wisdom to preserve.

THE LEGACY TODAY

Geological history did not end with our arrival. The forces and processes continue, at times mocking our folly when we ignore the geological evidence. Global climate change, both the periodic fluctuations and the massive human-caused changes in solar-radiation balance, will dramatically alter the snowpack and runoff. Species redistribution both from climate change and from humans transporting nonnative plants and animals to new areas will change the appearance of the forests and foothill shrub communities. Changes in plant communities cause changes to erosion patterns.

The Wasatch continues to rise, and the Great Basin continues to stretch. Fault scarps are clearly visible in the gravel moraines between Little Cottonwood and Bells Canyons, recording an earthquake scarcely more than a century old. Avalanches, landslides, and rockfall onto trails and highways all serve to remind us that the canyons are still cutting into the uplifted block. Likewise, the unstable nature of the unconsolidated foothill soils makes some areas permanently unsuited for development. In August 1945, for example, a cloudburst caused a major landslide in Perrys Hollow that washed debris across Eleventh Avenue and on into the cemetery. Subdivisions climb farther up the foothills than they did forty years ago, increasing the risk of major damage.

The Wasatch geology presents us with hazards but also provides unparalleled opportunities. The scenic beauty of the Wasatch is unsurpassed for a location adjacent to a major city. The abrupt mile-high uplift is an efficient water collector for the thirsty city. The foothills provide a bountiful supply of sand, gravel, lime, and quarried stone for constructing a technological civilization. In the last century the mountains yielded fortunes in silver and base metals. Today, recreation and the tourist industry are not only major employers, but also a significant factor in the quality of life available to persons living in Utah.

TREES AND WILDFLOWERS*

Hikers travel through an environment shaped by the terrain and the vegetative cover. Geologic history has created the terrain. Contemporary patterns of sun, rain, wind, and soil along with human activities such as logging, ski-area development, and fire

*Adapted from the unpublished manuscript "Wildflowers of the Wasatch" by Mike Treshow.

suppression determine the vegetation found along the trails. Learning about the trees and other plants adds to hiking enjoyment and helps in understanding the complex ecological relationships that exist in natural places. Wildflowers play vital ecological roles and are a delight for hikers. A casual glance at a summer hillside reveals a carpet of color, but the beauty is even greater when you see and recognize the individual flowers.

PLANT ASSOCIATIONS

The concept of "plant associations" or "plant communities" is very useful in understanding what you see along a trail. Each type of plant needs specific conditions of temperature, moisture, soil, and exposure to the sun for best growth. Because these conditions vary with elevation, the plant life at any given elevation will be much the same from one site to another. The resulting plant communities are named for the most prominent plants in any given area.

The dominant plants form the habitat for the other plants, as well as for birds, mammals, and insects. The plant associations also determine the "feel" of a trail. Walking an open sunbaked ridge with only a few mountain mahogany trees is totally different from hiking a stream-bottom willow thicket with birch and cottonwood overhead.

Starting in the lower foothills at five to six thousand feet, the "grasslands" association is most prominent. This is also known as the plains or prairie zone. This zone is dominated by various grasses, with some sage and other species present. In April and May, numerous wildflowers bloom here, including our state flower, the mariposa or sego lily. But these areas soon dry out, and by the end of June they have turned brown and the plants now wait for the next winter's moisture to resume their growth.

The "mountain brush" or chaparral association, dominated by Gambel oak, appears at about fifty-five hundred feet and extends one to two thousand feet higher. We also find a few other woody shrubs or trees, including mountain mahogany, with its gray bark and small dark-green leaves, and junipers. Big-tooth maple appears in shady or moist sites, mostly along streams. The draws and ravines found here lend to varied habitats that support a rich diversity of wildflowers.

Passing through the mountain brush community, more and more fir trees and aspen begin to appear, first in ravines and on north-facing slopes, and finally providing a full cover of trees at sixty-five hundred to seven thousand feet. The conifers and aspen can occur as much as fifteen hundred to two thousand feet lower in elevation on moist north-facing slopes than on more arid south-facing slopes. This "needle-leaf" community, characterizing the montane zone, is typically represented by Douglas fir, white fir, and blue spruce. Areas of deciduous forest, dominated by the aspen association, occupy the moister sites. Beneath the shaded canopy, we find several other woody plants such as the low-growing mountain lover, currants, elderberry, and mountain ash. Mountain lilac, characterized by thick evergreen leaves, grows in more open areas, while along streams we find big-tooth maple, river birch, alder, and dogwood with its distinctive red bark.

The species of fir and spruce change at roughly eight thousand feet, but the forest looks much the same. Now we have Engelmann spruce and subalpine fir, which form the principal components of the subalpine zone. Aspen may continue to appear near the streams, which are often bordered by flowering meadows. By the time we reach nine thousand to ninety-five hundred feet, again depending largely on the exposure, the trees become less frequent, the forest opens up, and we begin to leave the subalpine community. Here we find shrubby species and an occasional subalpine fir, with limber pine on the harshest sites of rocky outcrops.

We must get above ten thousand feet before all the trees have disappeared and we have entered the distinct Wasatch alpine zone or community. Here we find mostly short grasslands and rock fields, intermixed with patches of sedge in the marshy spots, and gardens of wildflowers on the drier sites. The flowers are often short stemmed and form a cushion or carpet. At the very highest elevations in the Wasatch, near the summits of such peaks as the Twins or Lone Peak, we find mostly the rich flora of lichens covering the otherwise bare rock and an occasional sprig of grass and small perennial plants between the rocks.

PLANT IDENTIFICATION

The local flora is easy and fun to recognize. With only a little background, you will be able to identify most of the trees and many of the wildflowers along the Wasatch trails.

Space does not permit providing adequate information for identifying individual species. Excellent regional field guides ranging from colorful picture books to scholarly tomes are listed in the bibliography.

A few hints will help you get started in plant identification. Learning the common trees is the best way to get started. This will enable you to recognize the major plant associations on sight and will also help you understand the effects of slope direction, angle, soil conditions, and other factors on the distribution of species. Also, learning the trees is relatively easy, as there are few species within the limited geographical area of the Wasatch. For example, only one pine, one oak, and two maples are common in the Wasatch. Because the number of species is so limited, trees can be identified by any of several characteristics such as the leaf, the bark texture, or the overall shape.

The small herbaceous plants can occasionally be identified by secondary characteristics, but the best approach is to identify them by the flowering parts. These parts change more slowly than characteristics such as leaf shape, color, and size, which can vary widely even within a species. The flower is the key to recognizing the deeper evolutionary relationships of the plant families. Learning to recognize the major wildflower families rather than memorizing individual species organizes your growing knowledge, makes using the technical books much easier, and enables you to make a

Wildflowers can be enjoyed throughout the hiking season.

partial identification with difficult specimens. Identify only a few (four to six) species on a single hike and then review them by looking for additional specimens along the trail.

Wildflowers can be studied throughout the hiking season. Plants found at lower elevations early in the spring often make a later appearance higher up. Once you become familiar with a plant—say, in the grasslands zone—you will recognize it a month or two later as it comes into bloom along a trail in the fir forest.

VEGETATION ZONES OF WASATCH TRAILS

The predominant zones and the best season for wildflowers for some of the more popular trails can be categorized as follows:

Trails mostly in the grassland and mountain brush zones. Best wildflower season: April or May.

Mount Olympus to stream	Ensign Peak
Little Black Mountain	Bonneville Shoreline Trail (BST)
Big Beacon	Grandeur from West

Trails mostly in the mountain brush and conifer or montane zone. Best wildflower season: June.

Grandeur from Church Fork	Thayne Canyon
Terraces to Elbow Fork	Mount Olympus
Mule Hollow	Ferguson Canyon
Bells Canyon to waterfall	Bowman Fork

Trails beginning in the montane zone and climbing into the subalpine zone. Best wildflower season: June and July.

Mill B North Fork	Mineral Fork
Mill D North Fork	Lake Blanche
Butler Fork	Days Fork
Box Elder Peak	Broads Fork

Trails predominantly subalpine and leading to the alpine zone. Best wildflower season: July and August.

Brighton–Twin Lakes	White Pine
Peruvian Gulch	Secret Lake (Albion Basin)
Lake Catherine	Red Pine
Collins Gulch	Lone Peak Cirque

WILDLIFE IN THE WASATCH

The land and the ecological relationships in the area have been drastically altered by human activity—often in ways not noticeable to the casual forest visitor. Loss of winter range to foothills urbanization limits the population of deer. The elk heard is also sensitive to human disturbance, both on their winter range and in their spring calving areas. Large carnivores such as bear, lynx, bobcat, and cougar are rare due to disturbance and predator-control efforts. Highways impair migration routes, destroy and alter streams, and result in road kills.

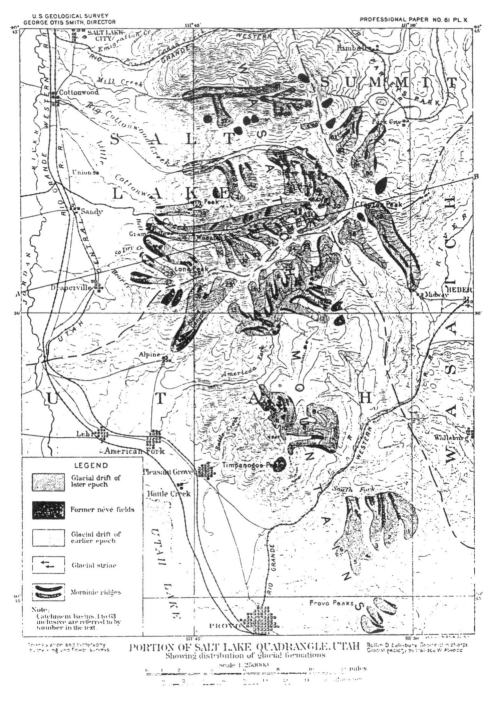

Map from Wallace W. Atwood, "Glaciation of the Uinta and Wasatch Mountains, 1909," showing both the extent of Pleistocene glaciation and the extent of human settlement at the beginning of the century.

3

History and Environmental Protection

When the pioneers arrived in Utah, the canyons offered a wealth of water, minerals, timber, wildlife, grazing, and open space. Since then our technology has stripped the canyons of old-growth timber, depleted the mineral deposits, and built dams, roads, cabins, condominiums, and ski lifts. The Wasatch, like all natural places, is finite and fragile, yet the demands of the adjacent urban area are enormous and growing. The opposing forces of development and conservation have shaped the Wasatch for 160 years. The foresight of early conservationists created the forest preserves that evolved into the national forests and wilderness areas of today. For persons who know and love the Wasatch, the challenge of the next century will be to manage this unique resource wisely by setting priorities and resolving use conflicts.

HUMAN HISTORY AND THE RESULTS

Only wildlife witnessed the highest level of Lake Bonneville lapping the flanks of the mountains while glaciers pushed from the canyons onto the beaches. The earliest evidence of humans in northern Utah is the 11,000-year-old debris in Danger Cave near Wendover. Only a few local sites survive from the Fremont culture, which flourished in Utah from AD 400 to about 1300. From 1300 until the arrival of the mountain men and government explorers in the early 1800s, the Wasatch was a sparsely populated area between the Shoshone, Ute, and Goshute lands.

The Mormon pioneers arrived in July 1847 and immediately began using the water and timber to build Zion. They also introduced a conservation ethic and publicly controlled the water, timber, and grazing land for the good of the community. Communal ownership was followed by privatization and increased exploitation. The main influences on the mountains during the 1800s were grazing, hunting, lumber cutting, mining, and development of transportation routes.

Grazing had an amplified effect on the mountains because Utah has a very limited supply of upland summer range compared to the greater supply of winter range in the desert. Wildlife was overexploited for meat and fur and to reduce depredation of livestock and crops. The numbers of large mammals were substantially reduced, and some species such as Rocky Mountain bighorn sheep, elk, and grizzly bear ceased to inhabit the area.

Lumbering, which began at the mouth of City Creek, had reached all the way to Tanners Flat in Little Cottonwood Canyon by 1851. About fifty sawmills operated in the canyons adjacent to Salt Lake City at various times, leaving behind names such as Alexander Basin and Mill A Gulch. Mining brought increased demand for large timbers, and the Alta and Brighton areas were denuded. By 1900 the timber near the Wasatch Front had run out, and lumber began to arrive by railroad.

Mining in Utah began in Bingham Canyon in September 1863, and the Wasatch Mining District was organized the next year. The greatest production occurred between 1870 and 1880, followed by a second maximum between 1901 and 1910. Mining claims quickly covered the mineralized parts of the Wasatch, resulting in today's landownership pattern in the canyons. The overlapping claim locations were defined by trees and piles of rock, and today many of the boundaries between private and Forest Service lands are still not surveyed.

Many trails began as wagon roads that were carved up the side canyons to reach mine sites. Some logging roads were also constructed, but most trees were horse-skidded to the mills in winter. A narrow-gauge railroad, with snow sheds across avalanche paths, reached Alta in the early 1870s. Horses pulled the empty ore cars up the tracks, and descent was by gravity, with a brakeman attempting to control the cars. About 1915, passengers were transported up the canyon in a GMC truck mounted on railroad-car wheels, a precursor of today's transit proposals. The decline of mining made the railroad obsolete, and the tracks were removed from Little Cottonwood in 1935.

BEGINNINGS OF PRESERVATION

Throughout the West, the mountains were unable to withstand the grazing, logging, and mining. Concern about hillside erosion and decreasing water quality led to public concern, restrictions on grazing of watersheds, and the beginning of protection for public lands.

As chief grazing officer in the Department of the Interior, Albert E. Potter visited the Wasatch during the summer of 1902 while conducting a personal survey of the condition of forestlands. His diary records the deforestation around Brighton:

"It would be difficult to find a seedling big enough to make a club to kill a snake."
Regarding grazing, he wrote, "The transient herd cutting feed and mountain cover to
ribbons as it rushed the season to beat some other tramp to a bit of grass was a common phenomenon."

The contrasting conservation attitudes that we see today between the urbanized
Wasatch Front and the sparsely populated counties were already evident. Cache Valley
welcomed Potter's survey and requested that a forest preserve be quickly established.
Meanwhile, Beaver County, which had experienced neither a timber shortage nor
watershed damage, was opposed to the entire concept of conservation. At the April
1902 General Conference, the Mormon Church voted to support federal withdrawal of
public lands for watershed protection.

In 1891 Congress provided for forest reserves, and in 1897 a presidential order designated part of the Uinta Mountains as Utah's first reserve. By the end of 1902, four
million acres of additional forest reserves, including much of the Wasatch, had been
established in Utah. In 1905 the forests were transferred from the Interior Department to the new Forest Service within the Agriculture Department.

Bringing herd sizes in line with the summer-range capacity was the Forest Service's initial priority. The 1930s brought new programs, including the Soil Conservation Service and the Civilian Conservation Corps. The terraces constructed on local
peaks to stabilize and revegetate overgrazed slopes and the realigned automobile roads
up the canyons are a result of these programs. The Forest Service eventually became
aware of the recreational potential of the mountains, and by 1935 the agency was pro-
moting ski development at Brighton.

Conservation efforts were changing ownership of the Wasatch Mountains. Salt
Lake City purchased much private land, including numerous sections of railroad land,
for watershed protection. In 1937 George Watson sold eighty mining claims to the Forest Service for one dollar to help create the Alta ski area. In the early 1970s the Forest
Service acquired surface rights to twenty-five hundred acres of patented mining claims
that covered most of the Brighton Basin using two million dollars from the Land and
Water Conservation Fund. After the mid-1970s the acquisition of critical lands slowed
drastically due to political shifts in Washington that dried up funding.

CONTEMPORARY ISSUES

The legacy of these conservation efforts is a mountain resource that provides high-
quality water, hiking, mountaineering, world-class skiing, and three superb wilderness
areas overlooking an urban area. Now, more than a million people live within twenty
miles of the mountain area covered by this book. The exploding population requires
more water, housing, transportation, and recreation. Watershed protection, control of
canyon development, preservation of access to public lands, and wilderness protection
are a few of the issues facing the Wasatch.

WATER AND RECREATION DEVELOPMENT

Since pioneer times watershed protection has been emphasized, and Salt Lake now has excellent drinking water. The economic benefits of a nearby watershed far outweigh timber, grazing, minerals, or even skiing. The stream quality ranges from pristine in Red Butte Canyon, to acceptable in Big and Little Cottonwood Canyons, to irrigation quality in Millcreek, to heavily polluted in Emigration Canyon.

Increased human activity on a watershed often results in lower-quality water. Coliform bacteria count is a measure of direct fouling with human waste. The runoff from roads and parking areas contains salt and oil products. Soil erosion resulting from construction, devegetation, or even trail erosion causes both silt and bacterial contamination of the streams. Pets and domestic animals add to the burden.

Fortunately, human impacts can be mitigated. Healthy ecosystems produce high-quality runoff, as natural processes decompose wastes and riparian zones act as filters for silt and other pollutants. Proper sanitation practices by backcountry users and appropriate technology in developed areas can decrease the contamination resulting from a given level of use. Sewer lines have been installed in Big and Little Cottonwood Canyons, protecting the water, but also facilitating further development.

Early water developments diverted streams after they left the mountains, but dams to capture the runoff and conduits to convey water to the city were soon built farther up the canyons. Today, in-stream flow is a major issue. The lower sections of Big Cottonwood and Little Cottonwood creeks are often dry in late summer because all the water disappears into pipelines. Proposals are still on the drawing board for diverting water from Lambs Canyon and upper Millcreek into the Little Dell Reservoir.

Protecting the riparian habitat in the local canyons while providing water to the city requires balancing objectives. Well-placed small dams reduce the peak runoff and extend it into the summer. Also, depending on local water resources is less costly and damaging than importing water from the Uintas.

ACCESS TO PUBLIC LANDS

Large areas, in both the foothills and in the upper canyons, have historically been reached by routes that cross a strip of private land between the public road and the public land. Changes in landownership, the escalating market value of scenic properties near the national forest, and irresponsible activity by a few users have resulted in more "No Trespassing" signs and fences.

The years since the first edition of this guidebook brought repeated challenges to trail access along the foothills, but they also brought the first signs of real progress. Landowners put up fences and posted signs on traditional access routes to Mount Olympus, Hounds Tooth, Deaf Smith Canyon, and Bells Canyon. New foothill developments have continued the irreversible loss of open space, recreational opportunities, and winter wildlife habitat.

The past two decades have also been a sign of progress. Open space and trailhead access are now issues being considered by municipal governments in their planning process. The Bonneville Shoreline Trail is now complete from Davis County to Emigration Canyon, and a second long section is being constructed through Draper into Sandy. The Bonneville Shoreline Trail is both a wonderful hiking and bike route and an access to many foothill trails. For the future, the community is embracing the vision of the Bonneville Shoreline Trail, and the Forest Service has completed the environmental assessment for extension of the trail from I-80 to Sandy. Some additional sections are likely to be completed in the next five years. There is also a long-range vision of a county-wide network of urban trails and bike paths linking the Jordan River with the mountains.

Salt Lake City, Sandy City, and Draper City have constructed new trailheads that are managed as city parks but offer access to the Bonneville Shoreline Trail and to Forest Service lands. A new trail alignment was constructed from Wasatch Boulevard onto Mount Olympus, resolving a private-owner conflict. Two new trailheads and an access trail have opened Bells Canyon to recreation. The first edition praised the land exchange that resulted in the Forest Service acquiring the south side of lower Little Cottonwood Canyon as a model for future conflict resolution. Cooperation between the Whitmore estate, which had owned the land for many years; the Trust for Public Land, a private conservation organization skilled in negotiating land transfers; Salt Lake City, which provided temporary financing; and the Forest Service, which sold several other parcels to pay for the land, finally preserved these pinnacles and buttresses. Now the Little Cottonwood Creek Trail and Temple Quarry Trail are on the formerly private land.

Since the first edition there have been many other public-private partnerships to acquire key land parcels as public open space. Some of the recent projects include the area around the H-Rock above Foothill Drive, the west side of Grandeur Peak, the Z-trail above Mount Olympus Cove, and the Corner Canyon area in Draper.

Trailhead protection requires strong public support. Hikers must express this support to elected and administrative officials at both the federal (congressional delegation and Forest Service) and the local (Salt Lake and Utah Counties, Salt Lake City, Sandy City, Draper, and Alpine) levels.

Good previous relations between recreational users and adjacent landowners will be an advantage when negotiating trailheads. Parking congestion, noise, litter, and travel off the designated trail are typical conflicts that we should all strive to prevent.

CLIMATE CHANGE

The extent of summer snow cover and the distribution of plants are already changing noticeably due to global climate change. Large areas of dead trees are the result of drought combined with milder winters that allow bark beetles and other insects to survive to attack again the next season. Regardless of year-to-year variations, there will be long-term changes to the local mountains. Legacy CO_2 emissions have altered the planet's solar-energy balance. The driving forces of population growth and fossil fuel energy will continue for the foreseeable future because there is insufficient political will to change. Adaptation to climate change will be a major challenge.

WILDERNESS PROTECTION

Wilderness represents many things: scenic natural vistas, intact ecosystems with abundant wildlife, pure water, and unconfined recreational opportunities; or locked-up resources, a threat to one's livelihood, and a restriction against taking a motorcycle up every hill it can climb. To some, wilderness means any undeveloped land, and to others it means only the most isolated and remote places on earth. With a capital *W* it usually refers to a designated wilderness area, with protection guaranteed by an act of Congress. The Wilderness Act of 1964 created the Federal Wilderness Preservation System and serves as the basis for the subsequent laws that designate specific areas.

A wilderness area was defined as "an area where the earth and its community of life are untrammeled by man, where man himself is a visitor who does not remain." The Wilderness Act further defined wilderness as an area at least five thousand acres in size that has outstanding opportunities for solitude or for primitive and unconfined recreation. The act directed that these areas are to be managed for "the public purposes of recreational, scenic, scientific, educational, conservation, and historical use."

Wilderness areas are protected by prohibiting roads and structures and by restricting motorized transportation to emergencies and similar essential uses. Contrary to popular misconceptions, grazing and hunting are identified as allowable uses of wilderness. Exceptions also exist for water projects, mining claims, oil leases, and private inholdings that predate the wilderness designation.

Wilderness is not an exclusive playground for elite backpackers. Much wilderness is readily accessible to anyone willing to walk. This book includes many hikes into wilderness areas that require less than two hours round-trip.

Wilderness is used by and is valuable to everyone—including persons who never enter a wilderness. First, there is the emotional and intellectual satisfaction of knowing that wild places exist and are preserved for future generations. Wilderness areas are ecological reservoirs where species that are intolerant of human disturbance can thrive. Wilderness users include anyone who looks up from the road and watches a soaring eagle or sees mountain goats perched on a cliff. Actually, everyone along the Wasatch Front who looks up at Lone Peak, Twin Peaks, or Mount Olympus and enjoys the view of unscarred land is a wilderness user.

There is also the global perspective. The health of our planet depends on natural systems, especially the tropical rain forests, for genetic diversity, winter habitat for

Conflict between different groups of recreational users is one of the major issues in the Wasatch.

migratory species, and climate regulation. How can we justly encourage poor, overpopulated nations to preserve their rain forests if we, a rich nation, do not set an example by preserving our own wild places? Wilderness designation is a way of saying that we value preserving the earth more than we value a few more barrels of oil or truckloads of lumber.

UTAH'S WILDERNESS AREAS—NOW AND TOMORROW

After a long battle by local environmentalists, the thirty-thousand-acre Lone Peak Wilderness was included in the Endangered American Wilderness Act of 1977 and became Utah's first wilderness area. An extensive public relations campaign was required to educate the public and local officials about the concept of wilderness and its compatibility with other land uses such as watershed.

Wilderness preservation is a slow process. The Wilderness Act of 1964 required an inventory of all roadless areas on national forest lands and a report to the president on their suitability for designation as wilderness. The inventory process in Utah began in 1971 and climaxed with the Utah Wilderness Act of 1984 that designated twelve Forest Service wilderness areas statewide. The Alexander Basin controversy illustrates how complex wilderness issues can become due to differing priorities and objectives.

Protection for Alexander Basin, on the magnificent north side of Gobblers Knob, was a high priority throughout the inventory and review process. But this area is also coveted by helicopter skiers. To obtain the wilderness designation, many groups and individuals were willing to accept a special clause that would have allowed continued helicopter skiing "subject to Forest Service regulation," believing that any protection was better than none and that the helicopter issue could be resolved later through regulation. Others, concerned about national priorities, feared that this nonconforming use would set a bad precedent for future wilderness legislation. The issue split the local environmental groups when a united effort was needed. The last days of the legislative process were hectic, and the final bill was a compromise that resulted in the peculiar shape of the Mount Olympus Wilderness boundary. The north-facing bowls were excluded, and a few more acres around Dog Lake were added in exchange. Which is more important—protection or precedent?

In the first edition I wrote, "Wilderness battles are not over. There are still roadless forest areas which do not have the protection they deserve." A noted local wilderness advocate disagreed and felt that what we got in 1984 was what we were going to be able to preserve. In April 2010 Congressman Jim Matheson introduced the Wasatch Wilderness and Watershed Protection Act that would expand the existing local Wilderness Areas. The bill was the result of discussions among stakeholders, including environmental organizations, city and county governments, the Salt Lake Public Utilities Department, ski resorts, mountain bikers, private landowners, and transportation officials. The ultimate fate of this renewed protection attempt is still uncertain. In 2013 the fate of the Willow Lake area depends on the ultimate outcome of Matheson's protection bill versus the pro-ski-area idea of SkiLink.

PLANNING AND DEVELOPMENT

The Forest Service responds to numerous influences, including political decisions in Washington, executive actions, technical input from professional staffers, and comments from local agencies and forest users. Citizen input is vital throughout this process.

These influences become codified in laws, in Forest Service regulations, and in management plans. The forest plans allocate lands for various uses (developed recreation, timber harvest, primitive areas, and so on) and set specific management objectives for a ten- to fifteen-year period. The plan for the Salt Lake Ranger District was issued in 1979, and the plan for the entire Wasatch-Cache National Forest was issued in 1984 and most recently revised in 2003. Generally, the plans are sensitive to environmental protection issues and try to balance the competing interests of various users. Continued citizen monitoring and input are needed, as the plan only sets goals and many specific actions, such as the location of an access road or the extent of trail reconstruction, need to be worked out year by year.

The primary responsibility over private lands in the canyon is with the county commission acting through the planning and zoning function. When the county commission candidates were asked, at a 1986 preelection meeting, what their vision was for the canyons in twenty years, each answered that they wanted to see the canyons remain as they were at the time. Achieving this vision has been difficult due to legal, environmental, economic, and social issues, but nearly thirty years later the canyons have survived and prospered. This preservation vision needs to be renewed for the next two decades and beyond.

There are also conflicts between various recreational users. Each expansion request by a ski area raises the question of how to allocate land between developed and dispersed recreation. Snowbird continues to covet the area to the west of its current operation and has proposed more summer amenities like a mountain coaster ride. The owner of the Canyons ski resort has proposed a gondola link over the ridge and down to Solitude. Because nearly all of the gentle terrain in the canyons is already developed, the issue is more than one of relative acreage. Ski development also affects hikers, since ski roads, ski lifts, and ski-run clearing drastically alter the character of an area in summer.

TRAIL CONSTRUCTION

Building trails is hard work. Many of the trails in the Wasatch are remnants of roads cut for mining, logging, or irrigation pipelines prior to establishment of the National Forest. Other old trails are a legacy from the Civilian Conservation Corps, a 1930s-era program that put people unemployed by the Great Depression to work and has greatly benefited the public lands ever since. More recently, trail construction and maintenance have been done by a mix of paid crews and volunteers. Events such as National Trails Day are nice, but volunteers who commit multiple days to a project are the ones who get things done.

Now when trails are constructed there is a lengthy planning and design process. Rights-of-way across private and municipal lands need to be acquired, water companies need to be satisfied that their supply will not be contaminated, environmental assessments are needed on federal land, and for urban foothill trails there are municipal issues, including home-owner concerns, traffic, parking, and law enforcement. Civic-minded volunteers are what make things such as the Bonneville Shoreline Trail and Corner Canyon Regional Park happen. Sitting through Planning Commission meetings is even less fun than working with brush clippers on a hot summer afternoon, but there is a lot of satisfaction in seeing new trails being opened to the public.

Hikers today should be grateful for the legacy of local trails created over the past century. They should also be willing to contribute time, labor, and money to the maintenance and expansion of the trails for the future.

WILD AND NATURAL PLACES TOMORROW

Can wilderness coexist with urban areas? Trampling of vegetation is causing severe erosion on popular trails and at heavily used and developed forest sites. Many do not yet understand the devastation caused by mountain bikes and all-terrain vehicles (ATVs) climbing hills and consider limiting travel to designated routes to be an infringement on their freedom. A new appreciation and ecological consciousness must be developed. Our local challenge of preserving our mountains is truly an experiment in low-impact living on earth that will have to be repeated elsewhere many times if future generations are to appreciate healthy ecosystems and the freedom of natural places.

Public education and involvement are essential if natural areas are to be preserved. If people know the area only from a distance and do not understand it at close range, the protection effort will have no support. Getting people walking the Wasatch trails is one step in building a constituency for preservation. Protection of the mountains requires letters to agencies and to elected officials to reinforce the commitment to preservation. Sensitive ecosystems cannot be saved solely through political action. Much more remains to be done. Concerned individuals can become involved in many ways, ranging from volunteer work on trail-clearing projects to active membership in several local conservation and environmental organizations.

4

Trailhead Directions and
Trail Recommendations

This chapter answers two important questions: where should I hike, and how do I get to the start of the trail? I have tried to include the information I look for when I visit an unfamiliar area and pick up a local guidebook.

This book covers the Wasatch Mountains within Salt Lake County and is generally organized going from north to south and from the mouth of the canyons east to the Wasatch Crest Ridge. Because the county line follows ridge crests but hikes start from roads, this book also includes the most important routes leading into the area of coverage from Davis County to the north and Utah County to the south.

TRAILHEADS

The driving directions to all the trailheads are consolidated here. Organizing trailhead directions this way saves repetition, as multiple trails often start from the same place. It also makes it easier to see the relationship between nearby trailheads. Trails are crowded on popular summer weekends, and parking is an access constraint everywhere except at the closed ski resorts. Whenever possible, meet your friends in town or at the canyon mouth and carpool to the trailhead.

LOCAL ROAD NAVIGATION

Directions to trailheads all start from a nearby highway or major arterial street that can be found on any local road map. All of Salt Lake County uses addresses based on the distance north, south, east, or west from the corner of South Temple and Main Street in downtown Salt Lake City, with addresses incrementing 100 to a block and eight blocks per mile. Street names like "13th East" and "1300 East" mean exactly the same thing, and both refer to a north-south street about 1⅝ miles east of Temple Square. Davis and Utah Counties use the traditional system where each city has its own grid, typically numbered outward from the intersection of Main and Center Streets. The roads up the canyons are described in road logs giving cumulative mileage from a well-defined and obvious landmark near the canyon mouth.

DAVIS COUNTY TRAILHEADS

The foothill trails leading from Davis County toward City Creek are all reached from the foothill arterial road known as Bountiful Boulevard in Bountiful and Eagle Ridge Drive in North Salt Lake. The street is continuous, but the name changes when you cross the city line. Eagle Ridge Drive winds downhill to US 89, and Eaglepointe Drive continues south to two trailheads. From the north, take Exit 317 from I-15 and turn east on 400 North in Bountiful. This will take you past Main Street and up the hill where 400 North feeds into Bountiful Boulevard, which turns south past the temple.

From the south, take Highway 89 to the south end of North Salt Lake and turn east to the traffic circle where Orchard Drive and Eagle Ridge Drive join. Follow Eagle Ridge Drive 1.6 miles up the hill to the intersection with Eaglepointe Drive.

MUELLER PARK

Follow Bountiful Boulevard, described above, or Orchard Drive to 1800 South in Bountiful, turn east, and continue toward the mountains. The eastward extension of 1800 South becomes Mueller Park Road, going 1 mile into the mouth of the canyon.

NORTH CANYON

Follow Bountiful Boulevard, described above, to Canyon Creek Road (approximately 3400 South). Go 0.8 miles and park on the street near the end of the pavement. A dirt road continues up the canyon and provides access for the next half mile through private land.

WILD ROSE TRAILHEAD

Take Bountiful Boulevard to where it becomes Eagle Ridge Drive in North Salt Lake and continue 0.3 miles south on Eaglepointe Drive to Sky Crest Lane. Turn left and go 100 yards to the city park and parking lot.

BONNEVILLE SHORELINE TRAILHEAD

Continue a half mile south from the intersection of Eagle Ridge Drive and Eaglepointe Drive. Look for the trailhead signs near the intersection with Parkway Drive. At the time of field checking, Kern River pipeline construction disturbed the area, but the permanent trailhead will be restored.

SALT LAKE CITY TRAILHEADS BETWEEN
THE STATE CAPITOL AND PARLEYS CANYON

From the intersection of State Street (State Road 186) and North Temple Street in downtown Salt Lake City, head north on State Street to the capitol and turn right onto East Capitol Boulevard. Continue for 1.4 miles and turn left on Ensign Vista Drive, which is just before the gated area at the end of East Capitol.

ENSIGN PEAK TRAILHEAD

Go west 0.25 miles on Ensign Vista Drive to the top of the hill. The trailhead is a tiny park on the north side.

ANTENNAS ROAD

Continue west and then south on Ensign Vista Drive to Dorchester Avenue, turn right, and go to the end of the street. The start of the nonmotorized right-of-way is the sidewalk past the gate.

SALT LAKE CITY TRAILHEADS FROM THE AVENUES

The Avenues Section of Salt Lake City is the area north of South Temple Street between downtown and the university. South Temple is the major collector street between State Street (100 East) in downtown and 13th East near the university. In the Avenues neighborhood, numbered "avenues" run east-west and alphabetical "streets" run north-south. I street and Virginia Street are the main routes uphill.

CITY CREEK CANYON

Bonneville Boulevard is a one-way street that gives access to the Bonneville Shoreline Trail and the road up City Creek Canyon. The only way to get onto Bonneville is from the intersection of B Street and 11th Avenue. Bonneville Boulevard descends the steep walls of City Creek Canyon and makes a hairpin turn at the bridge over the creek. Here the road into City Creek Canyon branches north. Limited parking is at the hairpin bend, and a larger parking area is on the City Creek Road just before the gate. Bonneville Boulevard ends at 500 North on East Capitol Boulevard, which can be used to return to downtown. Pedestrians can reach the mouth of City Creek by walking up through Memory Grove Park from downtown. Trails from the mouth of City Creek Canyon include the Bonneville Shoreline Trail, the canyon road and footpath, and several options to climb to the north ridge of City Creek.

UPPER CITY CREEK (ROTARY PARK)

Hikers can drive up to the trailhead at the end of the City Creek Canyon Road only on holidays and odd-numbered days during the summer period from Memorial Day to the last even day in September. The canyon gate opens at 8:30 a.m. The fee for driving to the trailhead is three dollars, exact change only. Follow the directions above to the mouth of City Creek, pay your fee at the gate, and take the paved road 5.75 miles to a large turnaround at Rotary Park. Access is to the upper canyon, Smugglers Gap, Rudy Flats, and the Great Western Trail.

MORRIS RESERVOIR

From South Temple, ascend I Street to the top where it feeds into North Hills Drive, which bends to the west. Continue curving uphill 0.75 miles to the first street on the left, Hill Top Drive. A trailhead parking area is at the end of this short street.

TERRACE HILLS DRIVE

From South Temple, ascend either I Street or Virginia Street (1250 East) to 11th Avenue. Proceed to 11th Avenue Park (890 East) and turn uphill on Terrace Hills Drive. Go about a mile to the end and park where you will not disturb home owners. Gates mark city trailheads going northeast to the Bonneville Shoreline Trail at the water tank above Morris Reservoir and northwest to the BST below Avenues Twin Peaks.

PERRYS HOLLOW TRAILHEADS

For the west side, follow the directions above to Terrace Hills Drive, go uphill 0.5 miles, turn right on North Bonneville Drive, and continue 0.5 miles to the end. A neighborhood trailhead starts from the short street going north and ascends a steep ridge on constructed steps. For the east side, follow the directions below for Tomahawk Drive, go east to the intersection with Perrys Hollow Drive, turn right, and then turn left at the T. A trailhead gate is at the west end of the spur road. Access is to the Bonneville Shoreline Trail and Avenues Twin Peaks.

TOMAHAWK DRIVE TRAILHEADS

There are three neighborhood trailheads on this street. From South Temple, ascend Virginia Street past Popperton Park and continue north on Chandler Drive, which leads to Tomahawk Drive. Narrow access points between lots are located at about 1400 East Tomahawk Drive and at Limekiln Gulch (about 1550 East). Park on the street and avoid blocking driveways. This street provides access to the Bonneville Shoreline Trail, Avenues Twin Peaks, and the block U and can also be used for hikes into the Dry Creek area.

POPPERTON PARK

This trailhead gives access to the Bonneville Shoreline Trail, Dry Creek, Avenues Twin Peaks, and Little Black Mountain. From South Temple and 13th East, go one block east to Virginia Street, turn north, go past the Shriners Hospital, and turn on Popperton Park Way (360 North). A pedestrian right-of-way leads east from the park through the subdivision to connect with the foothill trails below the block U. It is 0.75 miles to Dry Creek, and a steep connector leads to the end of Tomahawk Drive above.

SALT LAKE CITY TRAILHEADS FROM FOOTHILL DRIVE

Foothill Drive (State Route [SR] 186) is the arterial route between I-80 at Parleys Canyon and 400 South Street through downtown Salt Lake City.

DRY CREEK

The service road into the mouth of Dry Creek was once a popular access point, but is now a marginal access point due to limited parking and extensive hospital construction. Dry Creek is east of the Jewish Community Center and north of the Huntsman Cancer Center, which are both at the upper end of North Campus Drive. From 100 South 1300 East, continue east up the hill and bear left where 100 South becomes North Campus Drive. Parking on the university campus is restricted on workdays. The University Trax line, the buses going to the hospital, and the free campus shuttle are alternatives. The service road to Dry Creek and the Bonneville Shoreline Trail can be reached by walking through the community center parking lot.

MEDICAL CENTER UPPER PARKING LOT

This long parking lot extends from directly south of the Huntsman Cancer Center to Red Butte Garden. From the stoplight on Foothill Drive near the Veterans Medical

Center, take Mario Capecchi Drive into campus and continue past the Trax station to the University Guest House. Turn right on South Medical Drive and follow it uphill as it winds around the buildings to eventually reach the parking lot at the upper edge of campus. Parking on the university campus is restricted on workdays, but there are some pay visitor areas. After 6:00 p.m. and on weekends, parking is free. Several spur trails lead from this parking lot up to the Bonneville Shoreline Trail, which provides access to Dry Creek, Cephalopod Gulch, and Mount Van Cott.

RED BUTTE GARDEN

The Bonneville Shoreline Trail is interrupted by a short stretch of sidewalk as it passes Red Butte Gardens (fee area) at the south end of the medical center parking lots and then resumes again above Colorow Drive in Research Park.

RESEARCH PARK

From Foothill Drive, turn at the stoplight for Wakara Way and go east through Research Park, cross Chipeta Way, and turn south on Colorow Drive just below the Utah Museum of Natural History. Park near the north end of Colorow Drive and look for the signs marking a route up through the oak brush to connect with the Bonneville Shoreline Trail. This trailhead may get redefined after the museum construction is completed, but permanent public access in this area is planned. A spur road about 1,000 feet south branches uphill from Colorow Drive to reach an office building. Another BST access is from the parking lot behind this building. Research Park trailheads provide access to the Bonneville Shoreline Trail, the loop around Red Butte Garden, and the Georges Hollow Trail up Big Beacon.

THIS IS THE PLACE HERITAGE PARK

This gives access to the south route up Big Beacon (F-06) and the southeast end of the Bonneville Shoreline Trail from City Creek Canyon. From Foothill Drive, turn at the stoplight on Sunnyside Avenue and go east one mile. Look for the trailhead parking area on the north side of the street across from Hogle Zoo. A marked trail goes outside the fee-area fence to reach the BST above.

H-ROCK

This gives access to the ridge between Emigration Canyon and Parleys Canyon. There is city-owned access at both ends of the short trail below the H-Rock. For the south access, take 21st South east from Wasatch Boulevard, which curves and becomes Hyland Hill Road. Turn left onto Lakeline Drive, continue past gated Carrigan

Canyon Drive, and park near the end of Lakeline. The north access is at the end of Devonshire Drive.

EMIGRATION CANYON

Emigration Canyon is a patchwork of private, Salt Lake City, and Forest Service lands. The trail system here is still very limited. The road up Emigration Canyon is the extension of Sunnyside Avenue, 850 South, going east from Foothill Drive (State Route 186). The upper end of this road connects with State Route 65 from Interstate 80 to East Canyon.

MOUTH OF EMIGRATION CANYON

See "This Is the Place Heritage Park," above.

EAST SALT LAKE COUNTY

KILLYON CANYON

Drive east for 7 miles from Foothill Drive. Turn left at the fork and go 0.3 miles on the road toward Pinecrest. Turn right at the fork onto Killyon Canyon Road and go another 0.4 miles, going past the end of the pavement and following the narrow lane to the obvious end. Park on the right and avoid blocking driveways.

LITTLE MOUNTAIN SUMMIT

This is access to the ridge route between Emigration Canyon and Parleys Canyon and the trail north toward the saddle between Killyon Canyon and Affleck Park. Drive east for 8.7 miles from Foothill Boulevard to the large parking area on the crest of the ridge where the highway starts down toward Little Dell Reservoir.

PARLEYS CANYON–MOUNTAIN DELL CANYON

Take I-80 to Exit 134 and head north on State Route 65, following signs to Emigration and East Canyons. This road is closed in winter beyond the junction with Emigration Canyon.

ALEXANDER SPRING TRAILHEAD

Go north for 0.4 miles from the off-ramp and look for a small parking area and gate on the right, just past the golf course. A service road heads east.

CLOSED ROADS

Avoid the temptation to explore the roads below Little Dell Reservoir, including the
now-closed old highway alignment leading to the dam and the historic Sheep Trail.
Salt Lake City patrols this area and enforces watershed-protection closures.

EMIGRATION CANYON

For an alternative approach to the head of Emigration Canyon and the Little Mountain
Summit trailhead, go 2.3 miles on SR 65, turn left at the sign for Emigration Canyon,
and continue 1.5 miles to the summit parking area.

LITTLE DELL RESERVOIR

Go 3 miles on SR 65. Turn at the fee-station entrance. Ask to be directed to the free
parking area for trail users. This is the lowest trailhead for the Mormon Pioneer Trail,
which parallels the road.

AFFLECK PARK

Go 3.5 miles on SR 65. Affleck Park is managed as a reservation-only campground, but
is also an access point to the Mormon Pioneer Trail and the trails to Killyon Canyon
and Lookout Peak. There is a small parking area on the left side of the highway, a short
way above the gate to Affleck Park. Park there and walk back to the driveway down
into Affleck Park.

BIG MOUNTAIN PASS

Go north 8.3 miles on SR 65 to the large parking area with restrooms on the right
where the road crosses into East Canyon in Morgan County. This gives access to the
Great Western Trail and the Mormon Pioneer Trail.

PARLEYS CANYON–LAMBS CANYON

Take I-80 to Exit 137 and go south on the narrow paved road. The Lambs Canyon Trailhead is a parking area on the right 1.5 miles from the off-ramp. This is the access to the
Lambs Canyon Trail–Great Western Trail to Millcreek. The canyon road dead-ends in a
private cabin area.

SALT LAKE COUNTY FOOTHILL TRAILHEADS AND MILLCREEK CANYON

This group of trailheads is reached from Wasatch Boulevard, the major road along the foothills south of I-80 and east of I-215.

WASATCH FRONT SOUTH OF PARLEYS CANYON

PARLEYS CANYON, SOUTH

This gives access to the west side of Grandeur Peak and to the foot and bike bridge system that carries the Bonneville Shoreline Trail across the freeways. From I-215, take the 3300 South exit, turn east across the overpass, and then immediately turn north on Wasatch Boulevard. There is a trailhead parking area at the end of this street.

CRESTWOOD DRIVE

Hikers are currently allowed on a private road starting at about 3401 Crestwood Drive and leading up to the water tanks. From the 3300 South exit on I-215, go south on Wasatch Boulevard and turn uphill on Eastwood Drive. Crestwood is the top street in this subdivision. Just south of the tanks, a user-created trail continues up toward the S-shaped rock outcrop high on the southwest ridge off Grandeur Peak.

MILLCREEK CANYON (SEE ROAD LOG)

From I-215, take the 3900 South exit and go east to Wasatch Boulevard, which is the frontage road between the 3300 South and 4500 South exits. Turn north at the stop-light and then turn east at the next stoplight at 3800 South Wasatch Boulevard. The road into Millcreek Canyon is straight ahead, and at the four-way stop sign the right turn leads to the Neffs Trailhead. The road-log mileages start from the intersection of 3800 South and Wasatch Boulevard.

NEFFS CANYON

This is the access to the northwest portion of the Mount Olympus Wilderness. Follow the directions for Millcreek Canyon above. Turn right onto Parkview Drive (3700 East) at the four-way stop sign 0.3 miles from Wasatch Boulevard. Follow Parkview Drive around a left and then a right bend, heading generally southeast until it meets

Parkview Terrace (4175 East 4245 South). Turn left on Parkview Terrace; the second
street on the right leads to White Park, where there is a trailhead parking lot.

Z-ROAD (THOUSAND OAKS DRIVE)

From the 3900 South exit from I-215, go straight at the stoplight on Wasatch Boulevard and take Jupiter Drive southeast for 1.1 miles, turn left on Adonis Drive, and
then take the first right onto Thousand Oaks Drive. The trail starts as a set of steep
steps up the hill and quickly joins the Z-road, a historic mining road that leads up into
the one of the couloirs on the north side of Mount Olympus. This access connects with
the Bonneville Shoreline Trail section between Neffs Canyon and the Mount Olympus
trail. This is a neighborhood trailhead, so park respectfully.

MOUNT OLYMPUS

A trailhead sign is on Wasatch Boulevard at about 5700 South, and the parking area
is above the road. From the 4500 South exit from I-215, go east to Wasatch Boulevard
and head south for 1.5 miles. Alternatively, from I-215 take Exit 6 and follow the signs
for 6200 South, Wasatch Boulevard, and the ski areas. At the top of the hill, there is a
stop sign where a left turn puts you on Wasatch Boulevard going north, and straight
ahead leads to the mouth of Big Cottonwood Canyon. Turn left and go about a mile to
the Mount Olympus Trailhead on Wasatch Boulevard.

HUGHES CANYON

This trailhead is in the Canyon Cove subdivision above Wasatch Boulevard 1 mile
south of the Mount Olympus Trailhead. Turn east onto Canyon Cove Drive, continue
0.1 mile, and turn north onto Oak Canyon Drive. The public right-of-way is near the
intersection of Oak Canyon Drive and Berghalde Lane. Park on Oak Canyon Drive.

BIG COTTONWOOD CANYON, COTTONWOOD HEIGHTS, AND SANDY FOOTHILL TRAILHEADS

All these trails are reached from Wasatch Boulevard, south of I-215. From I-215, take
Exit 6 and follow the signs for Wasatch Boulevard and the ski areas. In 0.7 mile at
the top of the hill, there is a stoplight where continuing straight ahead leads south
to the junction of Wasatch Boulevard (State Route 190) and Fort Union Boulevard
(7000 South). Here the Big Cottonwood Canyon Road heads east into the canyon, and
Wasatch Boulevard (State Route 210) continues south. At a stoplight 2.2 miles south
of the mouth of Big Cottonwood Canyon, there is a stoplight and Y intersection where
Wasatch Boulevard heads right and the road to Little Cottonwood Canyon goes left.

BIG COTTONWOOD CANYON (SEE ROAD LOG)

The canyon road-log table starts from the stoplight at the intersection of Fort Union Boulevard and Wasatch Boulevard. A recreation and commuter parking area is located on the northeast corner of this intersection. Additional carpool parking is available along the north side of Fort Union Boulevard.

FERGUSON CANYON

From the stoplight at the mouth of Big Cottonwood Canyon, head south on Wasatch Boulevard 0.3 miles, turn left onto a short street connecting with Prospector Drive (3835 East), turn right and go south 0.3 miles to the intersection with Timberline Drive, where you turn left. The trailhead parking is 0.1 miles up Timberline Drive, where a service road heads up the hill.

LITTLE COTTONWOOD CANYON (SEE ROAD LOG)

Continue south 2.2 miles from the stoplight at the mouth of Big Cottonwood Canyon and take the left branch at the stoplight, where the road divides. Continue another 1.6 miles along North Little Cottonwood Road (State Route 210) to the mouth of Little Cottonwood Canyon, where there is a Y intersection with Little Cottonwood Road (State Route 209), which is the extension of 9400 South through Sandy. The road up the canyons continues east from the Y intersection, and the road-log table for Little Cottonwood starts at the electric road sign.

TEMPLE QUARRY

A marked spur road branches from Little Cottonwood Road (State Route 209) 100 feet west of the Y intersection at the mouth of Little Cottonwood Canyon and leads to the parking area. This is also access for the lower end of the Little Cottonwood Creek trail.

WASATCH BOULEVARD, SOUTH OF LITTLE COTTONWOOD CANYON ROAD

From I-215, take Exit 6, follow the signs for Wasatch Boulevard and the ski areas, continue south on Wasatch Boulevard, and go straight at the stoplight at the mouth of Big Cottonwood Canyon. At a stoplight 4 miles south of the I-215 exit and 2.2 miles south of Big Cottonwood Canyon, there is a Y intersection where Wasatch Boulevard heads right and the left branch follows the foothills into Little Cottonwood Canyon. Continue another 1.1 miles to the stoplight where Wasatch crosses Little Cottonwood Road (State Route 209). Little Cottonwood Road is also the continuation of 9000 South, 9400 South, the major route that crosses through Sandy City from Exit 295 on I-15.

GRANITE TRAILHEAD, BELLS CANYON

From the intersection of Wasatch Boulevard and Little Cottonwood Road, turn right. The Granite Trailhead for Bells Canyon is 0.1 miles east on the south side of the bend in the road. If you continue east, you will come to the Y intersection at the mouth of Little Cottonwood Canyon and the Temple Quarry Trailhead.

BOULDERS TRAILHEAD, BELLS CANYON

From the intersection of Wasatch Boulevard and Little Cottonwood Road, continue south 0.7 miles to the parking area on the east side of Wasatch Boulevard at about 10245 South.

ROCKY MOUTH CANYON

From the intersection of Wasatch Boulevard and Little Cottonwood Road, continue 2.1 miles to a small parking area on the east of Wasatch Boulevard at 11300 South. A footpath leads up to Eagle View Drive, but trail-access parking is prohibited on this residential street. Walk south along Eagle View Drive to the bend in the road. The trail starts at a marked gate located between two residential lots.

HIDDEN VALLEY TRAILHEAD

From the intersection of Wasatch Boulevard and Little Cottonwood Road, continue 3.1 miles to Hidden Valley Park at about 11600 South. The park is immediately south of the Latter-day Saints (LDS) Temple. The Hidden Valley Trailhead provides access to the Bonneville Shoreline Trail going south to Draper, the mouth of Little Willow Canyon, and the Sawmill Trail up the west side of Lone Peak.

Beyond the Hidden Valley Trailhead in Sandy, it is necessary to detour west to 1300 East if you want to continue farther south into Draper.

DRAPER FOOTHILL TRAILHEADS

These Draper trailheads are all reached from Highland Drive, the main foothill road in the southeast part of the valley. Highland Drive in Draper does not yet connect with Highland Drive to the north in Sandy. Two routes to Highland Drive in Draper will be described.

From the north, take Exit 291, 12300 South, from I-15 and go 1.8 miles east to the major intersection at 1300 East. Turn south, go down the hill to the traffic circle, and exit the circle going east onto Pioneer Road. Follow Pioneer Road 1.1 miles to the intersection with the north end of Highland Drive at 2000 East. From the west or south, take the Bangerter Highway exit from I-15, turn east, and follow the main road going uphill to reach the stoplight at the intersection with Highland Drive where Bangerter Highway ends and Traverse Ridge Road continues straight ahead.

ORSON SMITH TRAILHEAD

The trailhead parking area is at 12600 South on Highland Drive in Draper. This is 0.8 miles south of the Pioneer Road intersection and 3.4 miles north of the Bangerter Highway intersection. The Orson Smith Trailhead gives access to the Bonneville Shoreline Trail and the routes up Lone Peak.

CORNER CANYON ROAD

This unpaved road gives vehicle access to the Jacobs Ladder route up Lone Peak and several of the Corner Canyon Regional Park trails. The road starts at the gate on the south side of the Orson Smith Trailhead. The road is rough but generally okay for two-wheel-drive vehicles that have reasonable clearance. The Corner Canyon Road is closed seasonally.

GHOST FALLS TRAILHEAD (JACOBS LADDER)

Drive 2.6 miles up the Corner Canyon Road from the Orson Smith Trailhead. The parking area serves both the Ghost Falls Trail going down hill and the Jacobs Ladder Trail to Lone Peak. The Jacobs Ladder Trail is across the road, 200 feet south of the parking area.

COYOTE HOLLOW COURT (DRAPER TEMPLE)

From the intersection with Highland Drive and Bangerter Highway, go straight ahead onto Traverse Ridge Road and continue for 1.3 miles. Turn on Mike Weir Drive, and go another 1.3 miles to Pinyon Hills Lane, a short divided street leading straight into the LDS Temple parking. Immediately, 100 feet ahead, turn left (south) for one block and then turn right on Grey Fox Drive. Follow Grey Fox around the corner, and turn left on Coyote Hollow Court. A small trailhead parking area is located on the circle at the end of this short street. Draper has posted small brown signs with arrows to the trailhead.

CORNER CANYON REGIONAL PARK

This section describes multiple urban trails and trailheads. A major urban trailhead is the access to the Lower Corner Canyon Road from Andy Ballard Equestrian Center, 2.5 miles northeast on Highland Drive from the stoplight at the end of Bangerter Highway. Trailheads have excellent signboards and usually a supply of small trail maps. The Draper trail system is still under development. See the Draper City website for recent additions.

CANYON ROAD LOGS

MILLCREEK CANYON TRAILHEADS (FEE AREA)

The road into Millcreek Canyon starts at 3800 South on Wasatch Boulevard. This is between the 3300 South and 3900 South exits from I-215 and a block north of the Olympus Hills Shopping Center. A good carpool meeting point is the Park-and-Ride lot just north of 3900 South on Wasatch Boulevard. All mileages to Millcreek trailheads are measured from the stoplight on Wasatch Boulevard. The road is narrow, especially the upper portion beyond Elbow Fork. During the winter the Millcreek road is plowed only as far as the Terrace Picnic Area. Currently, the fee is three dollars per vehicle or forty dollars for an annual pass, and bicycles are free.

Miles	Elevation	
0.0	4,960	Wasatch Boulevard and 3800 South
0.3		Parkview Drive, street to Neffs Trailhead
0.7		Fee station
1.4		Wasatch National Forest boundary
1.6	5,320	Rattlesnake Gulch Trailhead
3.2	5,680	Church Fork Trailhead (Grandeur Peak)
3.4	5,720	Desolation Trailhead (Desolation and Thayne)
4.1		Log Haven Inn
4.4	5,956	Porter Fork
4.5	6,020	Lower end of Burch Hollow Trail (Pipeline Trail)
4.7	6,200	Terrace Picnic Area (Bowman Fork and Terrace to Elbow Fork)
4.8		Accessible fishing platform and boardwalk
4.9		Parking area and gate; road is closed above here until mid-June
6.4	6,547	Elbow Fork (Mount Aire, Lambs Canyon pass, Pipeline Trail)
7.8	7,080	Alexander Basin Trailhead
9.2	7,500	Wilson Fork
9.5	7,600	Big Water Trail (lower trailhead) and Soldier Fork
9.6	7,640	End of Millcreek road, large parking lot; access to Big Water Trail, Little Water, and Upper Millcreek

BIG COTTONWOOD CANYON TRAILHEADS

The road into Big Cottonwood Canyon starts at the stoplight on Wasatch Boulevard at 7400 South (Fort Union Boulevard). The large parking lot and bus staging area on the northeast corner is a popular meeting point. Big Cottonwood mileages are measured from the stoplight at the intersection.

Miles	Elevation	
0.0	4,960	Intersection stoplight
2.9	5,800	Storm Mountain picnic area (Stairs Gulch)
3.2		Mule Hollow Trail
4.5	6,200	S turn (Mill B North Fork, Lake Blanche, and Broads Fork)
6.1	6,709	Mineral Fork
7.1	6,960	Mill A Gulch (no cleared trail)
8.5	7,080	Butler Fork
9.3	7,268	Cardiff Fork Road Turnoff; new Mill D North Trailhead
9.9	7,320	Mill D North Fork old trailhead
10.1	7,360	Spruces campground and Days Fork Trail
11.3	7,560	Beartrap Fork Trail
12.2	7,850	Willow Creek
12.7	8,120	Solitude lower lot (Silver Fork and Honeycomb Fork Trails)
13.1	8,200	Solitude Ski Area upper lot
13.4	8,300	Redman campground
14.3	8,600	Guardsman Pass Road turnoff
14.7	8,730	Start of Brighton one-way loop
14.8		Silver Lake Trailhead
15.1	8,760	Brighton Ski Area parking lot

LITTLE COTTONWOOD CANYON TRAILHEADS

The road into Little Cottonwood Canyon is reached either by driving south from the mouth of Big Cottonwood Canyon (State Route 210) or by driving east on 9400 South, Little Cottonwood Canyon Road (State Route 209). All mileages to Little Cottonwood trailheads are measured from the electric road-condition sign at the Y junction at the mouth of the canyon.

Miles	Elevation	
0.0		Entrance to Temple Quarry parking area
0.0	5,400	Start, electric road sign
0.2		Forest Service boundary sign
1.3		Gate Buttress rock-climbing area
1.9	6,040	Hydro power station (Coalpit Gulch area)
2.9	6,400	Lisa Falls
4.4	7,200	Tanners Gulch, Tanners Flat campground

Miles	Elevation	
6.0	7,700	White Pine Trailhead (also access to Red Pine, Maybird Gulch, Hogum Fork, and beyond)
6.4	7,850	Snowbird lower parking lot
6.6	8,040	Snowbird upper parking entrance; Snowbird tram
7.1	8,300	Bypass road lower end
7.7		Town of Alta boundary
7.9	8,460	Bypass road upper end
8.1	8,560	Alta Ski Area main parking lot
8.3	8,650	Alta town office (Cardiff Pass, Mount Superior, Grizzly Gulch road)
8.7	8,800	End of paved road, Albion information booth (direct access to Grizzly Gulch, Albion Meadows Trail)
9.2	8,920	Gate on right to ski-area service road (walking route to Albion Basin)
11.2	9,400	Side road on left, start of Catherine Pass Trail
11.3		Albion Basin campground (Catherine Pass, Secret Lake, Devils Castle, Sugarloaf)

UTAH COUNTY TRAILHEADS

DRY CREEK–ALPINE TRAILHEAD

From Interstate 15, take the Alpine exit, Utah 92 East, 5.5 miles, then turn north on Utah 74, continue to a traffic circle, and exit the circle onto Main Street in the town of Alpine. To reach the trailheads, you need to get onto Grove Street. One way is to drive to the four-way stop at 2nd North and Main in Alpine, turn right, go to 2nd East, and turn north onto Grove Drive, which curves northeast. Alternatively, stay on Main Street until it becomes Heritage Hills Drive, which winds around to join Grove Street. This area has become urbanized since the first edition. Back in 1987 the pavement ended just beyond the sharp turn on Grove Street.

Miles	Elevation	
0.0	4,957	Intersection of Main Street and 2nd North in Alpine; turn right at stop sign
0.1		Turn left onto 200 East, which becomes Grove Street
1.2		Heritage Hills Drive joins Grove Street
1.6	5,200	Sharp right turn
1.7	5,240	Alpine Cove Drive to Schoolhouse Springs Trailhead

Miles	Elevation	
TO SCHOOLHOUSE SPRINGS TRAILHEAD		
1.7		Turn left on Aspen Cove Drive
2.0		Turn left on Aspen Drive
2.1		Gravel road on right is Schoolhouse Spring Trailhead; park near pavement or continue on rough road to park near water tank
2.4		Water tank and gate; foot trail continues
CONTINUING EAST ON GROVE STREET		
1.7		Continue east
2.0	5,340	Grove Drive jogs right, crosses a bridge, immediately turns left, and continues past the Rodeo Grounds
2.1		Box Elder Drive ahead leads to trailheads in Lambert Park
2.6	5,420	Dry Creek Trailhead

AMERICAN FORK CANYON TRAILHEADS (FEE AREA)

American Fork Canyon, in Utah County, is reached by State Highway 92. Coming from the Salt Lake Valley, take Interstate 15 south across the Traverse Mountains and take the first exit in Utah County, which is marked with signs for Alpine and Timpanogos Cave. Turn east and follow Utah 92 for 7 miles directly to the mouth of the canyon. Highway 146 from Pleasant Grove approaches American Fork Canyon from the south. The fee is currently six dollars for a three-day pass.

Miles	Elevation	
0.0	5,044	Mouth of canyon, junction of Utah 146 and Utah 92
0.1		Uinta National Forest boundary sign
2.7	5,600	Timpanogos Cave visitor center
5.2	6,073	North Fork Road (Utah 144) branches left
LOG CONTINUES UP NORTH FORK		
7.4	6,360	Tibble Reservoir; fork to Granite Flat Campground and Silver Lake Flat
8.3	6,720	Granite Flat campground; Silver Lake Flat road branches right
8.4	6,760	Deer Creek Trailhead in campground
8.5		Box Elder Trailhead in campground

Miles	Elevation	
LOG OF SILVER LAKE FLAT ROAD		
8.3	6,720	Begin dirt road to Silver Lake Flat
9.0	7,000	Upper access to Deer Creek Trail
10.8	7,440	Summer-home area
11.2	7,520	Silver Lake Flat Reservoir
11.8	7,550	Silver Lake Trailhead and upper parking area; four-wheel-drive road fords stream and continues northeast

TRAIL RECOMMENDATIONS

When I visit an unfamiliar mountain range, I buy the maps and guidebooks and start thumbing through descriptions of challenging trails and interesting destinations. But choosing is difficult. There are many routes and so little time. Worse, the descriptions are confusing to someone who is unfamiliar with the area and who must sift through the entire book looking for routes appropriate for the time available and desired level of difficulty. When I listen to hikers talking to a ranger at a visitor center, the second question always seems to be, "What do you recommend?"

This chapter sorts through the descriptions and recommends hikes by length, level of difficulty, and the best season. For beginning hikers and newcomers to the area, there are trails for the first few hikes. For those who are busy, there are many worthwhile hikes that require three hours or less round-trip from the car. Experienced hikers will find new areas to explore, including rarely visited summits and interesting bushwhacks.

SHORT HIKES AND EASY HIKES

BEGINNER HIKES

All of these hikes are relatively short and ascend gradually on a maintained trail. The trails are well marked and easy to follow.

Beginner Hikes	Trail
Bonneville Shoreline Trail–Avenues section, multiple options	F-01
Desolation Trail to the Salt Lake Overlook	M-04
Church Fork and Pipeline	M-01 and M-02
Stairs Gulch	B-01

Beginner Hikes	Trail
Lake Mary or Dog Lake from Brighton	B-24
Twin Lakes from Brighton	B-22
White Pine Trail to the canyon overlook	L-05
Secret Lake from Albion Basin	L-13

POPULAR EASY HIKES

These trails are easy but are not necessarily as well maintained as the beginner hikes.

Popular Hikes	Trail
Elbow Fork to Terraces Picnic Area	M-11
Big Water Trail to Mill D Pass and Dog Lake	M-16
Lake Solitude	B-21
Catherine Pass from Albion	L-14
Willow Lake	B-16
Mill B North to Overlook	B-05

FAMILY HIKES

The hikes marked "Family" are easy, have interesting features along the way, have no cliffs or dangerous stream crossings, and are recommended for families hiking with small children. Of course, any adults who are hiking with children should be sufficiently experienced to recognize hazards and to evaluate trail and weather conditions.

Family Hikes		Trail
City Creek Canyon Road		
Lower Bells Reservoir		WF-6
Temple Quarry Trail	Very short	
Rocky Mouth Canyon	Very short	WF-7
Silver Lake loop at Brighton	Level	B-20
Lambs Canyon from Elbow Fork		M-10
Lake Mary or Dog Lake from Brighton		B-24
Twin Lakes from Silver Lake		B-22
Secret Lake from Albion Basin		L-13

♿ ACCESSIBLE DESTINATIONS

Everyone can enjoy the mountains. Here are some ADA-accessible places you can go if you have an elderly relative, a friend recovering from an injury, children in a stroller, or any other special needs. These are obviously worthwhile destinations for anyone.

Canyon	Trail Name	Location
Millcreek Canyon	Fishing platform and boardwalk	Just past Terraces Picnic Area
Big Cottonwood Canyon	Mill D South Interpretive Trail	S-turn trailhead
Big Cottonwood Canyon	Silver Lake boardwalk	Brighton area
Little Cottonwood Canyon	Temple Quarry Trail	Canyon mouth
Little Cottonwood Canyon	Barrier-Free Trail	Snowbird base area

NO ROUTE-FINDING PROBLEMS

Trail maintenance has improved in recent years, but some Wasatch trails are still full of false branches and overgrown sections where the trail nearly disappears. If you want a longer hike than the beginner trails but prefer trails that are easy to follow, try these roads. Vehicles are restricted, so walking is pleasant.

Hike	Trail
Lower City Creek (road along stream)	CC-2
Mineral Fork (abandoned mining road)	B-06
White Pine Trail to lake (dam-access road)	L-05
Collins Gulch to Germania Pass (ski-area road)	L-11

SHORT HIKES—REQUIRING LESS THAN THREE HOURS

One of the greatest benefits of living in Salt Lake is the wealth of readily accessible short hikes. You can go hiking after work on summer afternoons, or you can go hiking on a Saturday morning and be home before lunch. All the routes listed here are short enough that an average hiker can do the round-trip in one to three hours. Many of these short hikes follow a longer trail only as far as a meadow, an overlook, or another feature that makes a logical destination. There are enough suggestions for one hike per week from May through September. Hiking distances are in fractions throughout, as a decimal such as 1.75 conveys false precision.

Short Hikes	Miles Round-Trip	Feet Elevation Gain	Standard Time Round-Trip	Trail
FOOTHILLS				
City Creek, North Rim	2	500	1h 25m	CC-1
Mount Van Cott	2	1,148	1h 50m	F-04
Avenues Twin Peaks	1 to 2	1,100	1h 55m	F-01
Olympus to Tolcat stream crossing	3	1,100	2h 20m	WF-2
MILLCREEK				
Elbow Fork to Terraces (one-way)	1¾	−430	1h	M-11
Pipeline Trail (one-way)	2	630	1h 20m	M-07
Church Fork to start of switchbacks	2	880	1h 40m	M-01
Elbow Fork to Mount Aire Pass	2	1,170	1h 50m	M-09
Bowman Trail to White Fir Pass	3	1,240	2h 30m	M-06
Elbow Fork to Lambs Pass	3	1,490	2h 40m	M-10
Alexander Basin	3	1,640	2h 50m	M-12
Desolation to Salt Lake overlook	4	1,300	2h 50m	M-04
BIG COTTONWOOD				
Storm Mountain–Stairs Gulch	½	300	30m	B-01
Mineral Fork to canyon overlook	1½	450	1h 5m	B-06
Brighton to Lake Mary	2	760	1h 35m	B-24
Lake Solitude from Brighton	3	300	1h 45m	B-21
Mill B North to overlook	2¼	840	1h 45m	B-05
Twin Lakes Dam	2½	710	1h 50m	B-22
Mill D Dog Lake	3	1,010	2h 20m	B-09
Broads Fork to bridge	1¼	1,300	2h 20m	B-03
Greens Basin	3¼	1,050	2h 30m	B-14
Mule Hollow to mine	2¾	1,400	2h 30m	B-02
Lake Blanche Trail to meadow	3	1,600	2h 45m	B-04
Lake Catherine	4	1,200	2h 55m	B-24
Circle-All Peak	3½	1,587	3h	B-08
LITTLE COTTONWOOD				
Secret Lake from Albion	1½	420	1h 5m	L-13
White Pine to Overlook	2½	500	1h 40m	L-05
Red Pine to Overlook	3	500	1h 55m	L-01
Cardiff Pass from Alta	2	1,360	2h 5m	L-08

"EASY" SUMMITS

Reaching a summit is always a satisfying accomplishment, and the panorama makes the effort worthwhile. Easy is relative, and all summits require significant uphill hiking. The following are summits with well-defined trails all the way.

Summit	Trail	
Circle-All Peak	B-08.1	Just off the Butler Fork Trail
Mount Aire	M-09	Trail all the way
Grandeur Peak	M-01	Trail all the way
Clayton Peak	B-25	Trail all the way
Reynolds Peak	B-09.1	Short bushwhack up from Dog Lake
Sunset Peak	L-14.1	Easy from Catherine Pass
Mount Olympus	WF-2	Last 600 feet steep but well marked; some use of hands

HIKING WITHOUT A CAR

There are a few hikes that can be reasonably reached from the Utah Transit Authority routes. The UTA schedule can be obtained by calling 287-4636 (BUS-INFO) or at www.rideuta.com.

You can walk to City Creek Canyon directly from downtown Salt Lake City. It is a pleasant 1½ miles from Temple Square to the canyon road by walking the pathways along the stream up through Memory Grove Park.

The University Trax line or the no. 6 or no. 11 bus to the university hospital is actually the most convenient way to reach the Bonneville Shoreline Trail near Dry Creek on workdays. In addition, all of the Avenues-area foothill hikes are located within a mile or less of the no. 11 bus route. The no. 3 bus goes to This Is the Place Heritage Park, where there is access to the Bonneville Shoreline Trail and Big Beacon. Bus routes serve the 3900 South Park-and-Ride near Millcreek Canyon and the 6200 South Park-and-Ride near the Mount Olympus Trail. Buses run up the canyons only during the ski season, but there are frequent proposals for summer service to reduce canyon congestion. In addition, drivers in the canyons are usually willing to pick up hitchhikers, especially if you look like a serious hiker.

A HIKE FOR EVERY SEASON

The hiking season follows the retreating snow line up the mountain. The low, sunny foothills are snow free as early as March, while the ski season is still at its peak. By May the lower portions of the south-facing canyon trails are often wet and still have occasional patches of snow, but they are generally passable. June opens up many more trails and is also the best month for alpine hiking on consolidated summer snow. Nearly all trails are snow free by July, but snow lasts all summer in sheltered areas above about 10,500 feet. The high trails remain usable until the first heavy snowfall, which ushers in another ski season.

The limits of the receding snowpack vary with elevation and with the direction that the slope faces. The maps give a general idea of the snow conditions during the spring and early summer. The maps were based on typical conditions in the mid-1980s and can serve as an empirical indicator of climate change. Summer snow cover now is noticeably less that it was when the first edition was written.

EARLY- AND LATE-SEASON HIKES

March–April and November–December are the transitions between the hiking and ski and snowshoe seasons. These lower-elevation and south-facing trails stay snow free late into the fall and are the first to dry out in spring.

Bonneville Shoreline Trail–Avenues	Big Beacon from the south
Bonneville Shoreline Trail–Draper	Avenues Twin Peak
Ensign Peak	Grandeur from the West
Lower City Creek Canyon	Mount Olympus to the stream

EARLY-SUMMER HIKES

These mountain trails are generally snow free by late May or early June, but you may encounter small patches of snow, especially in shady locations at higher elevations.

Grandeur Peak	Elbow Fork
Ridge between Emigration and Parleys	Mill B North Fork
Mount Olympus	Lone Peak to the Cirque
Ferguson Canyon	Mule Hollow

EARLY-SUMMER SNOW HIKES

In June the higher basins develop consolidated summer snow, as the daily freeze-and-thaw cycle causes the snow to settle and recrystallize. In the morning you have firm, almost icy snow, allowing a steady ascent, and by afternoon the snow has softened, allowing rapid descent by plunge stepping or by glissading. Many areas are most easily visited at this time of year because the snow covers the loose rock and boulders that make summer travel exhausting.

Summer snow is not for the inexperienced. Anyone venturing onto the snow-covered cirque headwalls and ridges should be carrying an ice ax and should know

SNOW COVER BY MONTH

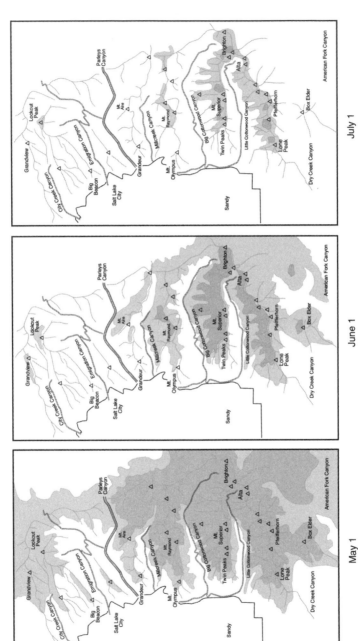

May 1

June 1

July 1

Snow Patches in Sheltered Areas

Continuous Snow Cover

how to use it. Also, some of the steeper areas are susceptible to afternoon avalanches. A basic mountaineering course is the best way to learn how to deal with these conditions.

The summer snow routes in the Wasatch are first-class alpine adventures, and the conditions are as exciting and as beautiful as climbs in the Tetons, in the Wind River Range, or in the Pacific Northwest. The finest snow routes are the following:

Pfeifferhorn	Beatout Hike (Red Pine to Bells)
Tanners Gulch–Triple Traverse	Hogum Cirque
Mount Superior from Lake Blanche	Broads Fork Twin Peaks

MIDSUMMER HIKES

In July and August you need to start early in the day and go high to avoid the worst heat. Shady north-facing trails with lakes and streams take advantage of cooler microclimates.

Alexander Basin	Maybird Lakes
Little Water to Dog Lake	Lake Blanche
Lake Solitude from Brighton	Broads Fork to Meadow

FALL AND EARLY-WINTER HIKES

Fall hiking offers the widest opportunities of the year, as all trails and routes are snow free and the cooler weather makes long, strenuous hikes more pleasant than in midsummer. The changing leaves make September and early October an especially nice time to be in the mountains. The best hiking area to see the fall foliage is along the Desolation Trail east of Gobblers Knob. By November or December hiking is again limited to the foothill and low south-facing trails.

LEGAL FOR DOGS

The Salt Lake City Watershed Department recommends the following as places to take your dogs. Please clean up—and take the bag with you. Seeing little bags along the trail that have been there for several days is not pleasant.

Bonneville Shoreline Trail—Davis to Emigration	Jordan River Parkway
City Creek Canyon below the water plant	Ferguson Canyon
Millcreek Canyon (fee area)	Park City Rail Trail
Mount Olympus Trail	American Fork Canyon (fee area)

Additional areas open to dogs include:

Bonneville Shoreline Trail south of Orson   Corner Canyon Regional Park—
    Smith Trailhead   except Ghost Falls area
Killyon Canyon west of Birch Springs Pass   Stansbury Range, Tooele County
National forest lands in Davis County   Uintas, Mirror Lake Highway

SUGGESTIONS FOR EXPERIENCED HIKERS

An unavoidable impact of a guidebook is increased use of the areas described. To help mitigate this concentrated impact, start doing a little exploring once you have gained experience with the popular trails in the Wasatch.

LITTLE-USED TRAILS THAT DESERVE MORE ATTENTION

The first edition referred to "constructed trails that have one hiking group on a summer weekend" and noted that "unofficial trails are disappearing into the undergrowth due to lack of foot traffic," but all the trails that I listed back then as needing more attention are now well used. Times change.

GO FARTHER AND HIGHER

The old "Yosemite Rule" states that the number of hikers declines with the square of the distance from the road and the cube of the distance above it. Many trails in the Wasatch share this hiker-distribution pattern. The first few miles are well used, but the higher reaches are seldom visited. If you want some solitude, then push all the way to the top of the trail and maybe beyond to the ridgeline. I rarely hike the exact trails in this book. Even after forty years in the Wasatch, I can still find new places within the area of this book that I have never hiked. The flurry of recent trail construction above Draper now creates new opportunities each season. Other first-time hikes for me involve off-trail hiking on the descent from a standard trail or bushwhacks to trailless, and often nameless, minor destinations. There is a lifetime of hiking in the Wasatch if you are willing to explore and have a sense of adventure. And, of course, there are marvelous hiking opportunities throughout the mountains and deserts of Utah.

HIGHEST SUMMITS IN SALT LAKE COUNTY

"Peak baggers" are hikers and climbers who set a goal of climbing most or all of some defined group of summits, be it all the peaks over 4,000 feet in New Hampshire or the highest summits on the seven continents. Peak-bagging gives an incentive to visit places that you might never otherwise consider.

Thirty-two summits in Salt Lake County are over 10,000 feet. For this list a point is considered a distinct summit if it is at least 200 feet above the saddle connecting it to the next peak on a ridge. Neither Sundial nor Flagstaff is included, as they are connected by continuous ridges to higher summits.

Highest Points in Salt Lake County	Elevation
1. American Fork Twins (West Summit)	11,489
2. Broads Fork Twins (East Summit)	11,330
3. Pfeifferhorn	11,326
4. White Baldy (between White Pine and Red Pine)	11,321
5. Sunrise (¼ mile west of Dromedary)	11,275
6. Lone Peak	11,253
7. Red Baldy (1 mile southwest of American Fork Twins)	11,171
8. South Thunder Mountain	11,154
9. North Thunder Mountain	11,150
10. Monte Cristo	11,132
11. Dromedary	11,107
12. Mount Baldy	11,068
13. Sugarloaf	11,051
14. Unnamed (½ mile east of Dromedary)	10,910
15. Upper Bells Peak/Bighorn Peak (½ mile east of Lone Peak)	10,877
16. Mount Wolverine	10,795
17. Clayton Peak	10,721
18. Sunset Peak	10,678
19. Unnamed (Reed and Benson Ridge north of Flagstaff)	10,561
20. Hogum Divide (¼ mile west of Maybird Lakes)	10,516
21. Bells Cleaver (northeast of Upper Bells Reservoir)	10,488
22. Honeycomb Cliffs	10,479
23. Pioneer Peak	10,440
24. Unnamed (between Clayton Peak and Guardsman Pass)	10,420
25. Kessler Peak	10,403
26. Unnamed (between Pioneer Peak and Snake Creek Pass)	10,316
27. Rocky Mouth Canyon Peak	10,292
28. Gobblers Knob	10,246
29. Mount Raymond	10,241
30. Scott Hill	10,116
31. Guardsman Peak (¼ mile north of Guardsman Pass)	10,026
32. Silver Peak (Wasatch Crest above Beartrap Fork)	10,006

CHALLENGES FOR THE EXPERT

These routes involve off-trail travel, route finding, and considerable elevation change. The reward is some of the most spectacular and remote areas of the Wasatch and the satisfaction of traveling an extraordinary route.

Mount Olympus from the north   Wildcat Ridge
Mule Hollow to Neffs Canyon   Upper Mill B North Fork Canyon
Dromedary Peak   Twin Peak from Ferguson Canyon
Alta to White Pine Canyon   Red Pine to Bells Canyon
Pfeifferhorn from Dry Creek   Box Elder Traverse

AUTHOR'S FAVORITES

Finally, to answer the question, "What do you recommend?" I will admit to having a few favorites. At the risk of overcrowding a few trails, my longtime favorites are as follows.

Mount Olympus   Grandeur Peak
Broads Fork   Mount Aire
Red Pine   Pfeifferhorn

5

Foothills and the Wasatch Front

The distinction between foothill hikes and Wasatch Front hikes is arbitrary and reflects seasonal preferences. The foothills are popular in spring and fall because they are snow free and relatively dry when the canyon trails are accessible only to skiers. The Wasatch Front hikes are longer and go higher than the foothill hikes and are generally considered summer hikes.

The foothill hikes are appropriately in the "foothill" or "transition" ecological zone. The dominant vegetation communities on the exposed slopes are open grasslands, Gambel oak, and mountain brush. Sheltered areas have stands of maple and aspen, and the drainage bottoms contain cottonwoods and willows. The foothills are vital winter habitat for deer. The Wasatch Front hikes start in the foothills and lead through successive ecological zones, finally climbing above treeline.

The experience of hiking from the suburbs to a wilderness summit is a unique and precious part of living in Salt Lake County, but this opportunity was once seriously threatened as subdivisions pushed closer to the mountains. In recent years there has been some loss of foothill hikes due to development on private property, but also great progress in establishing formal trailheads and easements that will protect future access. The most visible success has been the Bonneville Shoreline Trail, which provides both a nearly level urban interface hiking route and a series of trailheads that access major routes in the foothills.

Navigation on foothill trails is generally easy. Major drainages and ridges have either maintained hiking trails or, more commonly, user-created foot and bike routes. Off-trail destinations and major landmarks are generally visible from the valley, and the best routes follow terrain features such as ridges or gullies while avoiding areas of brush.

FOOTHILLS AND NORTHEAST AREA

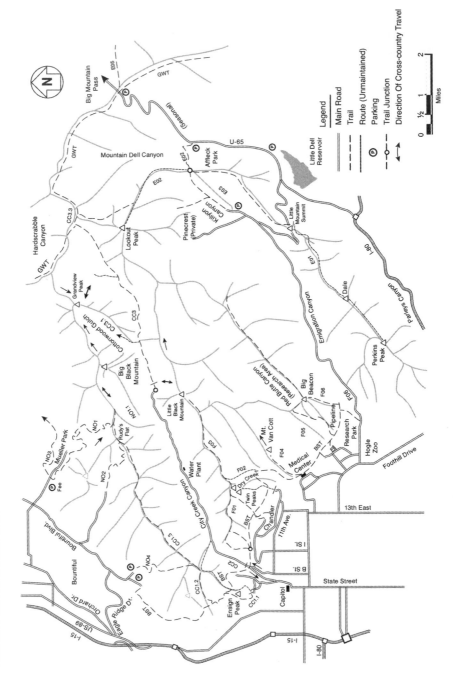

Legend

Main Road
Trail
Route (Unmaintained)
Parking
Trail Junction
Direction Of Cross-country Travel

Miles
0 ½ 1 2

The high peaks of the Wasatch Front, Mount Olympus, Twin Peaks, and Lone Peak are wilderness experiences even though the city is visible behind you. The huge vertical relief and the west-facing aspect make the hikes steep, sunny, and dry. Spectacular canyons incise the face of the Wasatch uplift. Neffs Canyon, Ferguson Canyon, Deaf Smith–Little Willow Canyon, and Bells Canyon all have trails climbing between steep walls through meadows and onto the passes and summits above. Draper City has created numerous new trails along the urban interface both in the foothills and leading high onto Lone Peak.

For general information regarding trails, see chapter 1. For driving directions to trailheads, see chapter 4. To cross-reference trail names, trailheads, and maps, see the "Hike Master List."

BONNEVILLE SHORELINE TRAIL (BST)

The long-range vision for this foothill trail is a recreational route for walking, running, and bike riding that extends from the Idaho border in Cache County to Santaquin in Utah County. The creation of this urban-wildland interface trail through Salt Lake County has been the greatest addition to the local trail system during the past three decades. The Bonneville Shoreline Trail serves many purposes: short foothill strolls from a neighborhood trailhead, an urban parkway, an access point for backcountry hiking on many foothill ridges and drainages, and an opportunity for long-distance rides and running. This trail offers incredible views in both directions: looking down at the metropolitan area and the Great Salt Lake and looking up at the peaks and ridges of the Wasatch.

The trail nominally runs on or near the bench formed by ancient Lake Bonneville's highest level. The Lake Bonneville maximum was about fifty-one hundred feet, but the remnant bench is often up to two hundred feet higher due to postglacial isostatic rebound (crustal uplift as the weight of water and ice is removed). Some trail sections go well above the Bonneville Bench level to bypass existing developments or terrain obstacles. Erosion has cut major drainages across the benchlands, requiring locally steep sections on the otherwise reasonably level trail.

The Bonneville Shoreline Trail concept began in 1990, and the trail is being built in sections as trailhead access, detail routing, and construction funding issues are resolved. There are currently two major foothill sections of the Bonneville Shoreline Trail within the area covered by this book. In the north there is a foothill trail from North Salt Lake to Emigration Canyon. In the south there is currently a foothill trail from the Hidden Valley Trailhead in Sandy to Corner Canyon Regional Park in Draper. In between, the currently constructed foothill sections are sometimes linked by marked routes following city streets. Creating a trail like this requires the cooperation

of private property owners, the municipal and county government bodies, and the
Forest Service, combined with generous private and foundation donations of cash lev-
eraged by huge amounts of volunteer labor. Trail users need to express their support
for continued expansion of the Bonneville Shoreline Trail.

CITY CREEK CANYON NORTH TO DAVIS COUNTY (BST)

Section	City Creek Road to Ensign Peak Trail	Ensign Peak Ridge to Antennas Road	Antennas Road to Eaglepointe Drive
One-Way Miles	1¾	1	1½
Gross Elevation Change	1,000	400	500
Hiking Time One-Way	1h 20m	40m	55m

This section is described south to north from the mouth of City Creek Canyon to
Eaglepointe Drive in North Salt Lake, and the reverse hike is described in chapter 9.
Intermediate access is from the road leading to the antennas on the north rim of City
Creek (see hike CC-1) and from the ridge continuing north from Ensign Peak (CC-1.1).
This section of the Bonneville Shoreline Trail was contentious due to the demand
for hillside-view lot development. After years of meetings and public hearings, the
planning process produced a route for the Bonneville Shoreline Trail and a recreational
right-of-way to Antennas Road. The process, though often emotional, was always conducted with mutual respect, and the result demonstrates what can be accomplished
when citizen groups, municipal planning departments, and developers seek a mutually
beneficial project design.

A trailhead sign is on the north side of the hairpin bend where City Creek Canyon
Road joins Bonneville Boulevard. The trail is on a constructed water-main cut and
goes parallel to the canyon road for almost a mile before the start of switchbacks up
to the ridge north of Ensign Peak. The start of the BST and the paved canyon road can
be combined to make a nice, nearly level loop hike. After the climb, the BST begins
a series of turns and switchbacks as it traverses the steep hillsides above the neighborhoods and gated developments that are behind the state capitol and eventually
crosses the Antennas Road partway up the main ridge. From here the trail descends
and crosses a broad, open, grassy bench with incredible views. The single-track trail
ends at the trailhead at the south end of Eaglepointe Drive in North Salt Lake City. See
chapter 4 for directions. Continuing north is a signed BST connector route that follows
city streets to the north end of Bountiful, where a trail resumes.

CITY CREEK CANYON SOUTH TO HOGLE ZOO (BST)

Section	City Creek to Terrace Hills Drive	Terrace Hills Drive to Dry Creek	Dry Creek to Pioneer Trails State Park
One-Way Miles	1¾	3¾	3½
Gross Elevation Change	1,200	1,000	600
Hiking Time One-Way	1h 20m	2h 15m	2h

A trailhead sign is on the south side of the hairpin bend where City Creek Canyon Road joins Bonneville Boulevard, marking the start of the BST section that climbs up the hillside from City Creek Canyon and continues by winding in and out of drainages above the Avenues before dropping to cross Dry Creek. Continuing south, the BST follows a petroleum pipeline above the University Medical Center, is interrupted by the road at Red Butte Gardens, then continues along the pipeline before dropping to Sunnyside Avenue, across from Hogle Zoo at the mouth of Emigration Canyon. This section provides trailhead access to popular foothill hikes, including Avenues Twin Peaks, Dry Creek, Black Mountain, Mount Van Cott, and Big Beacon.

Major trailheads are on Bonneville Drive at the mouth of City Creek, the top of Terrace Hills Drive, Red Butte Gardens, and Pioneer Trails State Park. Additional access points include Morris Reservoir, Perry Hollow, Limekiln Gulch, Popperton Park, Dry Creek, and Research Park. See chapter 4 for driving directions.

The trail toward the Avenues and university starts by the pond, crosses a bridge, and starts climbing the hillside to Morris Reservoir on the bench above. You soon emerge from the brush and are treated to views of the city and mountains. The area around the Morris Reservoir Trailhead is flat, and several side trails offer short, easy walks to viewpoints. The BST crosses the flats and climbs a long switchback to reach the ridge above, continues east past a water tank, and climbs still higher on the ridge. A service road leads from the water tank to the west trailhead at the end of Terrace Hills Drive. The BST stays high and contours in and out of side drainages, and another side trail connects with the east trailhead at the end of Terrace Hills Drive. This section of the BST goes well above the geological bench to stay on city-owned land and avoid housing developments. The BST continues around the Perrys Hollow drainage, passes south of Avenues Twin Peaks (F-01), and crosses high in Limekiln Gulch, before beginning to descend to Dry Creek.

From Dry Creek, the BST climbs the hill behind the Huntsman Cancer Center and then follows the hillside bench and pipeline right-of-way below Cephalopod Gulch and Mount Van Cott (F-04), eventually descending to cross the roads at the mouth of Red

Butte Canyon. The foothill trail is briefly interrupted by the fence around Red Butte Gardens, but begins again near the Utah Museum of Natural History, built in 2011. The trail continues above Research Park, traverses under Big Beacon and crosses Georges Hollow (F-05), stays high above the fee area for This Is the Place Heritage Park, and then descends to a trailhead on Sunnyside Avenue at the east end of the park fence.

EMIGRATION CANYON TO SANDY

Proposed alignments and trailheads have been suggested, but little exists yet on the ground. What is important is the vision and citizen support for continued development of the Bonneville Shoreline Trail. Construction of BST sections in the central section has the potential to provide both urban recreational opportunities and legal access to public land in the foothills.

BONNEVILLE SHORELINE TRAIL CONNECTOR

A short section of foothill Bonneville Shoreline Trail runs below the H-Rock between the ends of Devonshire Drive and Lakeline Drive.

A BST connector route continues on streets from Emigration Canyon to Parleys Canyon. From Sunnyside Avenue, take Crestview Drive to Wasatch Drive, which passes above Hogle Zoo and through the golf course. Head south on Wasatch Drive to Stringham Avenue and then go downhill to the bike path along Foothill Drive. The bike path and bridge system crosses the canyon mouth and I-80 and goes to the Parleys Canyon Trailhead on Wasatch Boulevard. An intersecting urban trail crosses I-215 to Parleys Historic Park. Eventually, this intersecting trail will provide a recreational route all the way to the Jordan River Parkway.

MOUNT OLYMPUS SECTION (BST)

At the time of this revision, the Forest Service was completing a BST section from the Neffs Canyon Trailhead, past the Thousand Oaks Drive access in Olympus Cove, and south to the Mount Olympus Trailhead.

LOWER CITY CREEK (CC-2)

This beautiful nature preserve is only a few minutes' walk from downtown. Starting from downtown by foot, it is a pleasant 1½-mile walk through a park to the vehicle trailhead. You walk Canyon Road (120 East North Temple) north into Memory Grove, continue up through the park on trails following the stream, and across Bonneville Boulevard. Cars need to take Bonneville Boulevard, a one-way road starting at 11th Avenue and B Street, to reach the City Creek Canyon Road, which starts where Bonneville Boulevard crosses the stream. There is parking just before the traffic-control gate.

City Creek Canyon is owned by Salt Lake City, and the canyon above the treatment plant is municipal watershed. Hikers should be careful to protect water quality—use the restrooms. Camping and wading in the creek are prohibited. Dogs are prohibited above Picnic Area no. 16.

Traffic is restricted on the City Creek Canyon Road, making the lower canyon a popular area for hiking and jogging. The current schedule is that foot traffic is allowed every day, bicycles on odd days, and limited private vehicles on holidays and even-numbered days. Picnic sites can be reserved by calling (801) 483-6705.

CITY CREEK CANYON ROAD

The narrow paved road follows the stream for 3.6 miles to the water treatment plant and continues for another 2 miles to end at Rotary Park. The stream and heavy forest along the canyon bottom are a pleasant contrast to the open hills above. The paved road is popular for walking, running, and bike riding.

CANYON HIKING TRAIL

A trail through the woods parallels the road from the mouth of the canyon to the water-treatment plant 3 miles up. The separation from the road makes this a good place to walk on days when the canyon is open to private vehicles. The first mile is part of the BST and follows the top of a buried pipeline on the north side of the canyon. You can start from the Bonneville Shoreline Trail sign on the north at the canyon mouth or take the ramp that connects the road and hiking trail a short way beyond the gate. At about Picnic Area no. 5, the BST heads uphill and the trail paralleling the road continues upcanyon as a footpath closed to bikes. There are multiple points where you can connect to the paved road below.

NORTH RIDGE ANTENNAS VIA PIPELINE ROUTE

Walk up the canyon road about 1¼ miles. A large blue pipeline valve station near the road and a large satellite dish hidden in a gully mark where a route heads up to the north ridge. Walk up open grassy slopes following user-created tracks. The ridge-crest trail is just beyond the microwave reflector that you can see high on the ridge.

UPPER CITY CREEK (CC-3)

The canyon above the water-treatment plant is covered in chapter 9.

NORTH RIDGE OF CITY CREEK CANYON (CC-1)

Destination	Ensign Peak	Antennas Loop	Ridge Exploration
One-Way Miles	½	6½	1 to 10
Elevation Gain	600	1,300	500 to 2,000
Highest Point	5,414	6,150	Varies
Hiking Time One-Way	40m	3h 50m	1h to 6h

The low ridge above the state capitol northeast of Salt Lake City is relatively low elevation, stays snow free for much of the winter, and can be hiked again very early in the spring. The area is open grass-covered hills, and many variations are possible, ranging from a short stroll to an all-day hike on the ridge. Even a short hike offers outstanding views. Few cities have such wonderful natural places so close to downtown.

The north ridge of City Creek can be reached from the trails coming up from Davis County (Mueller Park, N-01; North Canyon, N-02; Wild Rose, N-04), the Bonneville Shoreline Trail, or from lower City Creek road. Once on the ridge, you can hike for miles along the north side of City Creek Canyon. Beyond Rudys Flat the ridge degenerates into off-trail hiking, but it is possible for long-distance hikers to continue to connect with the east-area trails beyond Grandview Peak.

ENSIGN PEAK (CC-1.1)

Ensign Peak sits at the end of the ridge defining the north side of City Creek Canyon. This rounded hill with a prominent stone monument overlooking downtown has a long history as a site for commemorative events and casual hikes. The trail starts from a small commemorative park on the north side of Ensign Vista Drive. Take East Capitol Boulevard 1½ miles up from State Street and turn left onto Ensign Vista Drive. The trailhead is on the north, where the street tops the hill. A well-maintained but steep foot trail leads up from the park to the summit. Near the start a short spur leads to appropriately named Vista Mound. From the Ensign Peak summit, you can continue hiking along the ridge crest for ½ mile to the junction with the Bonneville Shoreline Trail.

THE ANTENNAS HIKE—ENSIGN PEAK TO CITY CREEK (CC-1.2)

A number of communication sites are located on the north ridge of City Creek. They are visible from a distance, making a distinctive landmark, and several hiking routes converge near the antennas. Access and hiking opportunities in the area have changed greatly in the past twenty years.

Historic access to the antennas area was by the service road for the communication sites. The Antennas Road is now an extension of Sandhurst Drive through a gated subdivision. Hikers and mountain bikes are allowed to continue on the sidewalk and up the road to reach the city-owned land beyond. To reach the start, continue downhill from the Ensign Peak Trailhead and turn west on Dorchester Drive to the gate. The Bonneville Shoreline Trail, either from North Salt Lake or from the mouth of City Creek, and the Ensign Peak Trail provide other ways to get to the Antennas Road. You can use the Ensign Peak Trail and the Antennas Road as a loop hike. Other possible loops to the antennas are to combine the Bonneville Shoreline Trail from North Salt Lake with the Wild Rose Trail (N-04) or the Bonneville Shoreline Trail and the Pipeline Route from lower City Creek.

Above the subdivision the Antennas Road traverses north to a junction where the left branch continues as the Bonneville Shoreline Trail to North Salt Lake and the right branch climbs to the antennas. After the third major antenna station, the road levels off and then drops a short way to a saddle. Beyond the saddle a set of vehicle tracks drops down to the City Creek road. A small square microwave reflector a short way below the ridge marks the correct turn to descend to City Creek. Coming up from lower City Creek, this is described as the Pipeline Route.

RUDYS FLAT FROM NORTH RIDGE OF CITY CREEK (CC-1.3)

This section can be done as a continuation of any of the trails that lead up to the Antennas Road. What was once a ridge-crest four-wheel-drive road continues east along the ridge and becomes faint in spots. The maintained trails coming up from North Canyon and Mueller Park in Bountiful meet the ridge at Rudys Flat, 3½ miles beyond the antennas. Motorcycles are allowed on this portion of the ridge if they come up from Davis County.

AVENUES TWIN PEAKS AREA (F-01)

Distance	1 to 2 miles to peak, depending on starting point
Elevation Gain	1,100
Highest Point	6,291
Hiking Time One-Way	45m to 1½h

A pair of small peaks, elevation 6,291 feet, on the ridge above the Avenues provides an outstanding view of the city and of City Creek Canyon. The summits are just south of the ridge crest and are obvious from any direction. The area has a network of trails, so many variations and loops are possible. These hillsides are a good place for viewing spring wildflowers.

TWIN PEAKS SUMMIT

All route to these peaks utilize the Bonneville Shoreline Trail for access. The shortest routes are from either of the Tomahawk Trailheads or the Terrace Hills Drive Trailhead, or you can make a longer hike by starting at any of the other trailheads above the Avenues and traversing along the BST. From the Tomahawk Drive Trailheads, you ascend about 350 feet in ½ mile to reach the Bonneville Shoreline Trail, which contours around the south side of Twin Peaks. Get onto the BST, hike to the small drainage just west of Twin Peaks, and then turn northeast on a spur trail that climbs to the ridge crest above City Creek and passes just north of Twin Peaks. Turn south and follow the ridge over both summits, enjoying the views. The ridge-crest trail north of Twin Peaks continues east past the head of Dry Creek toward Little Black Mountain.

LIMEKILN GULCH

From about 1550 East on Tomahawk Drive, a narrow trail passes between houses to reach the restored pioneer lime kilns and the Bonneville Shoreline Trail. The city-owned trail is between the brown concrete driveway and the fancy stone wall and is easy to miss. This is a nice area for a short hike, and the kilns are interesting for both children and those who like the history of technology. The trail ascends to the BST, and Limekiln Gulch is a good route to Avenues Twin Peaks.

PERRYS HOLLOW

This drainage is west of Avenues Twin Peaks. Trails connect neighborhood trailheads on North Bonneville Drive and Perry Hollows Road with the Bonneville Shoreline Trail. Perrys Hollow was the site of a massive landslide in 1945 that ran down to 11th Avenue, and the scars remain as a reminder of what a cloudburst combined with hillside devegetation can cause.

THE BOBSLED

Do not hike the bottom of Perrys Hollow from Chandler Drive up to the Bonneville Shoreline Trail. This is the Bobsled, a highly popular route for exciting downhill mountain-bike descent with a smooth surface and banked turns to promote high speed.

LOOP HIKES

A nice loop connects the Tomahawk Drive Trailheads, the Bonneville Shoreline Trail, and Dry Creek with only a short distance of on-street walking between Popperton

Mount Van Cott, just east of the university, is an easy foothill hike with excellent views.

Park and Tomahawk Drive. With two cars many other one-way hikes can be arranged between trailheads in the Avenues and university area.

DRY CREEK (F-02)

Distance	1 to 3 miles one-way
Elevation Gain	1,000 to 1,500
Hiking Time One-Way	1 to 2h

Dry Creek, directly northeast of the University Medical Center, offers nice canyon-bottom hiking and leads to the ridges above City Creek and Red Butte Canyons. Most of the land is owned by the university. Many options are possible, so time to destination is indefinite.

Dry Creek can be accessed from the Bonneville Shoreline Trail by parking at either Popperton Park or south of the Huntsman Cancer Center, as described in chapter 4. Alternatively, take Trax, a UTA bus, or the campus shuttle. From Popperton Park, take the constructed spur trail that drops down to the BST in Dry Creek. From the south, hike north behind the cancer center, past Cephalopod Gulch, and follow the BST down into Dry Creek. It is also possible to enter Dry Creek by walking east through the Jewish Community Center parking lot, past the substation, to reach a dirt road leading north for about ¼ mile that turns east into Dry Creek.

Petroleum and natural gas pipelines cross the mouth of Dry Creek, but it soon turns into a beautiful natural area. The official Bonneville Shoreline Trail continues up Dry Creek for a mile and then makes a switchback to the west and climbs up to the ridge above the Avenues. About ½ mile from the canyon mouth, a ridge divides the forks of Dry Creek. An unmaintained trail ascends the crest of the ridge dividing the forks of Dry Creek and can be followed all the way to Little Black Mountain if you are good about route-finding through oak brush. A secondary trail also ascends partway up the south fork of Dry Creek for about 2 miles to the head of the canyon. (The south fork is where Brian David Mitchell took Elizabeth Smart after the kidnapping.) The heavily used BST follows the north fork of Dry Creek. It is possible to continue up the north fork of Dry Creek beyond where the BST turns. Climb up onto the left hill and continue through aspen and several clearings to reach the ridge just east of Avenues Twin Peaks, providing the opportunity for a loop hike. The north fork route to the ridge involves about 1,000 feet of elevation gain in 1½ miles and is the most direct approach to Little Black Mountain.

LITTLE BLACK MOUNTAIN (F-03)

Distance	4¼ miles one-way
Elevation Gain	3,100
Highest Point	8,040
Hiking Time One-Way	3h 40m

Little Black Mountain is a high point on the ridge forming the south side of City Creek Canyon, and its forested slopes are a prominent feature as you approach Salt Lake City from the west. Little Black Mountain was my first hike with the Wasatch Mountain Club and has always been one of my spring hiking favorites.

There are two commonly used starting points for Little Black Mountain: Dry Creek from the University Medical Center and from the Bonneville Shoreline trailheads in the upper Avenues. From the Avenues, follow the directions for Twin Peaks and continue east on the ridge crest and continue past the trail coming up from the north fork of Dry Creek. Follow the ridge-crest trail for another 2 miles to the summit of Little Black Mountain. There is one steep section where the erosion damage caused by historic off-road vehicle use is evident, and the last ½ mile is a narrow limestone ridge with a little scrambling.

Most hikers stop at the first rock outcrop just before the ridge drops about 200 feet to a saddle. The Smugglers Gap Trail descends from this saddle into the second minor drainage above Rotary Park in Upper City Creek. Advanced hikers can continue east from Little Black Mountain and make a 15-mile off-trail hike above Red Butte Canyon, eventually reaching Big Beacon.

Dry Creek Ridge variation: Where the north and south forks of Dry Creek separate, a faint track makes a series of tiny switchbacks up onto the dividing ridge. This ridge merges with the main ridge ¼ mile west of the summit of Black Mountain. The best route is generally on the south slope near the ridge crest.

MOUNT VAN COTT AND CEPHALOPOD GULCH (F-04)

Destination	Head of Gulch	Mount Van Cott	Head of Dry Creek
One-Way Miles	½	1	3
Elevation Gain	700	1,148	1,800
Highest Point	5,900	6,348	7,000
Hiking Time One-Way	40m	1h 5m	2h 20m

This area is popular for lunchtime hiking for people working around the university and as an early- or late-season hike to view the Salt Lake Valley.

A distinct track on the ridge directly north of the upper University Medical Center parking lot is the route to Mount Van Cott. It is immediately south of where the Bonneville Shoreline Trail crosses Dry Creek. This area can be reached from the parking lot south of the cancer center or from any of the other nearby trailheads listed for the BST. The destination is an overlook 200 feet south from where the ridge climb levels off. The trail becomes fainter but continues northeast along the ridge. This is open grassland, and many longer hikes are possible, including continuing to the head of Dry Creek and returning along the drainage. Hikers often try the ridges going from Van Cott southwest toward Red Butte, but the ridges all become very steep slopes that are susceptible to erosion. These routes are discouraged.

A CEPHALOPOD. This ancestor of snails and squids is a common fossil in the Thayne Formation. The small gulch (F-04) is a collecting area used by geology students. From B. J. Sharp, "Guide Fossils for the Layman" in *Geology of Salt Lake County*, 53.

Cephalopod Gulch is the drainage immediately to the northeast of the Huntsman Cancer Center. The Bonneville Shoreline Trail crosses the mouth of this gulch, and a foot track leads up the dry streambed. The gulch soon closes in, and brush fills the bottom. Here, most hikers work their way up onto the more open side hills and climb to the ridges coming off Mount Van Cott above.

RED BUTTE CANYON

Red Butte Canyon, the major drainage between Dry Creek and Emigration Canyon, is managed as a research natural area. The Red Butte Gardens fee area is at the mouth of the canyon. Here the Bonneville Shoreline Trail is interrupted by a sidewalk connector, and a branch from the BST loops uphill around the outside of the fence around the gardens. A fence and gate block the canyon road ½ mile above the BST crossing, and the upper portion of the canyon is closed to recreational use. Red Butte Canyon was once part of Fort Douglas and now serves as an ecological research baseline, as it was never heavily grazed or developed and is also relatively free of human-transported invasive plants.

BIG BEACON

Approach Route	From Georges Hollow	From Sunnyside Avenue
One-Way Miles	2	1½
Elevation Gain	2,140	2,140
Highest Point	7,143	7,143
Hiking Time One-Way	2h 5m	1h 50m

The two large microwave reflectors once bounced telephone signals from downtown to Park City and made this summit between Red Butte Canyon and Emigration Canyon easy to identify from anywhere in the valley, but the reflectors were dismantled in 2013. The other structure on the summit is an abandoned aircraft beacon that was paired with "Little Beacon" on the hill directly south. The summit is called "Mount Wire" on the USGS maps, but that name is rarely used. The Georges Hollow and Southwest Ridge trails can be combined with the Bonneville Shoreline Trail to make a loop hike.

BIG BEACON FROM GEORGES HOLLOW (F-05)

This trail starts above Research Park from the Bonneville Shoreline Trail and goes up Georges Hollow. This route is slightly longer, but it has the same elevation gain and is more scenic. Start from the Utah Museum of Natural History trailhead on Colorow

Drive. Looking up from Fort Douglas Cemetery on Wakara Way, you will see two drainages immediately to the east. Georges Hollow is the left drainage with the small red rock outcrop on the north, but the trail actually starts in the right drainage. Follow the BST until you are northeast of the Neuropsychiatric Institute Building, ascend the side trail that loops up at the mouth of Georges Hollow, and take the footpath into the drainage to the southeast of Georges Hollow. Eventually, the trail turns north and continues to climb along the side of Georges Hollow. Route finding is necessary, as there are a large number of user-created bike routes in the area.

The trail follows the bottom of the south drainage for ½ mile and then crosses the ridge to the north and follows the Georges Hollow drainage. Just below 6,600 feet, a route branches back to the west and traverses to the top of Red Butte, while the main trail continues east to the minor pass overlooking Red Butte Canyon. Here, the trail makes a sharp right turn toward the summit of Big Beacon, ½ mile due south. The slopes are open, and the indistinct trail passes to the west of the minor summits.

Descending, remember that the trail turns down at the third saddle. If you turn down the wrong drainage, you will encounter dense oak brush.

THE LIVING ROOM

I would have preferred to keep this marvelous overlook a "secret," as the folk art is susceptible to vandalism, but it is now in other guidebooks. After climbing up from the BST about ½ mile, you will be near 5,800 feet, traversing the south side of Georges Hollow. A distinct spur trail can be seen branching left and going into the pinkish or orange rocks on the Red Butte ridge. This trail leads to the Living Room, a small level area on the ridge crest where hikers have arranged sandstone blocks to create a comfortable place to observe the valley below. Steep rough trails lead up and down the ridge.

BIG BEACON FROM SOUTHWEST RIDGE (F-06)

Start from the Bonneville Shoreline Trail access point on Sunnyside Drive east of the This Is the Place Heritage Park fence. Hike up to the pipeline road where the BST heads northwest toward the university.

Follow the pipeline road east over a couple of ridges until you are on the top of a ridge directly north of the condominiums on Donner Way. Here, a foot track branches left up the hill. This junction is on the last ridge before the power line crosses the pipeline. The distinct foot track follows the ridge crest to the summit. This is a pretty ridge with limestone outcrops, mountain mahogany, and an occasional cactus.

A service road that offers changing views down into Red Butte Canyon follows the ridge crest northeast from the summit. A track descends into Emigration Canyon after about 1½ miles along the ridge.

EMIGRATION CANYON TO PARLEYS CANYON

Urban development here preceded open-space planning. The foothills between Emigration Canyon and Parleys Canyon contain several historic hiking routes that are now almost inaccessible, and the Bonneville Shoreline Trail follows a paved connector route between Emigration to Parleys Canyons. In 2006 a well-designed trail system was proposed for Emigration Canyon, but the township planning commission rejected it. To quote the *Salt Lake Tribune* editorial, "In accepting the questionable arguments of a few who are wealthy enough to buy a piece of the canyon, the commission put up an arbitrary and unnecessary barrier to the public lands remaining in the beautiful hills between Summit and Salt Lake counties." The limited trail opportunities in Emigration Canyon will persist for decades to come.

H-ROCK AND RIDGE ROUTE, JACKS MOUNTAIN

The H-Rock is the landmark above Foothill Drive on the ridge between Spring Canyon and Carrigan Canyon. Start from the trailhead at the north end of Lakeline Drive. Informal trails head up to the communication site above. One route starts up the open slopes north of the Lakeline Drive trailhead, and the other is north of the H-Rock. Beyond, the route follows the ridge between Carrigan Canyon and Spring Canyon over several minor summits. Jacks Mountain has some mailboxes and a memorial

FOOTHILL HIKING. Ferguson Canyon (WF-4) in the center of the picture leads to Storm Mountain on the left skyline. The Hounds Tooth (F-10) is the flat-topped outcrop above Ferguson Canyon and is reached by hiking the slope to the right.

notebook. The H-Rock is the best, but brushy, current access to Perkins Peak from the west. There are currently no maintained trails between the Wasatch Front and the end of the Emigration Ridge trail from Little Mountain Summit trailhead, but there are plenty of opportunities for foothill exploration.

HISTORIC ROUTES

Perkins Peak (elev. 7,520) is the high point on the ridge east of Hogle Zoo. The direct route up the spectacular west ridge is now blocked by development at the bottom. Perkins Peak is best reached by traversing the ridge from Little Mountain Summit (see E-01). Pencil Point (elev. 6,130) is a sharp outcrop on the ridge between Carrigan Canyon and Parleys Canyon that was also once a popular foothill hike. These destinations are listed to encourage citizens to support continued foothill open-space protection and trailhead-access acquisition.

GRANDEUR FROM THE WEST (F-09)

Distance	1¾ miles one-way to summit
Elevation Gain	3,100
Highest Point	Summit—8,299
Hiking Time One-Way	2h 25m

Grandeur is the peak overlooking I-80 and I-215 between the south side of Parleys Canyon and Millcreek Canyon. The Parleys Canyon Trailhead is at the north end of Wasatch Boulevard, north of 33rd South. Public access to this area was enhanced in 2005 when the Salt Lake County Open Space Trust Fund, in cooperation with the Trust for Public Lands and Save Our Canyons, acquired a critical foothill parcel.

From the Parleys Canyon Trailhead parking area, the route goes up and quickly forks. The left branch goes to a utility site, and the right branch ascends past the end of Cascade Way to reach a trail heading south that is the access to the drainage between the first and second ridges south from Parleys Canyon. Distinct footpaths ascend both the bottom of the drainage and the second ridge south of Parleys Canyon. These trails join higher up. The ridge trail climbs rapidly and continues all the way to the summit, but it fades out in the oak brush when you get higher up. The lower slopes are very popular for short hikes, and there are numerous user-created and game trails. The hillsides are relatively open terrain, so many hiking possibilities exist.

The southwest ridge of Grandeur is marked by a dramatic S-shaped rock outcrop. This ridge can be reached from the access on Crestwood Drive. South of the outcrop, a foot track exists all to way to the ridge crest.

NEFFS CANYON (WF-1)

Destination	Meadow	Thayne Canyon Pass	Mill B Pass
One-Way Miles	2¾	3½	3¼
Elevation Gain	2,450	3,190	3,650
Highest Point	8,000	8,740	9,200
Hiking Time One-Way	2h 40m	3h 20m	3h 30m
Special Difficulties			No trail

Neffs Canyon is the west-facing bowl directly above Olympus Cove. This canyon is rarely crowded, even though it is within walking distance of homes. The lower canyon is heavily forested, and the upper canyon has jagged limestone cliffs and views of the city. The trail starts at the Forest Service trailhead at White Park (approximately 4300 East and 4300 South). See driving directions in chapter 4.

The trail starts to the south of the fence enclosing the water tanks and follows the road heading southeast into Neffs Canyon. After ½ mile there is an open area of unusually tall Gambel oak and a side stream coming from Norths Fork.

The Neffs Trail follows the old road for 1¼ miles, crossing the stream twice on improvised bridges, before entering the Mount Olympus Wilderness and becoming a foot trail south of the stream. The route climbs up the side of a small ridge and then drops back to a stream crossing. The trail becomes faint as it crosses a broad meadow 2¾ miles from the trailhead. When the grass is high, the trail can be found again by heading directly east across the meadow. Next, the trail climbs an aspen-covered hill and crosses an upper meadow with evidence of frequent avalanches. The trail now makes a long switchback, first heading south, then turning back north as it climbs the headwall of Neffs Canyon. The trail passes through a series of cliffs and then reaches a notch in the ridge where it joins the Thayne Canyon Trail.

NEFFS CAVE

I've been there, but the Forest Service does not want to publicize where it is. Some things should be left out of guidebooks.

NEFFS TRAIL TO MILL B PASS

Neffs Canyon provides access to Wildcat Ridge between Mount Olympus and Mount Raymond. At the extreme south end of the long switchback, leave the trail and continue southeast, climbing 450 vertical feet through wide-spaced trees to an open saddle at the head of Mill B Gulch. An old watering trough is partway up the hill. This saddle marks the end of the difficult scrambling when traversing Wildcat Ridge from the west. From here, an unmaintained trail heads east along the south side of the ridge to the junction with the Desolation Trail at the head of Porter Fork.

MOUNT OLYMPUS (WF-2)

Destination	Tolcat Canyon Stream	South Summit
One-Way Miles	1½	3
Elevation Gain	1,290	4,050
Highest Point	6,240	9,026
Hiking Time One-Way	1h 20m	3h 35m
Special Difficulties		Scrambling

The distinctive shape of Mount Olympus dominates the view from much of the valley's east side, and the summit is a popular objective. The trail has switchbacks up open foothills, a climb through dense forest, an easy rock scramble at the top, and spectacular views all along the way. This well-maintained trail is sunny and is a good choice for spring and fall, but is scorching hot on a summer afternoon.

The trailhead is a small parking area at about 5700 South on Wasatch Boulevard near the prominent rock outcrop known as Petes Rock. A lot of work by the Forest Service went into securing a trail easement at this location and in constructing this new trail after the historic route to the south was blocked.

The trail climbs steeply up switchbacks to the bench where it levels off before continuing up the hill and turning north along the alignment of the historic trail that started from Tolcat Canyon. The trail ascends in a series of switchbacks, passing through areas of Gambel oak, juniper, and mountain mahogany. It eventually enters Tolcat Canyon, where there is a seasonal stream. Formerly, the trail continued directly up the steep slabs known as Blister Hill, but now switchbacks to the left make the next section much easier. The trail continues east through the trees with the prominent west ridge of Mount Olympus on the left and a smaller rock rib on the right. Eventually, the trail reaches a saddle with a fine stand of Douglas fir and signs of picnic and camping use. On the way back down, be sure to watch for the top of the switchbacks.

From the saddle to the summit is 600 vertical feet in ¼ mile of easy scrambling, requiring occasional use of the hands. The trail turns north and heads for a couloir in the rock face directly ahead. Foot traffic has made a distinct track up the couloir. There is no exposure, and the major danger is that a careless hiker might kick rocks loose. If you find yourself overlooking a cliff or facing an unscalable wall, look around, and you will

see the correct route a few feet away. About two-thirds of the way up, the couloir runs
into an abrupt wall where the route jogs east for about 150 feet to a notch behind a pinnacle and then turns left and continues directly up. At the top, turn right and boulder-
hop along the ridge for about 200 feet to the summit. All routes from the summit other
than the ascent route involve at least basic rock-climbing skills (see chapter 11).

HEUGHES CANYON (WF-3)

Distance	1¼ to the waterfall
Elevation Gain	1,300 feet
Hiking Time One-Way	1h 20m

This is a steep, narrow, rocky canyon south of the Mount Olympus Trail. Since the first
edition, Holladay City has secured a recorded easement for a hiking route up Berghalde
Drive and into the mouth of the canyon. Berghalde Drive is a private road. Park on Oak
Canyon Drive or any of the other nearby public streets. A trail follows an old pipeline
route up the canyon bottom and continues to end at a viewpoint of a waterfall that can
be impressive during the snowmelt. It is possible to bushwhack and scramble all the
way up Heughes Canyon and eventually reach the Mount Olympus Trail far above.

DRY HOLLOW

A historic route starts from the water tank on the southeast side of the Canyon Cove
subdivision and follows vehicle tracks up the ridge between Heughes Canyon and Dry
Hollow. Currently, this has no official access, but may eventually be a popular trail
again if the Bonneville Shoreline Trail is constructed north of Big Cottonwood Canyon.
The trail traverses into the Dry Hollow drainage and then ascends the open slopes on
the north side of Dry Hollow to reach a pass overlooking Mule Hollow.

FERGUSON CANYON (WF-4)

Destination	Ridge Overlook	Upper Meadow	Storm Mountain Summit
One-Way Miles	1½	2¾	3½
Elevation Change	1,600	3,200	4,324
Highest Point	7,000	8,400	9,524
Hiking Time One-Way	1h 35m	2h 55m	3h 50m
Special Difficulties			Scrambling

Ferguson Canyon is the short, steep canyon located south of the mouth of Big Cottonwood Canyon and east of the Prospector Hill subdivision. The lower canyon is enclosed by granite walls popular with rock climbers, while the upper canyon contains open meadows. The access is from the trailhead on Timberland Drive in Cottonwood Heights. Trails that begin directly in urban neighborhoods create unique problems. Home-owner concern over late-night parties held in the canyon caused the Forest Service to institute a closure between 10:00 p.m. and 6:00 a.m. and a ban on fires and camping for the lower 2 miles of Ferguson Canyon.

Park at the designated area on Timberland Drive, walk up the service road to the water tank, and then descend into Ferguson Canyon. The trail soon crosses the Twin Peaks wilderness boundary. The trail stays in the canyon bottom and crosses the stream twice on logs and once on boulders as it climbs steadily. After about 1¼ hours, you will reach the bottom of the switchbacks that climb up the north side of the canyon.

In a sandy area near the top of the ridge, the trail to Storm Mountain makes a sharp switchback to the east, and a well-defined track branches left and heads west to a spectacular overlook on the crest of the narrow ridge above Big Cottonwood Canyon. A track continues down the crest of this ridge, but it is a very steep route on rock and gravel.

After the overlook junction, the trail continues east, traversing through brush high on the canyon side until it again approaches the now-dry stream bed. There is a trail from here all the way to the upper meadow. If you lose the trail (or are searching for it on descent), look for it 15 yards from the south wall of the obvious narrows at about 7,800 feet. Above the narrows the trail climbs on the south side of the drainage until it reaches an open boulder field, where it jogs to the north and then begins a very steep climb up an open slope. The easiest route here is along the stream; fragments of the old trail are seen nearby. The trail disappears soon after reaching the upper meadow, so locate landmarks for the return. Storm Mountain is visible ¼ mile ahead. To the right are a higher summit on the ridge leading around Stairs Gulch toward Twin Peaks and, farther right, a saddle overlooking Deaf Smith Canyon.

STORM MOUNTAIN

The best route to the Storm Mountain summit is to go up the center of the Ferguson Canyon bowl, aiming for the saddle south of the peak. An alternative is to ascend the north ridge and follow the crest, crossing one minor peak on the way. Both routes are enjoyable. Anything beyond Storm Mountain is a mountaineering scramble. The east face of Storm Mountain is a technical rock climb, and the north ridge is either a very difficult scramble or a technical climb, depending on the route. The traverse from Storm Mountain to Twin Peaks is long and involves route-finding along an exposed ridge.

HOUNDS TOOTH AND DEAF SMITH CANYON

These are foothill destinations where the historic access has been blocked by development and an official trail does not exist. Construction of the Bonneville Shoreline Trail between Big and Little Cottonwood Canyons is the most likely way that an official access will eventually be created.

HOUNDS TOOTH (F-10)

Distance	1¾ miles one-way to outcrop
Elevation Gain	2,600
Highest Point	7,800 at base of outcrop
Hiking Time One-Way	2h 15m

Hounds Tooth is the prominent granite outcrop high on the ridge above Golden Hills and immediately south of Ferguson Canyon. The Forest Service land starts about ¼ mile up the hill. The area can currently still be reached by traversing south from the Ferguson Canyon Trailhead. From the water tanks, look for a user-created trail up the slope to the southeast. Pick your way toward the main ridge that descends from the Hounds Tooth. The brush is less thick on the south side of the ridges, and game trails are plentiful. The hike stops at the base of the cliffs that looked so small from the valley. This outcrop has several technical rock routes, and the north side drops steeply into Ferguson Canyon. To climb higher on the ridge, pass south of the Hounds Tooth.

DEAF SMITH, ALSO CALLED LITTLE WILLOW CANYON (WF-5)

This is a very steep, narrow canyon leading from the Golden Hills subdivision to the summit of Twin Peaks. There have recently been emphatic "No Trespassing" signs and fences on the road leading from Kings Hill Drive into the mouth of the canyon. The alternative start traversing south from the end of Golden Oaks Drive also has No Trespassing signs. This is a magnificent canyon with a long record of use by the public. Purchase of easements for the Bonneville Shoreline Trail is the best opportunity for restoring public access.

A reasonably defined trail follows the stream up the north side of the north fork and then crosses to the south side before fading out 2 miles from the mouth at about 8,800 feet. Above here the terrain is open, and scree slopes in both branches of the drainage lead to the summit ridge of Twin Peaks.

BELLS CANYON (WF-6)

Destination	Lower Bells Reservoir	Lower Waterfall	Upper Waterfall
One-Way Miles	¾	2¼	3
Elevation Change	450	1,500	2,300
Highest Point	5,578	6,600	7,500
Hiking Time One-Way	35m	2h	2h 45m

This is a long canyon that rises from the sage-covered foothills, past two waterfalls and a popular rock climbing area, to reach an alpine cirque with Lone Peak and Thunder Mountain towering above. From high in Bells Canyon, the huge north face of Lone Peak dominates the view.

When the first edition was written, there was no legal public access to Bells Canyon. I urged readers to contact their public officials and express support for a Bells Canyon Trailhead. Now there are two official trailheads that are the result of Sandy City and the Forest Service working to resolve watershed-protection and landowner-ship issues and a lot of trail construction through steep rocky terrain. The Wasatch Front needs more trail-access successes like this.

Two Bells Canyon trailheads are operated by Sandy City. The Granite Trailhead to the north is on a bend in Little Cottonwood Road, just east of the intersection with Wasatch Boulevard. The Boulders Trailhead is at 10245 South Wasatch Boulevard. From the north, the trail makes a series of switchbacks up the glacial ridge on the south side of Little Cottonwood Canyon, crosses the crest, and traverses above the houses to join the service road at the north side of the reservoir. From Wasatch Boulevard, the trail climbs steeply past the houses and then continues up along the stream. The routes from both trailheads join at Lower Bells Reservoir, a pretty lake that makes a nice destination for hikes with children.

The combined trails follow the service road on the north side of Lower Bells Reservoir. Watch for the trail sign where the foot trail forks left from road. The trail crosses to the south side of the stream on a footbridge about ¾ mile from the reservoir. Beyond here the trail gets much steeper and rocky. Continue climbing another ¾ mile (it seems much longer) to reach the spur trail to the lower waterfall at about 6,600 feet. A landmark as you approach the lower falls is a spring-fed stream running across the trail. The trail to the falls is a well-used fork to the left from the main trail that crosses a minor ridge and then drops to the falls viewpoint. Remember that this is a wild area and there are no handrails or warning signs to keep the inexperienced and foolhardy away from danger. In the first three months of the 2010 hiking season, there were seven search-and-rescue calls for Bells Canyon.

BELLS CANYON ACCESS. *Top:* Bells Canyon entrance in 1993. *Bottom:* Bells Canyon Trailhead today. For years access was restricted and hikers entering this canyon were trespassing. Cooperation among citizens, the Forest Service, and Sandy City has now resulted in two official trailheads for this magnificent canyon.

DESCENDING BELLS CANYON ON CONSOLIDATED SNOW IN JUNE. The granite ridge ahead separates Bells Canyon from Little Cottonwood and is a popular rock-climbing area.

The main trail continues on the south side of the stream to about 7,500 feet, where there is a second waterfall. The landmarks as you approach the upper falls are an open area with large granite boulders, including a house-size slab, and the trail and stream getting quite close to the cliffs to the north. The trail on the south fades above the upper waterfall. The route on the north side of the stream beyond here is described as a mountaineering scramble in chapter 11.

ROCKY MOUTH CANYON (WF-7)

A trail leads into the bottom of rugged Rocky Mouth Canyon. Park at the designated Rocky Mouth Trailhead area at 11300 South Wasatch Boulevard, ascend the steps to Eagle View Drive, and go south on the sidewalk to the bend in the road where you will see a trail sign at a gate at the start of a fenced right-of-way between two lots. The trail goes southeast into the canyon. With a sealed mine shaft and spectacular scenery, this short trail is popular with children.

The gate on Eagle Drive is locked by Sandy City during the winter months. Eventually, the Bonneville Shoreline Trail between Bells Canyon and the Hidden Valley

Trailhead will connect with this trail, but watershed-protection issues need to be resolved before construction.

HIDDEN VALLEY TRAILHEAD AREA

Two trails lead from the parking area at 11600 South Wasatch Boulevard to the Bonneville Shoreline Trail. One goes northeast and leads to the end of the BST, where the Sawmill Trail starts, and the other goes south and connects with the BST near Little Willow Canyon. This is a watershed area, and dogs are prohibited.

SAWMILL TRAIL (WF-9)

Distance	4 miles
Elevation Gain	4,700
Highest Point	Pass into Bells Canyon, 9,900 feet
Hiking Time One-Way	4h 30m

This steep trail ascends the ridge between Big Willow and Little Willow Canyons on the west slopes of Lone Peak. From the Hidden Valley Trailhead, take the northeast path up to the Bonneville Shoreline Trail, go past the first gate, and continue north. In about ¼ mile you will come to a second gate with a watershed sign. The area north of the second gate is the Big Willow Canyon watershed and is currently closed to public access. The Sawmill Trail is marked by a sign just before this second gate. Even with switchbacks, the trail is steep and climbs rapidly. A climb of about 300 feet in the next ¼ mile brings you to a viewpoint looking up into Big Willow Canyon. The trail continues up the ridge, going through stands of thick timber. About a mile up a short side trail leads to a waterfall. The trail becomes less distinct higher up, but is marked by flagging nailed to trees. The Sawmill Trail enters the upper part of Big Willow Canyon as a faint but distinct track. At the top of Big Willow Canyon, a pass overlooks upper Bells Canyon, and Peak 10292 is on the triple divide between Bells, Big Willow, and Rocky Mouth Canyons. The views of the valley and the mountains above make this an interesting trail no matter how far you have the energy to climb.

BIG WILLOW CANYON

This canyon is closed for watershed protection. Some maps show the pipeline access road as a trail, but this is incorrect, according to Sandy City in 2011. Stay out until the rules change. The continued problems with dogs being taken into the Bear Canyon watershed from the BST in Draper will make resolving trail access for Big Willow much more difficult. Irresponsible behavior has consequences that affect everyone.

BONNEVILLE SHORELINE TRAIL—SANDY TO DRAPER (BST)

Section	Hidden Valley to Orson Smith	Orson Smith to Coyote Hollow
One-Way Miles	2	2¾
Hiking Time One-Way	1h	1h 20m

Currently, there are two long sections of the Bonneville Shoreline Trail in Salt Lake County: the section from Davis County to Emigration Canyon and the section from the Hidden Valley Trailhead in Sandy through Corner Canyon Regional Park in Draper. This southern section of the Bonneville Shoreline Trail has greatly improved public access to the drainages and ridges along the northwest side of Lone Peak, and much trail construction activity is taking place each season. The first edition of this book mentioned no trails between Bells Canyon and Corner Canyon.

From the Hidden Valley Trailhead, signs indicate the route up to the Bonneville Shoreline Trail. The trail heads south, crosses Little Willow creek on a bridge, and continues traversing the hillside above the houses. The trail becomes a narrow track that eventually climbs to cross the rocky ridge where Trail of the Eagle heads uphill. From the ridge, the BST drops to cross Bear Canyon on a bridge. Next is the double junction where Cherry Canyon Logging Trail heads uphill, and a spur trail drops down to the Orson Smith Trailhead. The area between Hidden Valley Trailhead and the Cherry Canyon Trail junction crosses privately owned watershed land and is closed to dogs. Recently, hikers taking dogs into the closed area at the Bear Canyon bridge caused serious problems with the water company. Ignoring closed-area signs threatens the access for everyone.

If you are starting from the Orson Smith Trailhead, a steep trail starts at the signboard on the north and climbs with well-constructed switchbacks to cross the aquaduct trail and continue up to the Bonneville Shoreline Trail in ¼ mile. Alternatively, you can head south past the vehicle gate and follow the Corner Canyon Road for ½ mile to the East Bench trailhead, where the BST crosses the road. The area south of Orson Smith Trailhead is open to dogs.

The Bonneville Shoreline Trail continues south from the junctions with the Cherry Canyon Logging Trail and the connecting trail down to the Orson Smith Trailhead, staying on the bench above both the Aquaduct Trail and the Corner Canyon Road. After about a mile, the BST crosses the Corner Canyon Road at the East Bench Trailhead and continues below the road into Corner Canyon Regional Park, where there is a growing maze of maintained trails. The BST continues past the bottom of the Ghost

Falls bike- and foot-trail network and continues to the Coyote Hollow Court trailhead, which is right behind the LDS Temple.

South of Coyote Hollow Court, the BST becomes an urban trail that roughly parallels Mike Weir Drive to the trailhead on Mike Weir Drive, loops below the homes near Oak Hollow, and then parallels Steep Mountain Drive to the current end at the Flight Park. A lot of trail work was going on in Draper at the time of field checking, and landmarks in this area are changing rapidly.

LITTLE WILLOW CANYON

Distance	½ mile
Elevation Gain	250
Hiking Time One-Way	30m

Take either of the trails south from the Hidden Valley parking area and join the Bonneville Shoreline Trail at the mouth of this side canyon. Just before the bridge over Little Willow Creek, a short side trail heads east and follows a pipeline route to a water diversion. The canyon mouth is narrow and rocky, so this is a nice destination for a short hike. Routes branching off the Sawmill Trail provide access to Little Willow Canyon higher up in the Lone Peak Wilderness.

ORSON SMITH TRAILHEAD

This is the main access to the west approaches to Lone Peak and the start of the Corner Canyon Road. The Bonneville Shoreline Trail and other Draper trails are also reached from here. The trailhead is at 2000 East and 12600 South in Draper. See driving directions in chapter 4, approaching from either Pioneer Road or Highland Drive. The trails onto Lone Peak are steep. This trailhead is at 4,800 feet, and the summit is 11,253 feet and 4 straight-line miles away, a 30 percent slope.

TRAIL OF THE EAGLE (WF-10)

Destination	From Orson Smith Trailhead to Trail of the Eagle Junction	Rock Outcrop	Cherry Canyon Logging Trail Junction	Outlaw Cabin
One-Way Miles	1	2	5½	6½
Elevation Change	600	1,100	3,500	4,500

Highest Point	5,300	5,800	8,200	9,200
Hiking Time One-Way	45m	1h 30m	4h 30m	5h 30m
Special Difficulties		Steep	Under construction	Faint route

This trail climbs the spectacular ridge between Bear Canyon and Little Willow Canyon with amazing views in all directions. From the Orson Smith Trailhead, head uphill on the well-marked route to the Bonneville Shoreline Trail and follow it across the bridge at Bear Canyon Creek and up the other side. The Trail of the Eagle branches off the Bonneville Shoreline Trail where it crests a rocky ridge on the north side of Bear Canyon.

This is another trail that is brutally steep even with the switchbacks, but the views make the effort worthwhile. The rock outcrop ½ mile beyond the BST junction is a popular objective. The trail climbs to a junction where a connecting trail traverses south across upper Bear Canyon and connects with the Cherry Canyon Logging Trail. At this point, your elevation gain is already comparable to hiking from the Cottonwood Heights to Alta, and Lone Peak is still above you. The Trail of the Eagle can be combined with the Cherry Canyon Logging Trail to make a loop hike from the Orson Smith Trailhead. Trail volunteers were working on this trail at the time of field checking, so route conditions high on the mountain are improving.

The Trail of the Eagle continues to climb easterly and eventually reaches the Outlaw Cabin, which is located in a bowl high in Little Willow Canyon north of Peak 9561 on the USGS map. From here it is possible to climb over the saddle to the southeast and descend to the Jacobs Ladder Trail, but this would be an inefficient route to Lone Peak Cirque.

LONE PEAK

This rugged summit, visible from North Salt Lake to Provo, was the centerpiece of Utah's first congressionally designated wilderness. The approach is steep, hot, and dry, but the experience of standing in an alpine cirque only a few miles from the city is unique. The cirque is ringed with near-vertical granite walls and angular summits; the view from the lower end of the cirque is one of the most photogenic in Utah.

This is a huge massif, and there are several major routes. Historically, the Jacobs Ladder route, and the nearby Movie Road variation, has been the most popular route up Lone Peak. The Cherry Canyon Logging Trail, the Jacobs Ladder Trail, and the now-closed Draper Ridge routes join near the minor peak marked 9322 on the topographic maps. The south summit of Lone Peak can be hiked from the Schoolhouse Springs

LONE PEAK CIRQUE— A RUGGED ALPINE WILDERNESS. The true summit is on the left side of the picture.

Trailhead in Alpine (DC-2). Mountaineers can approach Lone Peak from Bells Canyon or from the south face, but these are technical climbs, not hikes.

The Corner Canyon Road is closed in wet weather, but the cooler weather in early spring and late fall makes these the best times to climb these south-facing slopes. Although Cherry Canyon Logging Trail is a longer route to the summit than Jacobs Ladder, I suspect that Cherry Canyon will gain in popularity given the year-round access from Orson Smith Trailhead.

CHERRY CANYON LOGGING TRAIL (WF-11)

Destination	Traverse Trail	Jacobs Ladder Trail	Lone Peak Summit
One-Way Miles	3¾	5½	7¾
Elevation Change	3,700	4,600	6,700
Highest Point	8,500	9,200	11,243
Hiking Time One-Way	3h 20m	4h 30m	7h
Special Difficulties			Scrambling exposure

This trail starts from the Bonneville Shoreline Trail above the Orson Smith Trailhead and climbs the ridge between Bear Canyon to the north and Cherry Canyon to the south. From the trailhead, take the steps and switchbacks up to the BST. Immediately north of the junction with the BST on the flat bench south of Bear Canyon is the sign marking the Cherry Canyon Logging Trail. The BST continues toward Bear Canyon, and the Cherry Canyon Trail heads steeply uphill. The area is sagebrush and Gambel oak, making for good views, but a lot of sun. The trail climbs for 3¼ miles to a junction with the trail traversing above Bear Canyon between Trail of the Eagle and the historic Draper Ridge route. Turn south and aim for a rock pinnacle on the Draper Ridge at about 8,200 feet. To get to the Lone Peak summit, go southeast and continue following tracks up the Draper Ridge to the junction with the Jacobs Ladder Trail near 9,000 feet. Continue to the summit following the directions below.

JACOBS LADDER ROUTE (WF-8)

Destination	Lone Rock	Draper Ridge	Lone Peak Cirque	Lone Peak Summit
One-Way Miles	1½	2¾	3¾	5
Elevation Change	1,340	3,600	4,000	5,643
Highest Point	6,940	9,200	9,600	11,243
Hiking Time One-Way	1h 20m	3h 10m	3h 50m	5h 45m
Special Difficulties				Scrambling exposure

This route is scenic and direct, but steep. From the Orson Smith Trailhead on Wasatch Boulevard, drive 2.6 miles up the Corner Canyon Road to the Ghost Falls Trailhead.

The Jacobs Ladder Trail starts 200 feet beyond the parking area. The first part of the trail is popular with mountain bikes, so the route is wide and obvious as it climbs through oak brush and mountain mahogany. After about a mile, you reach a ridge overlooking Utah County where you get a nice view of the distant summit. The trail heads northeast for another ½ mile up the ridge called "Jacobs Ladder." Just before you reach the outcrop marked Lone Rock (elev. 6,939), the trail dips across the head of the drainage to your north and then starts climbing even more steeply up the mountain. Climb for about two hours to the junction with the Cherry Canyon Trail route.

The hardest part ends where the Jacobs Ladder Ridge meets the ridge at about 9,000 feet. The trail now heads east through a large meadow and crosses a small stream that is a reliable source of water as late as July. The unwary occasionally follow this stream by mistake, but the route continues east across a ridge and into the cirque. The trail gets faint as it crosses the granite ridge, but there are cairns all the way. The elevation gain is only 250 feet from where the trail first meets the ridge to the bottom of the cirque.

The trail ends soon after entering the cirque, and in early summer the route beyond here will be on snow. The prominent rock outcrop on the end of the ridge above marks where the trail enters the cirque and will be a landmark for the return. The true summit is the triangular point farthest left along the top of the sheer wall. The ridge on the right leads to a series of minor summits.

The normal route stays on the left of the stream (reliable most years) draining the cirque and heads north to the obvious saddle. The most energy-efficient route is to ascend the grassy slope to the granite dome on the far-left side of the cirque, staying about 200 feet from the cliffs. Next, traverse a boulder-filled cove and cross another area of exposed rock before reaching the short scramble to the saddle. From the boulder-strewn saddle, the route follows the ridge east toward the summit. The last few hundred feet involve scrambling with extreme exposure. Know your abilities and be very cautious if the rock is wet. The summit is a small flat-topped rock.

TRAIL TO SECOND HAMONGOG (DC-2.2)

A faint trail continues from Lone Rock and traverses east for 2¾ miles to the Second Hamongog, where it joins the trail coming up from Schoolhouse Springs in Alpine. The Pleasant Grove Ranger District does very limited maintenance on this trail.

FUTURE ROUTES IN CORNER CANYON

In November 2012 Draper City purchased twenty-four hundred acres of undeveloped land from Zions Bank. This will protect public access to open space along the ridge between the Suncrest development and Jacobs Ladder area in Corner Canyon.

HISTORIC ROUTES FROM CORNER CANYON

DRAPER RIDGE

This route, described as "incredibly steep jeep tracks carved into the hillside [where] 4WD adventurers have clawed their way directly up" in the first edition, has been closed and restored. The Cherry Canyon Logging Trail and Trail of the Eagle both are maintained trails going to the same ridge higher up.

MOVIE ROAD

This route variation followed the jagged ridge north of the current Jacobs Ladder Trail. The scar of the road made for filming the commando movie *Devil's Brigade* decades ago is still readily visible from the distance.

URBAN TRAILS

This is a guidebook to the mountains, but the major areas with urban trails will be briefly mentioned as they provide a venue for muscle-powered outdoor recreation. Urban trails are important to reduce the visitor demand on the National Forest. The Wasatch Front is a densely populated area, and urban trails can be hardened and managed for high use. If you want solitude, visit the wilderness, but if you just want fresh air and exercise, consider the following parks. The Salt Lake Valley is far behind other metropolitan areas such as Boulder, Colorado, and Portland, Oregon, in developing an urban trail network.

LEGACY PARKWAY TRAIL—FARMINGTON TO NORTH SALT LAKE

This 14-mile foot, bike, and horse trail parallels the Legacy Parkway and is managed by the Utah Department of Transportation as part of the environmental mitigation for the highway corridor. A 3¼-mile pedestrian-only section goes through the Legacy Nature Preserve between the highway and the Great Salt Lake. The nature preserve section is reached from the southern trailheads that are west of Redwood Road on Center Street in North Salt Lake, on 2425 South in Woods Cross, and on 500 South in Bountiful.

JORDAN RIVER PARKWAY—DAVIS COUNTY TO UTAH COUNTY

Several long sections of riverside trail are now constructed, and the vision is for a trail extending about 40 miles from the headwaters of the Jordan at Utah Lake to the Legacy Parkway Trail. A continuous trail now runs for 14 miles from 8500 South in

Sandy to 200 South in Salt Lake City. Trailheads are generally in small developed parks located near the bridges where major streets cross the river. The Jordan Parkway is a place where my wife and I go for a leisurely hike in midwinter or on summer evenings. The Jordan River Parkway is great for canoeing too.

RED BUTTE GARDENS—SALT LAKE CITY

This is a fee area with a paved interpretive trail inside the fence. The area is most noted for the formal gardens, but there are also several miles of paths through areas maintained in a more natural state. Also, a single-track trail on the south connects with the Red Butte Canyon road to create a loop around the outside of the fence. This exterior loop functions as an alternative route of the Bonneville Shoreline Trail.

PARLEY'S HISTORIC NATURE PARK—SALT LAKE CITY

This is a sixty-eight-acre creek-side area with county-operated Tanner Park to the west, Suicide Rock to the east, and a connection to the Bonneville Shoreline Trail. Parley's Historic Nature Park is at 2740 South 2700 East. At the east end, a paved trail and two bridges across the interstate connect this park to the Bonneville Shoreline Trail near the Parleys Trailhead on Wasatch Boulevard. The master plan is to eventually have trails connecting from this area west to the Jordan River Parkway.

DIMPLE DELL REGIONAL PARK—SANDY

This creek-bottom area was designated by the Utah County Commission as a nature park after a long battle between preservationists and golf course promoters. The trails in this 3-mile-long park are for walking, running, bicycling, and horse riding. The park is officially at 10400 South 1300 East, but there are other trailheads.

CORNER CANYON REGIONAL PARK—DRAPER

Citizen activists urged Draper City to build a high-quality system of foot, bike, and horse trails as the city developed. Today the Bonneville Shoreline Trail and the Jacobs Ladder route up Lone Peak are only a few of the many trails in this gem of an area. The trail system is developing so rapidly that I cannot provide all the details. During field checking, it seemed that every time I talked to Jack Earnhart, one of the trail leaders, he wanted to tell me about the mile of new trail that volunteers built the week before. Draper City publishes a map and keeps it updated. Major access points are the Equestrian Center and Orson Smith Trailheads on Highland Drive, Coyote Hollow Court behind the temple, Potato Hill on Traverse Ridge Road, and the seasonal trailheads high on the Corner Canyon Road.

6

Millcreek Canyon

Millcreek has a good system of maintained trails leading up from the narrow stream-cut gorge. The area was not heavily glaciated, and much of the area is covered by soft sedimentary rock, resulting in rounded summits and rolling ridges. Millcreek was logged in pioneer times, but the north-facing slopes are still heavily forested. Most of Millcreek Canyon is in the spruce-aspen zone, with higher portions in the montane zone with Douglas fir and white fir. None of this drainage is high enough to be in the alpine vegetation zone, but the north ridge has large treeless areas.

The Millcreek Ridge, on the north between Parleys Canyon and Millcreek Canyon, offers short hikes to Mount Aire and Grandeur Peak. The vegetative cover is mixed grass, mountain brush, and stands of aspen, with limited forest in sheltered areas. There are a few small cliffs but no serious obstacles to off-trail hiking. A herd of elk inhabits the area around Lambs Canyon, and they are frequently seen farther west.

The ridge on the south, between Millcreek Canyon and Big Cottonwood Canyon, is higher and has two topographically distinct portions. The western section from Mount Olympus to Neffs Canyon is called Wildcat Ridge. Narrow rock spurs separate nearly impassable couloirs and gulches. This rugged cockscomb formed by tilted layers of the Big Cottonwood and Mutual Formations is a place for mountain goats, alpinists, and adventurous hikers. Farther east, from Mount Raymond to the head of Millcreek, the Raymond Ridge is wider and much gentler. Here, the complex geology consists of layers that have been folded and shoved horizontally by the Raymond thrust fault. Trails lead up the main drainages and connect into a network of constructed trails, which run the full length of this ridge, from Neffs Canyon to Park City and Brighton.

CANYON MANAGEMENT

Millcreek Canyon is a fee area that is intensively managed for recreation. Currently, the fee is three dollars per vehicle, forty dollars for an annual pass, and bicycles are free. Since it was established in 1991, the access fee has provided funds for road, picnic-area, and general maintenance of the canyon. The paved road is popular for bike riding, but the upper canyon trails, like Big Water over to Desolation Lake, are open to mountain bikes only on even-numbered days. The canyon is not used as municipal watershed, so dogs are allowed, but dogs must be leashed in developed areas and throughout the canyon on even-numbered days.

 For general information regarding trails, see chapter 1. For driving directions to trailheads, see chapter 4. To cross-reference trail names, trailheads, and maps, see the "Hike Master List."

RATTLESNAKE GULCH (M-02)

Distance	¾ miles one-way
Elevation Gain	700
Highest Point	Pipeline Trail—6,000
Hiking Time One-Way	55m

I did not hike this trail for many years after it was constructed because I expected an uninteresting mountain-bike shortcut. When I finally tried the trail, I discovered a delightful climb up a tree-filled gully with a steady grade and well-designed switchbacks. This is the lowest trailhead in Millcreek Canyon, and it is only a short way above the entrance station. At the junction you can either continue west on the Pipeline Trail to a valley overlook or go east to Church Fork.

PIPELINE TRAIL (M-02, M-07)

Destination	Rattlesnake Gulch Junction to West Viewpoint	Rattlesnake Gulch Junction to Church Fork Junction	Church Fork Junction to Burch Hollow Trailhead	Burch Hollow Trailhead to Elbow Fork Trailhead
One-Way Miles	1	2	1½	3

Highest Point	5,920	6,000	6,000	6,700
Elevation Change	−100	Level	Level	700
Hiking Time One-Way	30m	1h	50m	1h 50m

This is a relatively level trail that is popular for both hiking and mountain bikes. It allows loop hikes between several trailheads and offers impressive views at many points along the way. The trail runs about 7 miles from its west end at a viewpoint high above the mouth of Millcreek Canyon to the paved road at Elbow Fork Trailhead. You can get on the trail at Elbow Fork Trailhead or by climbing up Burch Hollow (100-foot elevation gain), Church Fork (300-foot gain), or Rattlesnake Gulch (650-foot gain) Trail. Note that the above does not include the time to hike up or down from the Pipeline Trail at either Rattlesnake Gulch or Church Fork.

From the top of the Rattlesnake Gulch Trail, the Pipeline Trail goes west to a spectacular viewpoint, and this entire section is mostly open grassland and low brush. The trail currently dead-ends here, but eventually it may connect with the Bonneville Shoreline Trail toward Parleys Canyon. From the Rattlesnake Gulch junction, the trail also goes east to the junction with the Church Fork Trail, a short way above the top of the picnic area. The Pipeline Trail continues east, passing above Log Haven Inn toward the Burch Hollow Trailhead. Here a short spur trail drops to the highway, and the Pipeline Trail starts climbing in a series of switchbacks and then levels off. Going east, you are hiking through tall trees, but there are frequent open areas with views of the south side of Millcreek Canyon. The Pipeline Trail continues east past the junction with the trail to Burch Hollow Ridge. From here to Elbow Fork, the trail follows the level grade cut for the pipeline supplying a long-gone hydroelectric plant. It is free of brush and is easy walking. Remains of the pipeline can be seen where side drainages cross the route. Mountain-bike riders have provided much of the volunteer work to reconstruct this trail.

The Elbow Fork end of the trail can be found by leaving the road at the black rock outcrop that is 200 feet west of the Mount Aire trailhead.

GRANDEUR PEAK (M-01)

Destination	Pipeline Trail	Bottom of Switchbacks	Grandeur Peak
One-Way Miles	½	1	2¾
Highest Point	6,000	6,600	8,299
Elevation Change	360	880	2,619
Hiking Time One-Way	25m	55m	2h 40m

TRICANYON OVERVIEW

Grandeur Peak forms the west end of Millcreek Ridge and is prominent on the Wasatch skyline. It is the most accessible and the easiest of the major peaks overlooking the Salt Lake Valley. The trail starts from the Church Fork picnic area, on the north side of the road, 3.2 miles from Wasatch Boulevard.

Hike or drive the paved road north through the picnic area to a gate where the trail begins. A section of this trail passes through private land owned by the Boy

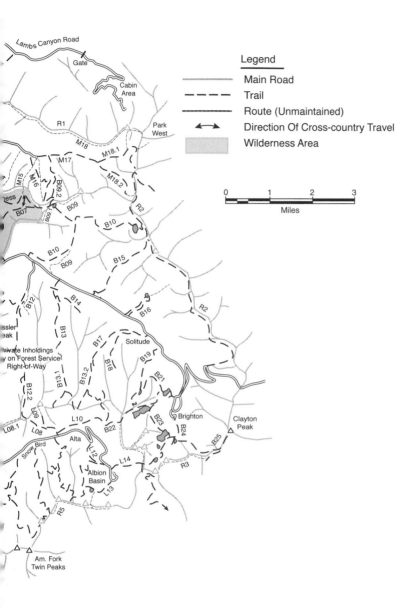

Scouts. A footpath continues up from the picnic area along the west side of the stream for ½ mile to a small clearing where the trail leaves the stream and turns sharply west. Well-constructed switchbacks lead up to a saddle on the Millcreek ridge crest where you get an outstanding view of Salt Lake Valley. The trail from the saddle follows the ridge west to the Grandeur summit ½ mile away and 680 feet higher.

Several trails branch from the trail to Grandeur. An unmaintained route follows Millcreek Ridge east toward Church Fork Peak and Mount Aire (R-1). An alternative descent is the west side of Grandeur Peak (F-09). The Lower Pipeline Trail (M-02) crosses from the Church Fork Trail just past the gate at the top of the picnic area and heads both directions near the 6,000-foot contour.

CHURCH FORK PEAK TRAIL (M-01.1)

The Church Fork Peak Trail is an old route that is now overgrown but follows a distinct constructed bench across the hillside. It branches from the Grandeur Peak Trail after the seventh switchback where there is a long curve to the west. The Church Fork Peak Trail leads in a straight line east to a meadow at the head of the Church Fork drainage. From the meadow, the route goes north through the trees and ascends the ridge to Church Fork Peak (elev. 8,316).

THAYNE CANYON (M-03)

Destination	Neffs Canyon	Thayne Peak	Desolation Trail
One-Way Miles	1½	2¼	2¾
Highest Point	7,950	8,760	8,676
Elevation Change	2,150	2,960	2,876
Hiking Time One-Way	1h 50m	2h 40m	2h 55m

This trail follows the Thayne Canyon drainage and offers a steep but easy climb to the upper portion of the Desolation Trail and a direct route to the pass at the head of Neffs Canyon. The trail starts at the Desolation trailhead on the south side of the road, 3.4 miles up Millcreek Canyon from Wasatch Boulevard. The trailhead is at the lower end of the picnic area just east of the Millcreek Inn. Head south past the outhouse and look for the Desolation Trail sign. After about 100 yards, the trails separate as the Desolation Trail makes a switchback to the right onto the hillside.

The Thayne Trail continues as a cleared path along the bottom of the drainage, and it eventually makes a short, sharp switchback to the left, immediately below a reliable spring and an old watering trough. A short distance above, the trail meets the Desolation Trail, which has been making endless switchbacks. The two trails combine for one long switchback, then separate again. The separation, marked by a cairn, is at the edge of a small ravine where the Desolation Trail turns back east. The Thayne Trail continues up along the east side of the ravine until the drainage opens into a bowl. Here the trail becomes less distinct. One route heads generally up and west, directly toward the

VIEW FROM THAYNE PEAK. This summit is a few minutes' climb from the Desolation Trail and offers excellent views in every direction. Mount Olympus is on the right skyline.

pass to Neffs Canyon, which is just to the left of a prominent rock outcrop. The more popular route goes higher and to the east but eventually curves to reach the pass.

Marine fossils are abundant in the limestone near the pass. The peak to the south (elev. 9,776) is a triple divide between the Millcreek, Big Cottonwood, and Neffs Canyons. This peak is most easily reached from the Big Cottonwood side. Thayne Peak (elev. 8,656) is visible on the divide between Thayne Canyon and Porter Fork. The Neffs Canyon Trail continues west from the pass down to Olympus Cove.

DESOLATION TRAIL—MILLCREEK PORTION (M-04)

Destination	Salt Lake Overlook	Thayne Trail Junction	Thayne Peak Junction	Porter Fork
One-Way Miles	1¾	3	4½	6¾
Elevation Change	1,250	2,150	2,906	3,570
Highest Point	7,000	7,900	8,656	9,320
Hiking Time One-Way	1h 30m	2h 35m	3h 40m	5h 10m

This well-maintained trail climbs by gentle switchbacks to a viewpoint overlooking the city. It is the beginning of the Desolation Trail, which continues east for 17 miles along the Raymond Ridge to Desolation Lake. The Desolation trailhead is just east of the Millcreek Inn, on the south side, 3.4 miles up Millcreek Canyon. Head south past the outhouse and look for the Desolation Trail sign. The Desolation Trail soon makes a switchback to the right and up out of the streambed.

DESOLATION TRAIL TO SALT LAKE OVERLOOK

This trail is an obvious constructed path, and the "Hiking the Wasatch" map accurately shows the series of easy switchbacks. The hillside is steep and susceptible to erosion, so avoid the temptation to shortcut the switchbacks. About 700 vertical feet above the trailhead, the Desolation Trail meets the crest of the ridge on the west, and a trail branches to the west and heads down into the Boy Scout camp. The Desolation Trail makes a long traverse and then continues climbing in another series of switchbacks to again reach the crest of the ridge on the west at the Salt Lake Overlook. There are excellent views both up and down the canyon from the overlook. To the north, just off the trail, there are a few sheltered resting spots. If you are using a topographic map, the overlook is on the end of the sharp ridge (elev. 7,000 feet) above Greens Canyon.

SALT LAKE OVERLOOK TO PORTER FORK

Beyond the overlook, the trail recrosses the ridge and begins a long, winding ascent of upper Thayne Canyon. It crosses the main stream drainage and meets the Thayne Canyon Trail after one hour of hiking. A spring and an old watering trough are located on the Thayne Trail a hundred yards below the junction.

From the junction, the Thayne and Desolation Trails combine for one long switchback. They then separate, and the Desolation Trail continues east to reach the small saddle just south of Thayne Peak (elev. 8,656). Beyond the saddle, there are endless switchbacks as the trail continues across Porter Fork, finally reaching the Porter Fork Trail a few switchbacks below the pass into Big Cottonwood. The Desolation Trail beyond Porter Fork is covered in the Big Cottonwood chapter.

Thayne Peak is a short scramble up deer trails. The summit has a panoramic view and is a popular destination.

Why does this foot trail have such gentle grades? The Desolation Trail was originally designed as a motorcycle trail but is now in the Mount Olympus Wilderness Area and is closed to motorized vehicles and to mountain bikes. Even prior to wilderness designation, the irresponsible behavior of a few motorcycle riders who could not resist the challenge of climbing the nearest hill led to trail closures to prevent serious watershed damage. Forest Service design standards resulted in a grade that makes sense for wheeled vehicles but is of limited interest to hikers. It simply takes too long to get anywhere—hence the continued popularity of the more direct Thayne Canyon Trail and the appearance of user-created switchbacks with a more realistic grade than the Forest Service trail.

PORTER FORK AND MOUNT RAYMOND VIEWED FROM BURCH HOLLOW. The Bowman Trail (M-06) climbs to Baker Pass on the left of Mount Raymond, and the Desolation Trail crosses the pass on the right of the peak and then continues west across Porter Fork toward Thayne Canyon.

PORTER FORK (M-05)

Destination	End of Road	Porter Fork Pass
One-Way Miles	1½	3¼
Highest Point	6,800	9,320
Elevation Change	1,140	3,660
Hiking Time One-Way	1h 20m	3h 25m

The route begins as a road through a summer cabin area on Forest Service leased land and continues into the Mount Olympus Wilderness to a junction with the Desolation Trail and the Porter Fork West Pass.

The Porter Fork road starts 4.4 miles up Millcreek Canyon. A small sign identifies Porter Fork, and there is a gate just after the bridge at the start of the side road. The road is a public right-of-way for foot traffic, but respect the cabin owners' privacy as you hike through the summer home area.

After 1½ miles, the road is blocked by the gate marking the wilderness boundary. A jeep trail continues up to a mine site that predates the wilderness designation. A mile beyond the wilderness boundary, the road turns west and the foot trail branches left. The junction with the Desolation Trail is about 400 vertical feet below

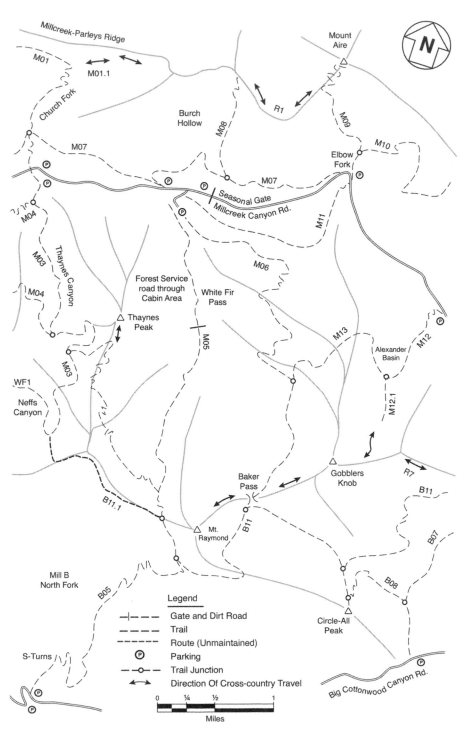

Millcreek-Parleys Ridge

M01

M01.1

Church Fork

Burch
Hollow

M07

M08

Mount
Aire

R1

M09

M10

Elbow
Fork

M07

Seasonal Gate
Millcreek Canyon Rd.

M11

M04

Thaynes Canyon

M03

M04

M07

M06

Forest Service
road through
Cabin Area

White Fir
Pass

Thaynes
Peak

M05

M13

Alexander
Basin

M12

M12.1

WF1

Neffs
Canyon

M03

Baker
Pass

Gobblers
Knob

R7

B11

B11.1

Mt.
Raymond

B11

B07

Mill B
North Fork

B05

B08

S-Turns

Circle-All
Peak

Big Cottonwood Canyon Rd.

Legend

—┼┼—	Gate and Dirt Road
— — —	Trail
· · · · ·	Route (Unmaintained)
Ⓟ	Parking
—o—	Trail Junction
↔	Direction Of Cross-country Travel

0   ¼   ½   1

Miles

MOUNT RAYMOND AREA

Mount Raymond viewed from the Bowman Trail just beyond Baker Spring.

the Porter Fork West Pass. A series of switchbacks takes you up the steep headwall to the pass on Raymond Ridge, where you can continue east on the Desolation Trail or turn west on an unmaintained trail that follows the Big Cottonwood side of the ridge to Neffs Canyon.

Porter Fork can be used in combination with the Bowman Fork Trail, Desolation Trail, or Mill B North Fork Trail to create a one-way outing.

BOWMAN TRAIL (M-06)

Destination	White Fir Pass	Baker Spring	Baker Pass
One-Way Miles	1½	3	3¾
Highest Point	7,520	8,880	9,320
Elevation Change	1,260	2,660	3,080
Hiking Time One-Way	1h 20m	2h 50m	3h 20m

The first part of the Bowman Trail up to White Fir Pass is an easy hike through dense forest. An intermediate hike takes you past Baker Spring, across open slopes, and on to the pass overlooking Big Cottonwood. Ambitious hikers can climb either Mount Raymond or Gobblers Knob, which are listed under "Summits from Baker Pass" (see B-08.2 and B-08.3).

The trail starts near the Terraces picnic area, which is on the spur road south, 4.7 miles up Millcreek Canyon. Drive across the bridge, take the right branch at the top of the hill, and park near the end of the road. A signboard marks the trailhead, which is the start of both the Bowman Trail and the trail to Elbow Fork. The Bowman Trail is the one to the right, heading south. The trail becomes a distinct constructed tread as it traverses a hillside and heads into the Bowman Fork drainage. This trail is shown on the USGS map, but the route location is inaccurate in several places.

A branch trail at the first stream crossing leads back north to the Porter Fork cabin area. After a mile, the Bowman Trail leaves the stream and climbs to White Fir Pass, a nice overlook with a good view of Porter Fork. A good place for lunch is just a few feet north of the pass along the ridge.

About 1½ miles beyond White Fir Pass, there is a junction with the connecting trail from Alexander Basin. The Bowman Trail continues up a lush gully to Baker Spring (a reliable water source) and then begins a long ascending traverse of the avalanche-swept slopes below Gobblers Knob to reach the saddle between Mount Raymond and Gobblers Knob.

There is a four-way junction at Baker Pass. Unmaintained trails lead to Mount Raymond and to Gobblers Knob. A short connecting trail descends the Big Cottonwood side of the pass to the Desolation Trail immediately below. For a longer return to Millcreek, you can follow the Desolation Trail west around Mount Raymond and descend by the Porter Fork Trail, making a 10-mile loop.

Baker Spring is a historical site where several mine workings were located. The miner's cabin burned down in the early 1980s. A stock watering trough was constructed here to service sheep grazing, which continued in Porter Fork until 1973.

BURCH HOLLOW TRAIL (M-08)

Destination	Trailhead to Junction	Lookout Rock	Millcreek Ridge
One-Way Miles	1½	1¾	3
Elevation Change	700	700	2,080
Highest Point	6,600	6,600	8,120
Hiking Time One-Way	1h	1h 10m	2h 40m

TRAILHEAD TO PIPELINE TRAIL

The Burch Hollow Trailhead is on the north side of Millcreek Canyon, just above the Porter Fork Road. The trail starts by heading downcanyon to a junction with the Pipeline Trail coming from Church Fork. From the Pipeline Trail junction, the combined trail climbs 600 feet in a series of switchbacks and then continues east on a level grade from a historic pipeline route. The junction where the Burch Hollow Trail separates from the Pipeline Trail is about ¾ mile after the top of the switchbacks and is easy to miss. The landmark is that the combined trail dips into the drainage formed by Burch Hollow Creek and then climbs back to the original grade and crosses the ridge for Lookout Rock, and in about 200 more yards the Burch Hollow Trail to the ridge makes a sharp switchback to the west. Look carefully for the trail starting up the hill. The trail ascends the east side of the Burch Hollow drainage with occasional switchbacks. A few spots have washed out and some areas are slightly overgrown, but the track is distinct all the way. The route passes beneath spectacular outcrops of Thayne Formation limestone and heads for the obvious saddle on the ridge. The saddle overlooks Mount Aire Canyon, a Y-shaped area of private land with roads and summer homes.

If you are hiking the ridge and want to descend Burch Hollow, the trail starts at the low point west of the prominent pinnacle on the crest and heads southeast, passing below the first cliff.

LOOKOUT ROCK

Where the combined Burch Hollow and Pipeline Trail climbs out of Burch Hollow drainage and turns east, a path through the woods following the old pipeline route can be seen heading southwest and slightly downhill to Lookout Rock. This outcrop, on the end of the ridge separating Burch Hollow from Millcreek, offers an outstanding view of Porter Fork. Although the road is clearly visible directly below, the best choice is to return the way you came, as the slopes below are steep and easily eroded.

HISTORIC BURCH HOLLOW ROUTE

The original Burch Hollow Trail started near the current trailhead, passed behind the guard station to the east, and went directly up the drainage. This route, described in the first edition, has now been closed and restored.

MILLCREEK FISHING DOCK AND BOARDWALK

There is an ADA-accessible streamside fishing dock and short boardwalk located on the south side of the Millcreek road, just above the road to the Terraces picnic area.

ELBOW FORK TRAILHEAD

Four trails start from this trailhead, located at the sharp right-angle bend 6.4 miles up the Millcreek Canyon road. Elbow Fork is the side canyon directly north of the bend, and the trails to Mount Aire and the Lambs Canyon Pass share a common route for the first ¼ mile up this drainage. The Pipeline Trail goes west along the north side of

MOUNT AIRE SUMMIT PANORAMA

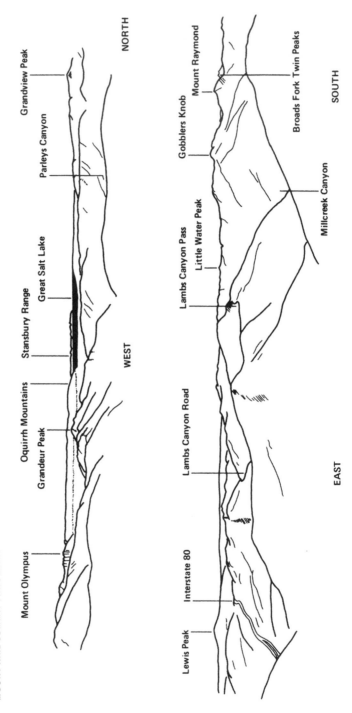

NORTH

Grandview Peak

Parleys Canyon

Great Salt Lake

Stansbury Range

Oquirrh Mountains

Grandeur Peak

Mount Olympus

WEST

Mount Raymond

Gobblers Knob

Broads Fork Twin Peaks

SOUTH

Millcreek Canyon

Little Water Peak

Lambs Canyon Pass

Lambs Canyon Road

Interstate 80

Lewis Peak

EAST

The Pipeline Trail in Millcreek Canyon is popular for hiking, running, and mountain biking.

the road, connecting with Burch Hollow, Church Fork, and Rattlesnake Gulch. On the south, a bridge across the stream is the beginning of the trail that winds up onto a spur ridge and then descends to the Terraces picnic area. The Pipeline and Terraces trails make good one-way hikes, or the two can be combined as a loop. Parking space along the road is limited and this is a popular trailhead, so park carefully.

MOUNT AIRE (M-O9)

Destination	Mount Aire Pass	Mount Aire Summit
One-Way Miles	1	1¾
Elevation Change	1,170	1,991
Highest Point	7,800	8,621
Hiking Time One-Way	1h 10m	1h 50m

When I want an outstanding view without too much hiking time or effort, I often choose the panorama from the summit of Mount Aire. The trail follows a pleasant south-facing slope and is especially good in the spring and fall, but it has enough shade to be a good summer trail as well.

The trail starts up the east side of the drainage from the Elbow Fork Trailhead. After about ¼ mile, the Lambs Canyon Trail branches east, and the Mount Aire Trail crosses the stream on a sturdy bridge. The trail becomes steeper, but you soon reach the saddle at the head of Mount Aire Canyon. The trail turns east and follows a series of well-defined switchbacks through the Gambel oak to reach the summit.

LAMBS CANYON FROM ELBOW FORK (M-10)

Distance	1½ miles one-way
Elevation Gain	1,490 feet
Highest Point	Lambs Canyon Pass—8,120
Hiking Time One-Way	1h 30m

Start at the Elbow Fork Trailhead and turn right just before the bridge where the Lambs Canyon Trail and the Mount Aire Trail separate. A sign marks the junction.

The trail follows the stream into a gully that is filled with moss and fallen logs and is reminiscent of the forests found in wetter areas. Near the head of the gully, the trail bends right and traverses to an excellent Millcreek overlook on the top of a minor ridge. Across the ridge, the terrain becomes more open, and you walk through a grove of small aspen before climbing a short hill to the pass.

At the pass is the junction with the Great Western Trail coming up from Lambs Canyon, a major side canyon of Parleys Canyon. The Millcreek Ridge trail (R-1) is the faint track heading east along the ridge crest toward Murdock Peak.

ELBOW FORK TO TERRACES TRAILHEAD (M-11)

Destination	Terraces Picnic Area	Return from Terraces
One-Way Miles	1¾	1¾
Elevation Change	−430	430
Total Ascent	690	1,120
Hiking Time One-Way	1h	1h 10m

This nice short hike has good views down Millcreek Canyon and up into Porter Fork and involves little elevation gain. The trail is on a north-facing slope and is shaded, so it makes a good summer hike even though it is at a relatively low elevation. You can start at either the Elbow Fork Trailhead, 6.4 miles up Millcreek Canyon, or at the Terraces Trailhead, 4.7 miles up the canyon.

The Elbow Fork end of the trail begins at the footbridge on the south side of the road, 200 feet upcanyon from the sharp turn. The trail climbs a series of steep switchbacks and reaches an excellent viewpoint after only 10 minutes of walking. From here, the trail continues generally south, as it gradually ascends to the crest of the ridge above Bowman Fork. The trail follows this mountain mahogany–covered ridge for ¾ mile before descending a series of switchbacks to the Terraces Trailhead.

It is an excellent trail for observing the effect of the direction of the slope on the microclimate and on the vegetation as you walk through dense stands of tall fir and more open areas of aspen and Gambel oak.

To get to the Terraces end of the trail, drive across the bridge and follow the picnic-area road to the top of the hill, take the right fork, and park at the end of the road. A signboard marks the beginning of both the Terraces Trail to Elbow Fork and the Bowman Trail heading south.

ALEXANDER BASIN TRAIL (M-12)

Destination	Alexander Basin	Gobblers Knob	Start of Trail to Bowman	Bowman Trail Junction
One-Way Miles	1½	2¼	1	2½
Elevation Change	1,640	3,086	1,040	1,440
Total Ascent	1,640	3,086	1,040	1,740
Hiking Time One-Way	1h 35m	2h 40m	1h	2h 5m

The Alexander Basin Trailhead is on the south side of Millcreek Canyon, 7.8 miles up from Wasatch Boulevard. A trail mileage sign and a wilderness boundary sign are located where the trail turns and climbs directly up the hill. The next section is one of the steepest official trails in the Wasatch. Soon, two well-graded switchbacks wind through stands of fir on the steep slope. After climbing 600 feet, the slope becomes more gradual, and the trail straightens out and heads southwest. To reach the Alexander Basin viewpoint, continue south up an aspen-covered hill, climbing another 600 feet in the next ½ mile.

The Mount Olympus Wilderness boundary has a strange shape excluding Alexander Basin. This 1984 Wilderness Bill outcome was the result of intense lobbying by both wilderness advocates who wanted protection and the helicopter ski interests who wanted winter terrain. Hike up to this beautiful glacial cirque and discover why local conservationists fought so hard to protect the area.

ALEXANDER BASIN TO GOBBLERS KNOB (M-12.1)

The first edition indicated that the official trail ended at the edge of the Alexander Basin cirque, but now the Forest Service trail continues all the way to the ridge. This route climbs 1,000 feet up steep and loose slopes to the east ridge of Gobblers Knob. Carefully pick your way and follow available switchbacks to avoid erosion. In June much of the route will be snow covered, and the ridgetop cornice will still be present. At the saddle, turn west and follow the ridge crest for ¼ mile to the summit.

ALEXANDER BASIN TO BOWMAN FORK (M-13)

Most hikers have not discovered the pleasant walking and spectacular views of Alexander Basin, Porter Fork, Mount Raymond, and the Salt Lake Valley that this underutilized trail offers. A maintained trail traverses the ridge and connects with the Bowman Trail about 1½ miles beyond White Fir Pass. The junction with this connecting trail to Bowman Fork is located in a small clearing, a mile from the Alexander Basin Trailhead, at about the 8,200-foot elevation.

From the junction, the trail to Bowman Fork heads west and drops a short way before beginning to climb across the first ridge. The trail rises and falls as it crosses a series of ridges and gullies but stays between 8,200 and 8,600 feet. The route alternates between open brush, wide-spaced aspen, and dense stands of fir. Soon, the huge Porter Fork basin comes into view, and you can see the Bowman Trail below. You can make a loop by descending the Bowman Trail to Terraces, then taking the trail to Elbow Fork, followed by walking a mile up the road from Elbow Fork to the start.

BIG WATER TRAILHEAD

This parking area at the end of the Millcreek Canyon paved road, 9.6 miles up the canyon, is the start of several official and unofficial trails that in some cases share common sections. These include the Big Water and Little Water Trails toward Big Cottonwood Canyon, the Great Western and Old Red Pine Road Trails toward Summit County, and the historic routes up Soldier and Wilson Forks. The upper parking often fills, necessitating parking in the overflow areas just downcanyon. The square mile of formerly private land just above the trailhead was recently purchased by Salt Lake County. Public support for acquisition of critical land parcels is important to improving trail systems.

If you dislike encountering downhill bikes while hiking, then go here on odd-numbered days. Bikes are allowed on the trails radiating from the Big Water Trailhead only on even days.

BIG WATER AND LITTLE WATER FORK

Destination	To Dog Lake Junction via Big Water, Official Trail	To Dog Lake Junction via Big Water, Direct Trail	To Dog Lake Junction via Little Water Trail
One-Way Miles	2½	1¼	1½
Elevation Change	1,200	1,200	1,200
Hiking Time One-Way	1h 50m	1h 15m	1h 20m

Note: All measurements are from the upper parking area to the Dog Lake junction.

Three options all lead from the Big Water Trailhead to the ridge where you can cross over into Big Cottonwood Canyon near Dog Lake.

BIG WATER, OFFICIAL TRAIL (M-16)

The combined Big Water Trail and Great Western Trail start at the southwest corner of the upper parking area. The trail heads west and joins with the alternative start coming from the lower parking area. The trail is a wide constructed path with frequent switchbacks, and there is no difficulty staying on the route. The trail turns back to the east and crosses the stream. Here the unofficial direct route can be seen going more steeply up the drainage. Near the top of a minor ridge, there is the junction with the Great Western Trail, which traverses east. The Great Western Trail soon crosses the Little Water Trail and then continues east toward the ridge crest, and the Big Water Trail heads generally south in a series of switchbacks until it reaches the four-way junction where it also crosses the Little Water Trail. Five more minutes from the four-way junction up either branch will take you to the Desolation Trail above Dog Lake.

BIG WATER, DIRECT ROUTE (M-16.1)

This is the foot track on the east side of the stream coming from Big Water Gulch. It follows a steeper grade, has signs of water-bar construction, and provides a faster way to the Desolation Trail while avoiding many of the bicycles. Avoid the meadow restoration just beyond the parking area. Start from the point where the official trail crosses the stream. The direct route continues up the drainage and rejoins the official trail one switchback below the four-way junction.

LITTLE WATER TRAIL (M-17)

The combined Little Water Trail, new Red Pine Road Trail, and historic road up the main drainage all start at the east end of the upper Big Water parking area. For the Little Water Trail, turn south in about 100 yards and follow the stream coming from Little Water Gulch. The Little Water Trail ascends through an open area, crosses the stream, and continues through forest and occasional small meadows until it reaches the four-way junction described above. Most of the way, there are an obvious track and evidence of a road bench in the hillside. This was treated as an abandoned or unofficial route in the first edition, but is now back on the Forest Service system trail map.

DOG LAKE JUNCTION AND BEYOND

All three routes converge at the Dog Lake junction on the Desolation Trail. From the junction, you can descend to Dog Lake or climb either Little Water Peak or Reynolds Peak.

The Desolation Trail (B-11) provides a connection to all the major trails from both Big Cottonwood and Millcreek, so many loops and extended hikes are possible in this area. Going east, the Desolation Trail connects with the Great Western Trail on the ridge above the Canyons ski resort, making a 9-mile loop back to the Big Water Trailhead. The 10-mile loop going from Dog Lake junction west and returning to Millcreek by the Bowman Trail is one of the best fall foliage hikes in the Wasatch. A shorter option requiring a car shuttle between canyons is to continue down into Big Cottonwood on either the Mill D or Butler Fork Trail.

OFF-TRAIL ROUTE—WILSON FORK (M-14)

The Wilson Fork route starts 9.2 miles up the canyon, a short distance below the Big Water Trailhead. A closed road starts up this drainage but ends in ¼ mile. From here, find your own route using a topographical map and staying on game trails on the left side or near the center of the drainage. The area is open forest with little brush. Use the surrounding ridges as landmarks and aim for the low point on the main ridge to the southwest. From the saddle, the head of Soldier can be reached by traversing the minor summit to the east. Also, the ridge going west is a nice route to Gobblers Knob.

OFF-TRAIL ROUTE—SOLDIER FORK (M-15)

The Soldier Fork route starts at the east end of the lower Big Water parking area, 9.5 miles up Millcreek Canyon. The well-graded Big Water Trail heads west from here and makes a wide loop before recrossing the Soldier Fork trail higher up. The unmaintained Soldier Fork trail goes directly up the drainage. Occasional fallen trees block the foot track. As you approach the head of the drainage, the slope becomes steeper and the game trails become as prominent as the human trail. The route makes several switchbacks just below the pass. If you lose the trail, work your way up through open forest. A trail continues from the pass to the Desolation Trail, about 200 yards downhill.

UPPER MILLCREEK CANYON (M-18)

Destination	Head of Millcreek via Red Pine Road Trail	Great Western Trail to Meadow	Great Western Trail to Cutoff to Ridge	Murdock Peak
One-Way Miles	4	3¼	6¾	3¼
Elevation Change	1,350	900	1,400	2,002
Highest Point	8,920	8,500	9,000	9,602
Hiking Time One-Way	2h 40m	2h	4h	3h

OLD RED PINE ROAD

This trail on the hillside north of the stream was constructed in 2011–12. The trail is named for the historic road that went from Millcreek Canyon across the ridge to Red Pine Lake in Summit County. The lands across the ridge are all part of the Canyons ski resort, formerly known as Wolf Mountain and before that Park West.

The trail starts at the east end of the upper Big Water parking area and in 100 yards takes the left branch where the Little Water Trail separates. Farther along is another fork where the Red Pine Road Trail heads uphill to the left and the historic road stays in the drainage. The trail is well designed to avoid sensitive riparian areas while maintaining a steady grade as it ascends along the slopes on the north side of the drainage. There is a junction with the Great Western Trail at the meadow near 8,500 feet, and the Red Pine Road continues east to the Wasatch Crest Ridge.

GREAT WESTERN TRAIL—MILLCREEK PORTION (R-2)

After descending to the road at Elbow Fork, the Great Western Trail follows the paved Millcreek Canyon road to the upper Big Water Trailhead. It becomes a trail again as it climbs up the south side of Millcreek Canyon to reach the Wasatch Crest Ridge above Desolation Lake. The official GWT routing is to the ridge south of Murdock Peak, but

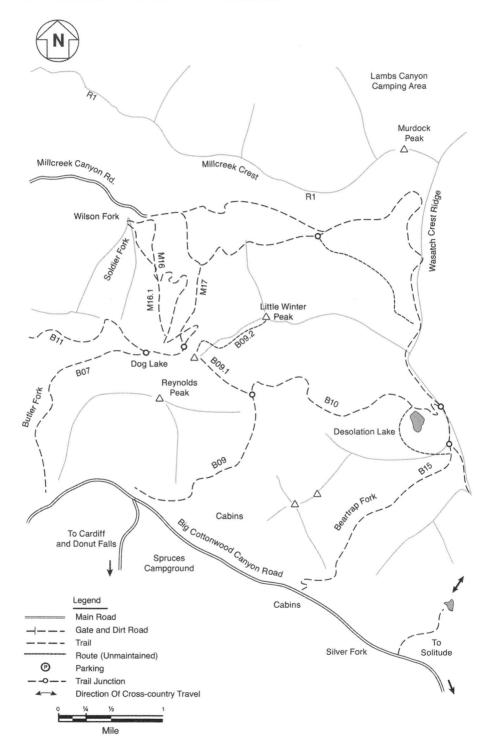

N

Lambs Canyon
Camping Area

Murdock
Peak

R1

Millcreek Crest

Millcreek Canyon Rd.

R1

Wasatch Crest Ridge

Wilson Fork

Soldier Fork

M16

M16.1

M17

Little Winter
Peak

B09.2

B11

B09.1

Dog Lake

Butler Fork

B07

Reynolds
Peak

B10

Desolation Lake

B09

B15

Beartrap Fork

Cabins

To Cardiff
and Donut Falls

Big Cottonwood Canyon Road

Spruces
Campground

Cabins

To
Solitude

Silver Fork

Legend

Main Road
Gate and Dirt Road
Trail
Route (Unmaintained)
Ⓟ   Parking
Trail Junction
Direction Of Cross-country Travel

0   ¼   ½   1

Mile

some maps show the GWT following the cutoff trail to the south and intercepting the Wasatch Crest Ridge above Desolation Lake.

The GWT leaves the south side of the upper Big Water parking area and initially follows the Big Water Trail, described above, for about a mile to the junction where the GWT turns east. This trail was originally constructed to get hikers and bikes around the section of private land at the head of the canyon. It traverses along the south side of the canyon and crosses the Little Water Trail. It stays nearly level until it meets the historic Millcreek road and new Red Pine Road Trail in the canyon bottom at around 8,500 feet.

The road enters a meadow where there is a junction. The GWT, Red Pine Road, and historic road continue east for another 1¼ miles to the Wasatch Crest Ridge, overlooking the ski area below. Most of the land on the east of the ridge is private, but managed for recreation. Consult the "Park City Trails" map, discussed in chapter 9, for options continuing into Summit County. Murdock Peak is on private land to the north along the ridge crest. Immediately before the pass, the GWT turns sharply south and follows the Wasatch Crest Ridge, staying on the Millcreek side around the head of Millcreek and following the Big Cottonwood–Summit County divide on toward Scott Hill and Guardsman Pass.

At the trail junction near 8,500 feet, the south branch is an unofficial trail that leads into the wide upper bowl, climbs to the ridge connecting Little Water Peak to the Wasatch Crest Ridge, and then connects to the GWT high above Desolation Lake. The ridge directly south of the bowl is the divide to the Mill D North Fork of Big Cottonwood Canyon.

HISTORIC ROAD

A two-track vehicle road once went all the way up the Millcreek drainage and crossed over into Summit County. Off-road vehicle closures and the phasing out of sheep grazing in the area resulted in this road degenerating into an overgrown track. The route along the canyon bottom has adverse impact on riparian areas, so the new Red Pine Road Trail on the north side and the Great Western Trail on the south side of the canyon are better hiking and biking options. The canyon bottom remains the logical route for cross-country hiking and winter ski tours such as the popular routes over the ridge from Big Cottonwood.

7

Big Cottonwood Canyon

This long canyon cuts east between Mount Olympus and Twin Peaks and then turns south as it approaches Brighton. The lower canyon is a narrow, stream-cut gorge with wild, steep walls that limit hiking. The upper canyon is a wide, glacier-carved valley with numerous side drainages leading to lakes and alpine cirques. The mouth of the canyon is flanked by hard, Precambrian metamorphic rocks forming spectacular red and pink cliffs and buttresses. The upper canyon is a geologist's nightmare of hard and soft, young and old rock that has been thrust, folded, and intruded into endless scenic variety. The canyon offers the full range of ecological transitions from foothill brush to alpine tundra and from swampy streambeds to forest zones to dry grasslands.

The trails near the canyon mouth lead into the wilderness areas on either side. The canyon has had a long mining history, and many of the trails, especially from Mineral Fork to Brighton, are actually on old wagon-road grades. The best easy hiking is in the Brighton area, where the glacier-scoured bowls have resulted in delightful lakes a short walk from the highway.

Raymond Ridge to the north is crossed by several trails, and the area is mostly gentle to moderate terrain. Cottonwood Ridge to the south is asymmetrical. The north side offers a long gradual ascent, but the south side drops sharply into Little Cottonwood Canyon, and, west of Cardiff Pass, there are no hiking routes across this ridge.

Big Cottonwood is in a cultural transition. It is far less developed than Snowbird or Park City, and most of the resorts, restaurants, and residences are remnants of a more low-key era. Older cabins and the folksy Brighton Store contrast with the fancy condominiums and restaurants of Solitude. Big Cottonwood has much private land, but restrictions on water hookups currently limit new development.

For general information regarding trails, see chapter 1. For driving directions to trailheads, see chapter 4. To cross-reference trail names, trailheads, and maps, see the "Hike Master List."

STAIRS GULCH (B-01)

STORM MOUNTAIN TRAIL

Distance	½ mile one way to end of trail
Elevation Gain	300 feet
Highest Point	Water intake—6,100
Hiking Time One-Way	20m

This short trail takes you into the lower portion of Stairs Gulch, an avalanche-swept couloir with the east face of Storm Mountain towering above. The cliffs, towers, and pinnacles combine with summer snowfields to provide an easily accessible glimpse of the conditions experienced by climbers on the upper portions of major peaks.

The trail starts on the south side of road directly across from the Storm Mountain picnic area, 2.9 miles up Big Cottonwood Canyon. Park 100 yards up the road near the geology sign. The trail follows the ramp up to the west and then turns directly south into Stairs Gulch. It follows the east side of the gulch along a water pipeline, and the constructed trail ends at the intake. The terrain beyond is suitable only for climbers or very experienced hikers and is described in chapter 11.

The snowfields in Stairs Gulch are frequently used by mountaineering classes for ice-ax training, and the cliffs have several intermediate to difficult rock-climbing routes. Rockfall from the frost-fractured quartzite walls accumulates to form the boulder-covered floor of the gulch. Stairs Gulch was a major obstacle to travel up the canyon before the modern graded road was constructed across the stair-like waterfall where the gulch meets Big Cottonwood Creek.

MULE HOLLOW (B-02)

Distance	1½ miles one way to the mine
Elevation Gain	1,400
Highest Point	Mine at 7,200
Hiking Time One-Way	1h 30m to mine

BIG COTTONWOOD, WASATCH BOULEVARD, TO MINERAL FORK

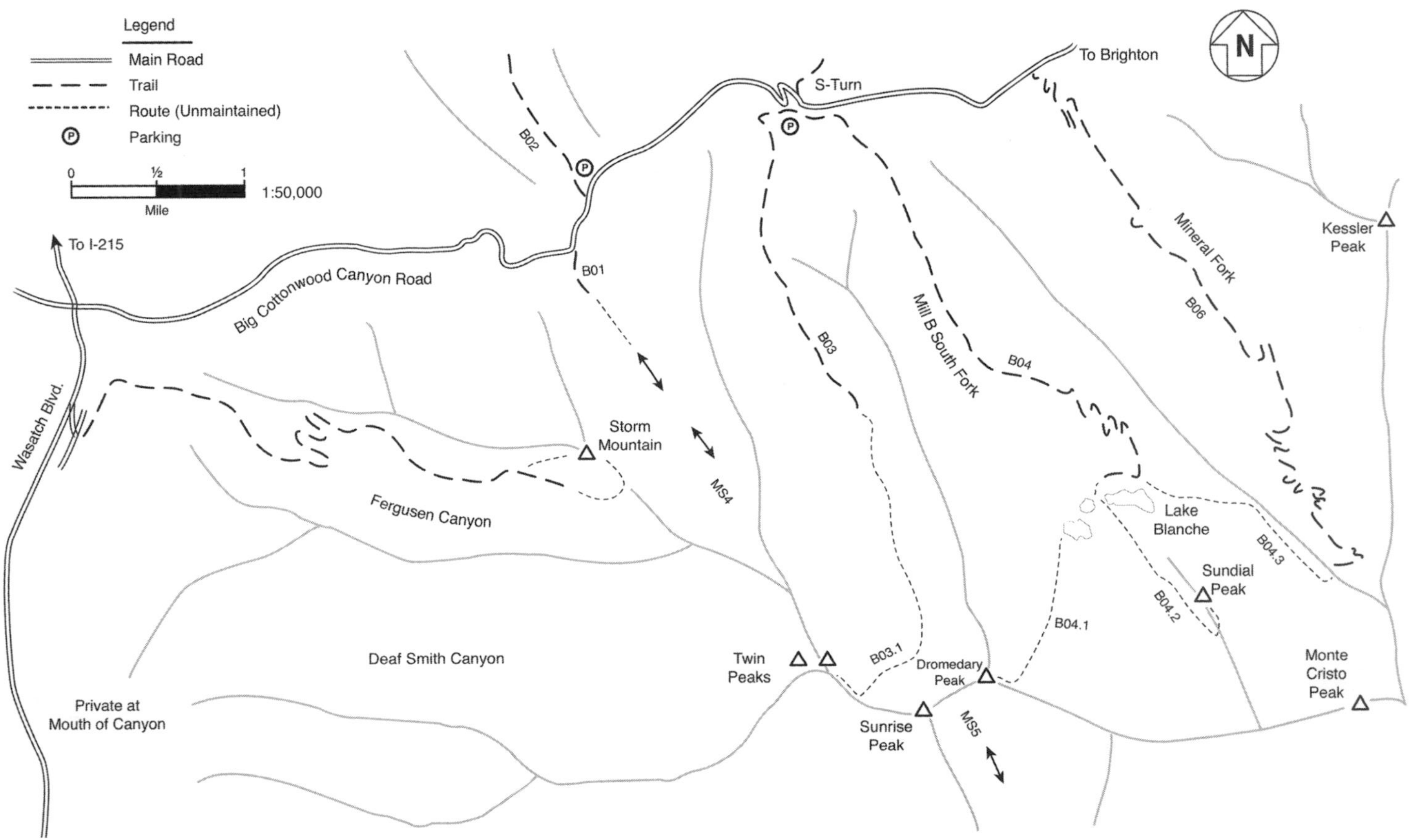

Legend

Main Road
Trail
Route (Unmaintained)
Parking

0   ½   1
Mile
1:50,000

To I-215

N

To Brighton

Kessler Peak

Mineral Fork

B06

B04.3

Lake Blanche

Sundial Peak

Monte Cristo Peak

B04.2

B04.1

S-Turn

B04

Mill B South Fork

B03

MS5

Dromedary Peak

Sunrise Peak

B03-1

Twin Peaks

MS4

Storm Mountain

B01

B02

Fergusen Canyon

Deaf Smith Canyon

Big Cottonwood Canyon Road

Wasatch Blvd.

Private at Mouth of Canyon

Mule Hollow is a nice hike to an abandoned mine in a seldom-visited side canyon. The trail is south facing and relatively low, so it is passable when other routes are snow covered. There are spectacular cliffs on both sides of this steep-walled canyon, and Stairs Gulch and Storm Mountain are visible from the mine.

The trail starts on the north side of the road, 3.2 miles up Big Cottonwood Canyon, just above the Storm Mountain picnic area. A small, unpaved parking area is on the north side of the road just after the bridge. The well-defined trail starts on the right side of the stream coming from Mule Hollow and climbs steadily up the drainage. The canyon is narrow, and the trail makes frequent stream crossings. The trail never gets far from the stream, and in several places the water overflows onto the trail during high runoff periods. Currently, the trail is badly eroded. The trail ends at the mine dump where there are a collapsed tunnel, the ruins of a cabin, and a few pieces of equipment. A short way farther up there is another tunnel on the west side of the stream that has a large flow of water coming out; numerous cascades can be heard inside. Another mine dump is a few hundred feet farther up.

Beyond the mines, Mule Hollow is filled with dense brush and loose rock, but deer trails and natural clearings can be used by adventurous hikers wishing to bushwhack higher. The west wall of the hollow can be climbed from the mine to a pass at the head of Dry Hollow, overlooking the Salt Lake Valley. An experienced hiker can scramble up the head of the drainage and reach Wildcat Ridge. Mule Hollow Wall, a rock-climbing area with many challenging routes, is on the west side of the hollow about ½ mile from the road.

S-TURN TRAILHEADS

The S-turn, 4.5 miles up Big Cottonwood Canyon, is the location of a very short walk to a waterfall and of three major trailheads. There are two parking areas, both on the right going upcanyon. The larger one is on the first bend, and the other is between the loops of the S-turn. Broads Fork Trail starts from the larger parking lot, just after the spur road crosses the bridge. The Mill B North Trail and the short walk to Hidden Falls start on the north of the road at the upper turn. The Lake Blanche Trail is reached by walking ¼ mile following the stream east from the parking area. With three major trails and two easy trails, this is one of the most popular trailheads in the canyon, and parking is very limited. Carpool if possible, and park carefully to utilize the available space.

MILL D SOUTH INTERPRETIVE TRAIL

This is an ADA-accessible paved trail. Park in the lot on the right at the first S-bend. An old paved road, now closed to vehicles, climbs for ¼ mile from the trailhead to where the parking for the Lake Blanche Trail was located when the first edition of this book was written. The pavement follows close to Big Cottonwood Creek, so you can see the pools and waterfalls. The evaporation from the stream and the shade from the trees on the steep hillside make this a pleasant place even on a hot summer day.

HIDDEN FALLS TRAIL (B-05.1)

Two trails start on the north side of the road on the upper loop of the S-turn, 4.5 miles up Big Cottonwood Canyon. A very short trail leads about 100 yards along the stream to Hidden Falls. The falls are out of sight of the highway, the stream rarely has a dangerous flow, and the area has a lot of interesting rock formations, making this a great hike for children.

BROADS FORK (B-03)

Destination	Stream Crossing	Meadow (Trail End)
One-Way Miles	1¼	2
Elevation Gain	960	2,200
Highest Point	7,160	8,400
Hiking Time One-Way	1h	2h 5m

This trail starts on heavily timbered slopes, follows a stream through open stands of aspen, and reaches an alpine meadow with fine views of Dromedary Peak (elev. 11,107) and Sunrise Peak (elev. 11,275). The trail starts from the lower loop of the S-turn. From the parking area, the Broads Fork Trail begins near the restroom and heads west up the hill.

The trail climbs around the end of the ridge into the Broads Fork drainage, making one switchback along the way. After a mile through fir and spruce forest, the trail crosses the stream on a sturdy bridge. Several small, shady clearings and the natural cooling of the stream make the bridge a nice destination on hot summer days. After crossing to the west side of the stream, the trail passes through open brush and stands of aspen. A couple of small ridges give the feeling of "we're there," followed by disappointment when the crest is reached and more trail comes into view. Finally, the trail curves around the left side of a small knob, and the meadow opens up beyond.

The maintained trail ends at the bottom of the meadow, but a footpath continues left across the stream and up the east side of the bowl toward Twin Peaks. Another faint footpath leads up the right side of the meadow, passing above the swampy and brushy area and continuing up the open west-side slopes. Both of these routes converge farther up. The upper part of Broads Fork is exposed to severe avalanches

BROADS FORK BASIN. The maintained trail ends at this viewpoint with Sunrise Peak ahead. The routes to Dromedary Peak and to Twin Peaks continue up the left side of the drainage.

coming off the steep, smooth slopes of Twin Peaks to the west. Massive ridges of avalanche debris remain through June.

If you enjoy route-finding and scrambling, you can cross the ridge to the east and descend to the Lake Blanche Trail. The notch north of the end of the Broads Fork Trail is probably the best, but all ridge crossings involve steep slopes of loose rock and gravel.

BROADS FORK TWIN PEAKS

Distance	5 miles one-way from trailhead
Elevation Gain	5,130 feet
Highest Point	East summit at 11,330 feet
Hiking Time One-Way	4h 45m to 5h 30m, depending on route conditions
Special Difficulties	Scrambling, snowfields, boulder-hopping

The beautifully matched summits of Twin Peaks form the west end of the rugged ridge separating Big Cottonwood and Little Cottonwood Canyons. Panoramic views, the magnificent alpine setting, the enormous vertical relief, and the prominent position on the Salt Lake skyline make this peak a popular objective for intermediate and advanced hikers. From the end of the Broads Fork Trail, there are several routes up Twin Peaks and all require some scrambling.

STANDARD ROUTE (B-03.1)

The standard route continues from the meadow up the main drainage to a notch on the Cottonwood Ridge and then follows the ridge west to the summit. Upper Broads Fork is a boulder field with much loose gravel and some brush. In May or June much of the route will be on snow, making travel easier, but an ice ax is advisable for climbing the steep headwall.

An unmaintained footpath continues east from the trail-end knoll, crosses the stream, and climbs up the east side of Broads Fork. After climbing about 1,000 feet, there is another, less distinct, basin, with Sunrise Peak directly ahead and the spectacular north face of Dromedary Peak to the left. Head toward the saddle to the right of Sunrise Peak. From this saddle, you can see most of the remaining route to the summit, ¼ mile to the northeast and 550 feet higher. There are two variations—the choice depends on the snow conditions and preferences for couloir versus ridge scrambling. Both routes have moderate exposure.

The high route follows the crest of the ridge until you come to an abrupt 20-foot cliff. This cliff is bypassed by traversing a series of ledges on the south side of the ridge for about 100 feet until you reach the crack, which can be ascended back to the ridge crest. This traverse involves difficult scrambling. Use caution! Continue along the ridge and then climb the switchbacks worn into the gravel of the summit cone.

The low route drops from the saddle and follows the slope on the Little Cottonwood side for about 200 yards to a couloir next to the cliffs that form the south ridge of the summit. Ascend this couloir, which may be snow filled early in the season, to the ridge crest and continue up the summit cone.

Deaf Smith Canyon (WF-5) is west of Twin Peaks. The best way to avoid the cliffs north of Twin Peaks is to descend southwest from the west peak into a rounded gully with steep rock ridges on both sides. Follow this drainage until it curves back north into the main canyon. Private property blocks the mouth of the canyon.

ROBINSON VARIATION (B-03.2)

An exciting variation of the Broads Fork approach is to ascend the wide, steep gully southwest of the end of the knoll at the end of the trail. The route looks forbidding, but with some route-finding a way can be found through the slabs to the ridge above. The right side of the gully leads to a saddle overlooking Stairs Gulch, and the left saddle overlooks Deaf Smith Canyon. There is considerable scrambling and exposure along the jagged north ridge to Twin Peaks but no technical climbing.

DROMEDARY PEAK

FROM BROADS FORK (B-03.3)

Distance	3¾ miles one way from Broads Fork Trailhead
Elevation Gain	4,907
Highest Point	11,107
Hiking Time One-Way	4h 30m to 5h, depending on conditions
Special Difficulties	Scrambling, snowfields, boulder-hopping

The route to Dromedary from Broads Fork is the shortest and easiest approach. Both this route and the route from Lake Blanche converge on the upper mountain. Starting from the end of the Broads Fork Trail, continue up the east side of the drainage as described for Twin Peaks. At about 9,800 feet, the Twin Peaks route turns southwest toward the notch and the route to Dromedary turns east. Aim for the shoulder of the mountain, about 200 feet above and south of the saddle on the ridge between Broads Fork and Lake Blanche Fork. At the shoulder, you are a few feet above the "sloping boulder-field" traverse described in the route from Lake Blanche. Traverse south on the Lake Blanche side, passing below the summit slopes, to the couloir leading up to the Cottonwood Ridge and then continue scrambling the east ridge to the summit.

LAKE BLANCHE TRAIL—MILL B SOUTH FORK (B-04)

Destination	Lower Clearing	Lake Blanche	Lake Lillian
One-Way Miles	1¾	3	3½
Elevation Gain	1,600	2,720	2,720
Extra Up and Down			120
Highest Point	7,800	8,920	8,920
Hiking Time One-Way	1h 40m	2h 55m	3h 10m

A well-maintained trail climbs past smooth rock slabs crowned with sawtooth spires to a photogenic basin containing Lake Blanche, Lake Florence, and Lake Lillian. The view of Sundial Peak above Lake Blanche is the emblem of the Wasatch Mountain Club, and the Salt Lake Valley is visible from the glacier-scoured rocks that ring the lakes. The USGS map calls this drainage "Mill B South Fork," but the name "Lake Blanche Fork" is commonly used.

LAKE BLANCHE AND SUNDIAL PEAK. This trail is fairly long, but these hikers managed the climb.

The trailhead parking is at the lower bend of the S-turn 4.5 miles up Big Cottonwood Canyon. Walk east on the interpretive trail for ¼ mile before turning uphill at the trail sign near the stream draining the Lake Blanche Fork. About ½ mile beyond the trailhead, the route crosses to the east side of the drainage on a bridge. For the next mile, the trail stays close to the stream and climbs steadily. Halfway to the lake, there is a clearing with fine views of the surrounding ridges and of Sundial Peak rising above the rounded red cliffs that rim the lakes.

The trail avoids the cliffs by leaving the stream and climbing the side slopes to the east. The Forest Service has done extensive trail work constructing switchbacks to bypass the erosion-prone steeper sections. Just before the lake, the trail crosses a short area of bare rock where the track disappears, but just keep heading in the same general direction. It helps to pick out a few landmarks here to help find the start of the trail on the return. The trail ends at Lake Blanche, which is the highest of the three lakes in the basin.

Footpaths head in various directions. Using these paths, you can follow the north side of Lake Blanche to reach Lake Florence and Lake Lillian, or you can make a circuit of the three lakes. Separate descriptions are provided for ascending each of the three peaks and for crossing the passes into Broads Fork and Mineral Fork.

ADVANCED HIKES FROM LAKE BLANCHE

Destination	Sundial Peak	Dromedary Peak	Mount Superior
One-Way Miles	4	5	5
Elevation Gain	4,120	4,907	4,932
Extra Up and Down			120
Highest Point	10,320	11,107	11,132
Hiking Time One-Way	4h 5m	5h 5m	5h 25m
Special Difficulties	Scrambling, exposure	Scrambling	Scrambling, exposure

Note: All distances and elevations are from the road.

DROMEDARY PEAK FROM LAKE BLANCHE (B-04.1)

Dromedary is a rugged and seldom-visited summit overlooking the major drainages on the far side of Little Cottonwood from White Pine to Hogum. The most direct route from Lake Blanche is to climb up the grassy gully that is south-southwest (200 degrees) from the Lake Blanche Dam. The gully headwall is an upward V of cliffs. On the left side, near the point of the V, there is a crack that requires about 20 feet of

THE SOUTH SIDE OF BIG COTTONWOOD CANYON VIEWED FROM WILDCAT RIDGE IN MID-JUNE.
Excellent trails lead up Mineral Fork, Lake Blanche Fork, and Broads Fork. The trail in Stairs
Gulch ends in ¼ mile; above is mountaineering terrain. *Top:* Lake Blanche to Stairs Gulch. The
skyline summits, from the left, are Dromedary, Sunrise, and Twin Peaks. *Bottom:* Mineral Fork
and Lake Blanche Fork. Mount Superior and Monte Cristo are on the skyline, and part of Kessler
Peak is visible on the far left.

easy rock scrambling with no exposure. After reaching the grassy slopes above, note landmarks so you can find the crack on your return. Continue directly up the slopes toward the couloir southeast of Dromedary and ascend to the Cottonwood Ridge. The summit is 300 vertical feet of moderate ridge-crest scrambling to the northeast.

The longer route up Dromedary is to ascend the wide scree-filled gully that is southwest (220 degrees) from Lake Blanche. Turn left just below the headwall into the steep couloir that takes you up 200 vertical feet through the cliff bands and onto the upper slope of Dromedary. An indistinct pass can be seen about 300 feet above the top of the couloir. This pass is the junction with the route to Dromedary from Broads Fork. From the top of the couloir, the route traverses for ½ mile south across a sloping boulder field. Traversing low is easier, while the high traverse from the pass is shorter. The traverse ends at the couloir leading to the Cottonwood Ridge, which was described above.

SUNDIAL PEAK (B-04.2)

The towering north face of Sundial is a difficult route for technical rock climbers, but hikers can scramble up the back side. Most hikers start by going around Lake Blanche on the north, crossing at the dam, and heading south up the rounded rock ribs ahead. When you are level with the talus slope at the base of Sundial, turn left and scramble up through the cliff band into the hanging canyon that is immediately on the west side of Sundial. Follow the side of Sundial southeast for ¾ mile, climbing 600 feet to a saddle on the Sundial ridge. From this saddle, scramble along the knife-edged ridge for 300 yards, heading back northwest to the summit. There are a few tricky spots with dangerous slabs below, so pick your route carefully and turn back if you question your ability.

An alternative to the hanging canyon is to continue up the rock ribs until the drainage curves to the southeast and you can turn back toward Sundial. This is a longer route, but the area is well worth exploring for its own sake.

EAST BRANCH—REGULATOR JOHNSON PASS, CARDIAC PASS, AND MOUNT SUPERIOR (B-04.3)

The east fork of the Lake Blanche drainage is a pair of glaciated canyons with sheer cliffs overlooking a spring-fed lake, meadows, moraines, and boulder fields. An unmaintained trail continues from the east end of Lake Blanche, traverses high on the wall of the east branch of the drainage, and leads to old mine workings just below the pass leading into Mineral Fork. This trail, which can be easily seen from the lake, avoids the cliff bands that make hiking the east branch a route-finding challenge. The start of the trail is lost among the tracks around the lake, so look for the distinct track leading east up between the first pair of rock ribs beyond the lake. After climbing

600 feet, the trail turns southeast and traverses through the dark cliffs and continues into the upper hanging canyon.

The trail ends above the ruins of a mine and near a small pond. The pass to the Regulator Johnson Mine in Mineral Fork is a 200-foot scramble directly up the slope from the trail end. The canyon beyond the pond is an open boulder field heaped into a series of moraines. The easiest way to continue up the east branch of Lake Blanche Fork is to drop down to the mine workings and then follow the drainage.

A steep, glacier-carved headwall rings the end of this drainage. The prominent notch on the left (east) is Cardiac Pass, which leads into Cardiff Fork. Mount Superior (elev. 11,050) is the indistinct high point to the south, while Monte Cristo (elev. 11,132) is the dark mass on the right. Superior can be reached by climbing to Cardiac Pass and then scrambling along the narrow ridge or by ascending the headwall directly below the summit. Monte Cristo is reached by continuing along the ridge from Superior. These summits offer a view of Snowbird's developments as well as a panorama of Big and Little Cottonwood Canyons.

The Twin Peaks Wilderness boundary follows the jagged ridge between Mineral Fork and Lake Blanche Fork to the summit of Mount Superior. The original conservationist proposal was to use the old mine road in Mineral Fork as the boundary, but this was opposed by helicopter skiing interests.

MILL B NORTH FORK (B-05)

Destination	Overlook	Desolation Pass	Porter Fork Pass	Baker Pass
One-Way Miles	1	3¼	3¾	4¾
Elevation Gain	840	2,960	2,960	3,120
Highest Point	7,040	9,160	9,160	9,320
Hiking Time One-Way	55m	3h 5m	3h 15m	3h 50m

Spectacular views of the wilderness to the south highlight this well-maintained trail as it winds upward through cliffs and across streams. Mount Raymond, Porter Fork, and Mill A Basin are reached from this trail, and it is often used as a descent from hikes starting at Butler Fork. The trail is named after the stream at the start, but it actually crosses both branches of the next drainage east before reaching the Desolation Trail.

The Mill B North Fork Trail starts on the north side of the upper S-bend and heads diagonally up the slope to the right of the Hidden Falls Trail. It makes a series of switchbacks and rejoins the stream above Hidden Falls. A half mile from the start, the trail passes the wilderness boundary sign. A few yards beyond, the trail makes a sharp 180-degree turn, leaves the stream, and heads south through open forest. Two more switchbacks bring you to the overlook. The viewpoint is on the rock outcrop, 20 feet south of the trail, just as the trail begins to turn back to the north. Cliffs drop 600 feet from the overlook to the road.

The trail now heads north along the crest of a ridge for another ½ mile to another overlook and a cliff band. Next it crosses into the Elbow Fork drainage, a remarkable area of riparian vegetation, follows this drainage a short way, and then begins a last series of switchbacks up the ridge to the east. The Desolation Trail makes a loop around Mount Raymond, staying between 9,200 and 9,400 feet. Maps are inconsistent regarding the location of the Desolation Trail junction due to trail relocation.

CONNECTIONS ALONG THE DESOLATION TRAIL FROM MILL B

The Desolation Trail can be followed west about ¼ mile to reach Porter Fork West Pass. From here, the Porter Fork Trail descends to the Millcreek road. The Desolation Trail crosses the ridge and traverses high across the Porter Fork drainage toward Thaynes Canyon. Immediately before the pass are the steep, open southwest slopes of Mount Raymond. Experienced hikers can ascend these slopes by staying well to the left, thereby avoiding the cliffs below the Mount Raymond summit. The easier route up Mount Raymond is to follow the Desolation Trail east 1 mile to Baker Pass and then climb the east ridge.

MINERAL FORK (B-06)

Destination	Overlook	Wasatch Mine	Regulator Johnson
One-Way Miles	¾	3	5
Elevation Gain	450	1,940	3,510
Highest Point	7,160	8,650	10,220
Hiking Time One-Way	35m	2h 30m	4h 15m

Mineral Fork has no route-finding problems and is well suited to large groups. A well-graded mining road leads to a spectacular overlook and then continues past the Wasatch Mine. This trail is currently open to ATVs and motorcycles. The Wasatch Mine is at the transition between forest and open alpine terrain. Above are the switchbacks across talus slopes to the Regulator Johnson Mine.

The Mineral Fork Trailhead is on the south side of the road, 6.1 miles up Big Cottonwood Canyon. Look for a heavy gate that marks the Mineral Fork road where it joins the highway. The dirt road crosses the stream and then heads west into the canyon. Both the USGS map and the "Hiking the Wasatch" map accurately show the road with all its switchbacks.

MINERAL FORK AND CARDIFF FORK. This rugged area is viewed from near Carbonate Pass. The old road climbing to the Regulator Johnson Mine is visible on the right in Mineral Fork (B-06). The Mount Superior area on the skyline is usually approached from the Alta side (L-08.1).

The road makes four switchbacks and then arrives at an overlook that provides a fine view down and across Big Cottonwood Canyon. The road eventually arrives at the Wasatch Mine, where a stream of rusty water discharges from the portal. From here you have a view back toward Kessler Peak and ahead toward the upper bowl of Mineral Fork. To reach the Regulator Johnson Mine, continue up the twenty-four switchbacks until you reach the scattered artifacts that mark the site. The upper portion of the fork is loose scree and is swept by winter avalanches, so there is little vegetation except low well-rooted or fast-growing species.

The pass 200 feet above the Regulator Johnson Mine is reached by scrambling up the boulders on the right of the mine. The route described for the east branch of Lake Blanche Fork is directly below the pass on the other side.

Mineral Fork is unusual in that the upper cirque is not on the main ridge line. The triple divide of Cardiff Fork, Mineral Fork, and Lake Blanche Fork is separated from the main canyon divide by a short, jagged ridge. This peak at the head of Mineral Fork can be reached by scrambling the ridge from the Regulator Johnson Pass. The area is broken by cliffs, narrow ridges, and rock pinnacles, so careful route-finding is needed.

BUTLER FORK TRAILHEAD

The Butler Fork Trail provides the best access to a large area on the north side of Big Cottonwood Canyon between Dog Lake and Mount Raymond. The east-branch trail climbs below the south slopes of Gobblers Knob to reach Dog Lake and Reynolds Peak. The west-branch trail climbs past a viewpoint on the ridge between Butler Fork and Mill A Gulch and then continues north. The Desolation Trail crosses high in the Butler Fork drainage, connects the east and west branch trails, and continues west below Mount Raymond.

The Butler Fork Trail starts on the north side of the road, 8.5 miles up Big Cottonwood Canyon. A small parking area is along the north side of the road, and a larger parking area is on the south, 100 yards up the canyon from the trailhead. The trail starts on the west side of the stream and then crosses on a bridge and climbs quickly up the steep-sided gulch. After ½ mile, the drainage widens and forks. A sign marks the junction where a maintained trail to Dog Lake turns east along the stream and the main trail continues left (west) toward the saddle above Mill A Basin.

EAST BRANCH OF BUTLER FORK (B-07)

Destination	Dog Lake	Loop via Desolation Trail
One-Way Miles	2½	6½
Elevation Gain	1,640	1,640
Highest Point	8,760	8,760
Hiking Time One-Way	2h	4h 10m

This route to Dog Lake passes through an incredible range of plant communities in a short distance. The mixture of sagebrush, stream-side willow, Gambel oak, aspen, and spruce-fir communities is an excellent example of the effects of microclimate and soil conditions.

From the trail junction ½ mile up Butler Fork, the trail to Dog Lake crosses a bridge and heads east along the stream. This side canyon between Gobblers Knob and Reynolds Peak is narrow, and the trail crosses the stream five times before the stream disappears in a meadow. The trail climbs to a saddle where it joins the Desolation Trail. The combined trail continues nearly level for ¼ mile along the head of Big Water Gulch, a side canyon of Millcreek, before crossing another saddle into the Mill D drainage just above Dog Lake.

The two branches of Butler Fork and the Desolation Trail can be combined into an excellent loop, or you can return to the Big Cottonwood Road by the Mill D Trail from Dog Lake. Another option is to climb Reynolds Peak from Dog Lake and hike cross-country west along the ridge and then drop back to the Butler Fork Trail.

RAYMOND RIDGE VIEWED FROM KESSLER PEAK SUMMIT.

The Desolation Trail (B-11) provides a high connection from Dog Lake, across Butler Fork, around Mount Raymond, and into Porter Fork. The routes up Mount Raymond and Gobblers Knob follow the ridge crest. Circle-All Peak is an easy hike with excellent views.

WEST BRANCH OF BUTLER FORK (B-08): CIRCLE-ALL PEAK, MILL A BASIN, AND MOUNT RAYMOND

Destination	Circle-All Peak	Desolation Trail	Baker Pass
One-Way Miles	1¾	2	3½
Elevation Gain	1,587	1,520	2,050
Highest Point	8,707	8,640	9,320
Hiking Time One-Way	1h 40m	1h 45m	2h 45m

At the trail junction ½ mile from the Butler Fork Trailhead, a well-maintained trail continues left and follows a small stream coming from the west branch for a short way. The USGS map shows the old route, now overgrown, continuing up the streambed, but the trail turns right and ascends switchbacks that were constructed to avoid trail erosion. The trail then crosses back to the left side of the drainage and makes another series of switchbacks up the steep, aspen-covered slope leading to the ridge crest.

Circle-All Peak (elev. 8,707) is 100 yards south from where the trail reaches the ridge. A foot track leads to this popular viewpoint. To the south, Kessler Peak dominates the foreground, with Cottonwood Ridge in the background. Mount Raymond and Gobblers Knob complete the panorama. This peak is named after the avalanche slide area below, but the origin of the slide-area name is obscure.

The trail continues north along the ridge above Mill A Basin for ¼ mile to the Desolation Trail. Several other tracks can be seen, including the now-abandoned trail that drops down into Mill A Basin and follows a moraine back up to Baker Pass. To reach the Mount Raymond area and Baker Pass, turn left on the Desolation Trail and follow an ascending traverse, gaining 450 feet in the next mile. Just below the saddle, the Desolation Trail continues east, and a short branch trail leads to Baker Pass and the junction with the Bowman Trail into Millcreek. The Desolation Trail stays on the Big Cottonwood side and may be followed on a nearly level grade for a mile southwest around the Mill A Basin to the Mill B North Fork Trail. Butler Fork and Mill B North can be combined to make a nice loop.

SUMMITS FROM BAKER PASS

Destination	Mount Raymond		Gobblers Knob	
Approach Route	From Butler Fork	From Bowman Fork	From Butler Fork	From Bowman Fork
One-Way Miles	4¼	4½	4	4¼

Elevation Change	3,161	4,041	3,166	4,046
Highest Point	10,241	10,241	10,246	10,246
Hiking Time One-Way	3h 40m	4h 15m	3h 35m	4h 10m

Note: Both summits are reached from Baker Pass, where the Bowman Fork and Butler Fork Trails join. Measurements are from the road.

MOUNT RAYMOND (B-08.2)

Mount Raymond overlooks nearly all of Big Cottonwood and Millcreek Canyons and is one of the most popular peaks in the Wasatch. Three well-defined ridges join at the angular summit, and cliffs drop to Porter Fork and Mill A Basin. The standard route heads up from Baker Pass and follows occasional switchbacks, keeping near the crest of the east ridge of Mount Raymond. Near the top, the ridge narrows to a knife-edge and there is some scrambling, but the route is suitable for most hikers. An alternative route is the steep slope on the west side of the mountain, which leads from the Desolation Trail near Porter Fork West Pass to the summit.

GOBBLERS KNOB (B-08.3)

This massive mountain is the highest point on the ridge between Millcreek and Big Cottonwood. From Baker Pass, a faint track heads northeast up the ridge toward Gobblers Knob. There is no scrambling, and there is little brush along the ridge. The true summit is the second high point on this route. The ridge continues east and is described as hike M-12.1, the route up Gobblers Knob from Alexander Basin. The upper portion of Gobblers Knob is largely treeless, creating excellent views and off-trail routes for hikers who like exploring.

MILL D NORTH FORK TRAILHEAD

DOG LAKE AND DESOLATION LAKE

The Mill D North Fork is one of the most popular canyons for easy hikes in summer and for ski tours in winter. These trails are also extremely popular with mountain bikes. The drainage is Y shaped, with maintained trails leading to both Dog Lake in the west branch and Desolation Lake in the east. Hiking in this valley gives an intimate, enclosed feeling. Connecting trails and routes continue beyond the lakes in all directions, and the easy peaks around the perimeter of the basin can be reached by short off-trail hikes. The Mill D Trail can be combined with the Butler Fork Trail to create a loop hike that requires only a short return walk along the road.

The trail starts from the Mill D Trailhead parking area, at the bottom of Reynolds Gulch and just across the highway from the road into Cardiff Fork, 9.6 miles up Big Cottonwood. The trail begins in the clearing east of the Reynolds Gulch stream and makes a gradual ascending traverse east across the south-facing slope between Reynolds Gulch and the Mill D drainage. It then turns north and continues almost level for ½ mile until it reaches the stream in Mill D Fork. The trail continues up the west side of the drainage. The now-unmaintained original trail starts 9.9 miles up the canyon. The historic route curves northwest into the drainage and then follows the west side of the stream across from the summer homes. This route crosses the stream twice before joining with the maintained trail.

DOG LAKE (B-09)

Destination	Y Junction	Dog Lake	Big Water Junction
One-Way Miles	1½	2	2¼
Elevation Gain	1,010	1,520	1,560
Highest Point	8,250	8,760	8,800
Hiking Time One-Way	1h 15m	1h 45m	1h 50m

Most Wasatch lakes are in alpine cirques, but Dog Lake is set in a forested area with rolling hills and grassy meadows. Several trails approach the saddle west of Dog Lake, providing connecting routes in every direction.

From the trail junction where Mill D North Fork branches, turn left and follow the wide trail along the bottom of the gully for ½ mile to the lake. This section is steep for a beginner hiker, but the trail is excellent and the steep section is short. There is a foot track all around the lake. If you want a little privacy, the meadow just south of the lake is off the main trails and drains into a gully that offers an interesting alternative return to the main Mill D Trail.

The trail continues along the north shore of the lake and climbs 50 feet to the junction on a small saddle. The Big Water Trail and Little Water Trail coming from Millcreek Canyon and the Desolation Trail converge here. The Butler Fork East Branch Trail separates from the Desolation Trail ¼ mile west of this saddle.

DESOLATION LAKE (B-10)

Destination	Desolation Lake	Beartrap Fork Pass
One-Way Miles	3½	4
Elevation Change	1,890	2,450

Highest Point	9,240	9,800
Hiking Time One-Way	2h 40m	3h 15m

Desolation Lake is a large mountain lake with no surface outlet—the water drains through the loose glacial deposits that formed the lake cirque. This was the last grazing allotment in the Tricanyon Area. Grazing was suspended in 1993. The area is popular with mountain bikes because the Great Western Trail is on the ridge crest above.

Starting at the Mill D Trailhead, hike 1½ miles to the junction where the canyon branches and take the right (east) branch to Desolation Lake. The trail makes a switchback at the start and then joins the east drainage near an overlook. There are excellent views of the Mount Superior and Cardiac Pass area on the far side of Big Cottonwood Canyon. The route follows the drainage through a meadow, up a short hill, then past a small pond. From the pond, the trail goes northeast through the woods and then climbs over the final moraine to reach the lake in an open cirque.

The trail continues past the north side of the lake and ascends 300 feet to the Wasatch Crest Ridge overlooking Summit County, where it joins the Great Western Trail from Millcreek to Scotts Hill. The trail to the ridge has switchbacks and is part of the Great Western Trail. Mountain-bicycle use has carved an eroded track up the slopes on the south side of the lake.

A good loop hike is to climb to the ridge and cross into Beartrap Fork, which is immediately south of Desolation Lake. Beartrap Fork can be followed back to the Big Cottonwood Road, where you will be only a mile from the historic Mill D Trailhead.

REYNOLDS PEAK (B-09.1)

Approach Route	Mill D Trail	Big Water Trail	Butler Trail
One-Way Miles	2¼	2	2¾
Elevation Gain	2,182	1,822	2,302
Starting Elevation	7,240	7,600	7,120
Hiking Time One-Way	2h 15m	1h 55m	2h 30m

Note: All measurements are from the indicated trailhead to the summit (elev. 9,422).

Reynolds Peak, an easy summit for hikers, is reached by a short off-trail ascent from Dog Lake. The summit panorama drawing identifies some of the features that can be seen from here.

The route to the summit starts on the low ridge southwest of Dog Lake and follows the north ridge of Reynolds Peak. A fairly obvious foot track goes from the south side of Dog Lake and passes the actual route up to Reynolds, before descending a drainage to eventually reconnect with the B-09 Dog Lake Trail. If you don't find the start of the unmaintained route up Reynolds, just head south from the lake, keeping near the crest of the ridge. From the saddle to the summit is ½ mile and 650 vertical feet. The climb is through open aspen with some brush.

This area is suitable for off-trail hiking. The southeast ridge of Reynolds Peak can be descended back to the start of the Mill D Trail. There is quite a bit of brush, but there are no other difficulties. Another alternative is to hike along the west ridge for a way and then drop down to the Butler Fork Trail and return to the road at the Butler Fork Trailhead. If you follow this ridge too far west, you get into an area with a lot of fallen trees, brush, and cliffs, so drop off the ridge while you can still see open areas among the fir trees below.

LITTLE WATER PEAK (B-09.2)

Approach Route	Mill D Trail	Big Water Trail
One-Way Miles	3	2¼
Elevation Gain	2,365	2,005
Starting Elevation	7,240	7,600
Hiking Time One-Way	2h 40m	2h 5m

Note: All measurements are from the trailhead to the Little Water Peak summit (elev. 9,605 feet).

This is another relatively easy summit for hikers. The route up Little Water Peak from Dog Lake starts as a track up the hillside on the north side of the lake and then turns right and follows the ridge northeast to the summit. There are several alternative tracks up the brushy hillside at the start. Once on the ridge, the terrain is open with grass and widely spaced aspen. Hiking is possible just about anywhere, but the game trails near the crest are the best route.

A good off-trail hike is to continue east from the summit to the Wasatch Crest at the head of Millcreek. If you get tired following the ridge, you can easily drop down to the Desolation Lake Trail.

DESOLATION TRAIL—BIG COTTONWOOD PORTION (B-11)

Trail Segment	Desolation Lake to Dog Lake Junction	Dog Lake Junction to Butler Fork West Trail	Butler Fork to Baker Pass	Baker Pass to Porter Fork
One-Way Miles	2½	3	2	2
Elevation Change	−400	−200	600	100

REYNOLDS PEAK SUMMIT PANORAMA

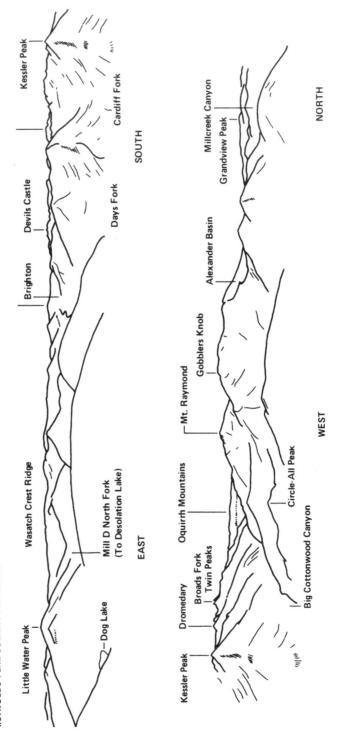

Highest Point	9,200	8,800	9,200	9,400
Hiking Time One-Way	1h 20m	1h 35m	1h 15m	1h 10m

The Desolation Trail was constructed by the Forest Service as a well-graded route from Thaynes Canyon on the Millcreek road to Desolation Lake. This long trail provides a nearly level connection among the numerous routes coming up from Millcreek and from Big Cottonwood, creating possibilities for extended hikes. The Big Cottonwood section is described going east to west. The section coming up from lower Millcreek is listed as trail M-04. If you like longer routes, a great hike for seeing fall foliage is to ascend Big Water Gulch and then follow the Big Cottonwood portion of the Desolation Trail west and return to Millcreek by either the Bowman Trail or the Porter Fork Trail.

DESOLATION LAKE TO DOG LAKE JUNCTION

Starting west from Desolation Lake, the Desolation Trail follows the drainage from down to the junction in Mill D North Fork and then back up the drainage to Dog Lake. The route is described as part of the Mill D North Trail, as that is how nearly everyone thinks of the route.

DOG LAKE JUNCTION TO BUTLER FORK

This section is wide, level, and in good condition. The trail provides a constantly changing view of Butler Fork and of the peaks on both sides of Big Cottonwood Canyon. From the junction with the Big Water Trail west of Dog Lake, this trail winds around the south side of Gobblers Knob, staying between the 8,600- and 8,800-foot contours. Five minutes after leaving the Dog Lake junction, the trail forks. The left trail leads down the east branch of Butler Fork, and the right trail is the Desolation Trail. The area west of this junction is in the Mount Olympus Wilderness. The slopes above are brushy, but a foot track leads to the head of Soldier Fork, and bushwhacking to the ridge above Wilson Fork is also possible. The trail descends 200 feet to a pleasant meadow and then climbs past a series of small cliffs to the junction with the Butler Fork west-branch trail.

BUTLER FORK TO PORTER FORK

From the junction with the Butler Fork Trail, the route continues west. It ascends 450 feet in 1 mile and then passes about 200 vertical feet below Baker Pass, the saddle between Mount Raymond and Gobblers Knob. A switchback leads up to Baker Pass and the Bowman Fork Trail junction. The Desolation Trail continues along a contour around the head of the Mill A Basin and hooks around the end of the sharp southeast ridge

DESCENDING KESSLER PEAK BY THE NORTH ROUTE (B-12.3). Mill A Gulch and Mount Raymond are visible across the canyon.

of Mount Raymond. After a mile the Desolation Trail reaches the small saddle above Maxfield Basin, where it joins the Mill B North Fork Trail. The nearly level trail continues another ½ mile to the pass west of Mount Raymond, leading down into Porter Fork. The continuation of the Desolation Trail on the Millcreek side is described as trail M-04.

PORTER FORK WEST PASS TO NEFFS CANYON (B-11.1)

There is a little-known route along the Big Cottonwood side of the ridge that leads to the pass between the head of Mill B Fork and Neffs Canyon. This is apparently an abandoned trail because some sections were obviously constructed while other sections are no more than game trails. Follow the ridge west from the Porter Fork Pass. The route traverses below some of the minor peaks rather than following the crest. Stay high and watch for the track and an occasional cairn.

DONUT FALLS (B-12.1)

Destination	Donut Falls
One-Way Miles	¾
Elevation Gain	280
Highest Point	7,200
Hiking Time One-Way	30m

This is an easy hike to a waterfall that drops through a hole in the rock. The road into Cardiff Fork turns south from the Big Cottonwood Road, 9.3 miles up the canyon. The road is paved to the Jordan Pines group picnic area and then becomes a gravel road that continues south through a summer home area. There is a trailhead for Donut Falls ¾ mile from the Big Cottonwood Road just before the stream crossing.

From the trailhead, follow the trail that starts on the east side of the creek. After walking ½ mile, you will come to a major fork. The left fork leads to the falls, and the right fork continues up to the mine. Continue along the stream to the falls. The trail gets rocky, and there are a few minor ups and downs as you approach the falls, which are somewhat hidden by boulders. If you want to combine a short approach with some more challenging terrain, it is possible to scramble to the top of the falls.

Donut Falls was in the first edition, but later access was blocked by "No Trespassing" signs. Eventually, Salt Lake City purchased 144 acres of private land and restored access to this treasure.

CARDIFF TO SPRUCES CONNECTOR

A ¾-mile trail leads through the woods between the Donut Falls Trailhead and the west end of the Spruces Campground. It offers a nice short, nearly level walk, but is probably used most by people staying in the campground.

UPPER CARDIFF FORK (B-12.2)

Destination	Cardiff Mine	Cardiff Pass
One-Way Miles	2½	3¼
Elevation Gain	1,660	2,720
Highest Point	9,140	10,200
Hiking Time One-Way	2h 5m	3h

Cardiff is a patchwork of private, Salt Lake City–owned, and Forest Service lands, and access to the canyon has been restricted in the past. In May 2012 the Forest Service completed an access agreement with the Cardiff Canyon Owners Association regarding access along the historic roads. This agreement gives the public year-round nonmotorized access across the road sections that are on private land. This means it is now possible to again hike up this scenic canyon and access the public land area.

The status of many of the historic trails and cross-country routes in upper Cardiff Fork are still uncertain. Some landowners, such as Snowbird, have historically been recreation friendly, while others may choose to manage their inholdings as a private retreat. That is their right. Observe any "No Trespassing" signs that restrict access off the main roads. Also, be aware that the agreement gave the property owners motorized access on the road sections that cross Forest Service lands. Share the road with authorized vehicles.

The Cardiff Fork access agreement was a major victory for the public, and I thank the agency staff and citizens who worked through the negotiation process. The agreement has a trial period for 2012–14. Public cooperation will be essential in preserving future access. Success of this agreement will be a major step to a long-range resolution of access to all the hiking trails, scrambling routes, summit destinations, and historic sites in this marvelous canyon.

Start from the Donut Falls Trailhead parking area, which is on the spur road that starts 9.3 miles up Big Cottonwood Canyon and passes through the Jordan Pines picnic area. You can either take the gated vehicle road that crosses the stream and makes an immediate switchback or start out on the Donut Falls Trail that intersects the road higher up. The Cardiff Fork road stays on the west side of the canyon as it follows the stream. There are several points where the road forks and rejoins, and there are branch roads that go to mines high on the canyon wall. Stay on the main road and observe any signs. The main road passes several mine dumps on the way to Cardiff Mine, where rusting machinery and buildings in various stages of collapse mark the site. Beyond the mine, the road soon degenerates into a trail that continues over Cardiff Pass at the head of the canyon and descends to Alta. Just below the mine, there is a major branch road that works its way up the west side of the canyon and passes through a meadow before it fades out near Montreal Hill on the west ridge.

KESSLER PEAK

The summit ridge near Kessler Peak is private property, and the historic routes to Kessler Peak were not addressed in the agreement with Cardiff landowners. Informal information indicates that as of 2012, the peak was not posted and no permission was required for noncommercial recreational use by the public. Access is subject to change at the owner's discretion.

Destination	North Route to Summit	Carbonate Pass Route to Summit
One-Way Miles	2¼	3
Elevation Change	2,953	2,953
Hiking Time One-Way	2h 40m	3h
Special Difficulties	Steep	Scrambling

Note: All measurements are from the stream crossing to the summit (elev. 10,403).

Kessler Peak, the high point on the north end of the ridge separating Cardiff Fork and Mineral Fork, is a challenging hike that offers a spectacular view of Flagstaff, Mount Superior, Dromedary, Twin Peaks, Mount Raymond, Gobblers Knob, and the entire upper end of Big Cottonwood Canyon. There are at least two well-defined trails up Kessler Peak from the Cardiff Fork road and several bushwhacking variations. Use a topographic map to supplement these descriptions.

NORTH ROUTE (B-12.3)

This route is the shortest and the easiest to follow. It climbs very steeply but involves no scrambling. The trail starts from the main Cardiff Fork road less than ¼ mile beyond the road to Donut Falls. An excellent landmark is a large, lone fir tree on the left, about 100 feet beyond where the north route trail starts by heading up the slope on the right. The USGS map shows the start of this trail. The start is on private land not covered by the owners' agreement, and the last section near the summit is also private.

The trail passes through a meadow and then continues climbing. About 9,200 feet, watch carefully for a distinct junction where the trail begins a traverse across an avalanche gully to connect with another trail on the far ridge. After crossing the gully, the trail crosses to the west side of the ridge and begins a very steep climb up a path that connected two mine workings. This brings you to the ruins of a cabin on the saddle between the north and main summits. From here, follow the west side of the ridge to the main summit.

CARBONATE PASS ROUTE (B-12.4)

If you find this trail, which is an old mining wagon road, the route is quite easy, If you miss the trail, you are in for brush and steep scrambling on loose rock. To locate the start of this trail, watch for the first mine dump on the right-hand side of the road. This trail starts on Salt Lake City land but crosses private land near the ridge.

SCRAMBLING BELOW DONUT FALLS. The rocks are slippery when wet. Use caution. A better view of the falls is not worth risking a fall.

Contour around the mine dump and you will see a trail starting up to the south that eventually curves back north and climbs to Carbonate Pass. As you walk up the road, note the prominent yellow spur ridge near the top of Kessler Peak. The trail goes on the south side of this ridge.

The trail ascends through the aspen and soon leads to a steep, grassy meadow. If you lose the trail, search for this meadow. The trail goes up the left side of the meadow, and at the top it traverses to the north. From here on, the route is a distinct track that follows switchbacks as it ascends past the huge mine dump to the south of the yellow spur ridge just before reaching the saddle between Cardiff and Mineral Fork. Several ruins of mine buildings are on the saddle.

From the saddle, a track heads north along the Mineral Fork side of the ridge, dropping about 100 feet before reaching the steep couloir leading to the summit. There are considerable scrambling and route-finding, but no difficulties that would stop an experienced hiker.

DAYS FORK (B-13)

Destination	Lower Meadow	Eclipse Mine	Silver Fork Pass	Flagstaff Peak
One-Way Miles	1½	2¾	3	3¾
Elevation Gain	850	2,250	2,570	3,180
Highest Point	8,200	9,600	9,920	10,530
Hiking Time One-Way	1h 10m	2h 30m	2h 45m	3h 35m
Special Difficulties				Scrambling

Days Fork is a long side canyon leading south from the Spruces Campground. The upper basin features a well-preserved boiler and steam engine and several old mine workings in a beautiful alpine cirque with a steep headwall. Mount Superior, Silver Fork, Twin Lakes Pass, and the Alta parking lot are all within a mile of the upper end of Days Fork.

The trail starts at the Spruces Campground on the south side of the road 10.1 miles up Big Cottonwood Canyon. Turn right on the side road to cross the bridge. At the concession booth, ask for directions to the hiker parking area. From the gate at the southwest corner of the hiker parking area, walk past the cinder-block toilet building and continue straight south toward the group picnic area. The Days Fork Trail starts as a jeep road beyond the locked gate ahead.

DAYS FORK TO THE MINE

After passing through the campground, the road enters a steep chute that is a nightmare for ski tours in the winter. After a climb of 300 feet, the trail levels off and climbs gradually for the next mile to the lower basin. The Greens Basin Trail branches left soon after the top of the steep portion. Ahead, the hiking trail goes left around a large wet area and then quickly rejoins the road.

The lower basin at 8,200 feet is a nice meadow with wooded cliffs on both sides. Here, the road loops to the right side of the drainage as the slope gets steeper. Looking back to the north, you can see much of the Mill D North Fork drainage and Reynolds Peak. After passing the remains of an old mine cabin, the trail continues on a long ascent along the west side of the stream. The road finally rejoins the stream after climbing about 1,000 feet from the meadow to the Days Fork Mine. The trail crosses the stream and then ascends a steep hill. Above, the slope levels off, and the trees give

UPPER DAYS FORK (B-13). The abandoned boiler at the site of the Eclipse Mine is a reminder of the era when the canyons were filled with mining camps.

way to an open bowl surrounded by steep, loose rocks mixed with smooth slabs. The road continues intermittently to the Eclipse Mine.

DAYS FORK TO SILVER FORK (B-13.2)

This trail follows an old mining road that leads to the crest of Cottonwood Ridge. The trail is easy to follow if you start at the right place, which is about 9,400-foot elevation and just a few minutes below Eclipse Mine. After making a long swing to the west, the Days Fork Trail crosses to the east side of the stream and then climbs a steep hill. Partway up the hill, the trail to Silver Fork branches left and heads back to the northeast.

The trail curves east, then south, as it makes an ascending traverse to the edge of a steep gully that drains into Days Fork. The route then runs parallel to this gully until it reaches a relatively wide and level pass in the ridge above Silver Fork. The route continues as a distinct track on the Silver Fork side, makes a traverse below an unnamed peak, and soon reaches Cottonwood Ridge. This destination overlooks Alta and Snowbird and is less difficult than the climb up Flagstaff. To continue along the ridge, see trail R-4.

FLAGSTAFF PEAK FROM DAYS FORK (B-13.1)

Experienced hikers can reach Flagstaff Peak by ascending the steep headwall of Days Fork, but the easiest route up Flagstaff is from the Alta side.

From the Eclipse Mine, one route continues along the drainage to the low point on the ridge east of Flagstaff. A faint foot track marks the best route. The steep, smooth rock slabs hold snow well into July, so careful route-finding and confidence in scrambling are needed.

The alternative route from Days Fork is up the slopes to the west of the mine. Remnants of a mining road head west toward the high point on the Reed and Benson Ridge. This route leads to the summit north of Flagstaff, which is slightly higher but does not have as good a view of Alta. To reach Flagstaff, you will need to scramble the difficult ridge connecting the peaks.

GREENS BASIN (B-14)

Distance	1¾ miles one-way
Elevation Gain	1,050
Highest Point	Basin at 8,300
Hiking Time One-Way	1h 25m

Greens Basin is a meadow hidden partway up the south side of Big Cottonwood Canyon on the ridge separating Days Fork from Silver Fork. A good trail through forest leads to this secluded spot.

Start from the Days Fork Trailhead at the Spruces Campground, 10.1 miles up Big Cottonwood Canyon. Follow the Days Fork Trail up the steep chute. About 100 yards after the slope levels off, watch carefully for a cleared, constructed trail heading back to the northeast. The trail makes two switchbacks as it climbs through the aspen on the east side of Days Fork; then it crosses a minor ridge and makes an ascending traverse along the south side of Big Cottonwood Canyon. A half mile after the second switchback, you arrive at the flat meadow. It is about 100 yards across and is walled in by the steep slope on one side and by a low ridge on the other. The trail ends in the meadow, but a faint track continues from the far side of the meadow and climbs up onto the ridge above Silver Fork.

Just before reaching the basin, there is a junction with a steep trail that comes up from a cabin area on private land down along the highway.

BEARTRAP FORK (B-15)

Destination	Upper Bowl	Desolation Lake Overlook
One-Way Miles	1¾	2
Elevation Change	1,940	2,240
Highest Point	9,500	9,800
Hiking Time One-Way	1h 50m	2h 10m

DESOLATION LAKE. The view from Beartrap Pass near the junction of hikes B-10, B-15, and R-2. Mount Raymond and Gobblers Knob are in the background.

Beartrap Fork is a short side drainage with an underutilized trail that joins the Great Western Trail (R-2), from Millcreek Canyon to Guardsman Pass. The lower part is in the trees, but higher up this trail offers great views of the peaks and ridges on the south side of Big Cottonwood Canyon, and it is a fast route to the ridge overlooking Summit County.

The trail starts at the watershed gate about 11 miles up the canyon. There is limited parking here. The "Rivers End Road" sign on the south across the Big Cottonwood Canyon road is a landmark. The route begins as a dirt road, and you take the uphill branch at the fork heading toward some cabins, make another switchback, and then begin a traverse toward the Beartrap Fork stream, where the trail begins climbing steeply along the east side of the drainage. The trail is in good condition and is easy to follow. Some of the stream crossings lack improvised bridges, but except during peak runoff, none will be a problem. The trail crosses to the west and fades out in the grassy upper bowl, but just continue up, staying in the drainage. The trail becomes more distinct as it approaches the Great Western Trail along the ridge crest. At the top, head a short way northwest to enjoy the view of Desolation Lake. Having made the climb, you can explore either direction along the Great Western Trail. The trail down to Desolation Lake is ¼ mile north.

If you are descending into Beartrap Fork, pick up the trail along the west side of the gully. The trail crosses to the east side of the drainage where the canyon bottom first narrows down and enters the trees. This trail is not heavily used by mountain bikes.

WILLOW HEIGHTS (B-16)

Destination	Willow Lake	Great Western Trail
One-Way Miles	¾	2
Elevation Change	640	1,960
Highest Point	8,480	9,800
Hiking Time One-Way	40m	1h 55m

This drainage is across the road and just upcanyon from Silver Fork and is a delightful hike through open aspen forest to a picturesque lake and several meadows. Gradual terrain leads to the ridges above. The terrain below the lake was recently placed in a conservation area through a public-private partnership.

A maintained hiking trail, marked by a low stone sign, starts on the north side of the road, 12.1 miles up Big Cottonwood Canyon, and follows the east side of the drainage to Willow Lake. The trail climbs steeply and then levels off about halfway to the lake. A user-created trail goes around the lake on the east. On descent from Willow Lake, be sure to take the trail on the east, not the jeep road shown on the USGS maps on the west side of the stream that descends into the cabin area at Silver Fork.

The terrain above the lake is open, rolling ridges. Foot tracks and game trails lead up from Willow Lake to Dry Lake and continue up to the Great Western Trail. The slope gets steep near the ridge. The proposed gondola skier connection from Canyons to Solitude is a major controversy at the time of the current revision.

SOLITUDE SKI AREA

The ski area consists of a lower parking lot 12.7 miles up Big Cottonwood Canyon and the restaurant and condominium complex at 13.1 miles. Solitude is the starting point for numerous trails, including Silver Fork, Honeycomb Fork, and the system of ski roads and constructed mountain-bike trails leading south toward the ridge and east toward Brighton. The area is a mix of Forest Service and private land. Solitude has a summer trail map that is available at the Solitude lodging information desk at the upper parking area and is also posted on signboards. Solitude welcomes summer visitors, and your buying refreshments after a hike will be appreciated in turn.

The developed ski areas are the best place to take large hiking groups and beginners. The open slopes provide distant views and abundant wildflowers. My preference is to walk the double-track dirt roads because they usually are more direct and have a more consistent grade than the single-track mountain-bike trails. Besides, the single-track routes are so narrow you often have to step into the vegetation to get around mountain bikes.

SILVER FORK (B-17)

Destination	Lower Mine	Upper Bowl	Grizzly Gulch	Days Fork
One-Way Miles	2¼	3	3¾	4
Elevation Change	420	1,500	1,940	1,740
Highest Point	8,520	9,600	10,040	9,840
Hiking Time One-Way	1h 20m	2h 15m	2h 50m	2h 55m

The hike up the Silver Fork road to the mine is easy but not exceptional. In contrast, the upper portion of Silver Fork is a spectacular bowl with dramatic geology, abandoned mines, and access routes to Days Fork and Little Cottonwood. Silver Fork is another patchwork of Forest Service and private land. Best access is from the lower Solitude parking area 12.7 miles up the canyon. Park along the highway if the parking-lot gate is closed, which is common in summer. Walk to the west end of the lot, pass the Eagle Express lift station, continue on the road ahead, and stay to the right where the ski trail from Honeycomb Fork heads uphill. You will immediately intersect the road that leads into Silver Fork.

SILVER FORK MINE

This is an easy, almost level walk along the road that starts at Solitude and passes along the upper edge of the summer home area in the mouth of the canyon. About ¼ mile of this road crosses private land, so stay on the road and respect the cabin owners' wishes. Follow the paved road until you pass a large building that was formerly a church lodge and is now called "Silver Hill." Here, the pavement stops, and a dirt road, which is closed to unauthorized vehicles, continues up the canyon. About ½ mile beyond the pavement, a jeep road branches left into Honeycomb Fork. The road to upper Silver Fork branches right less than ¼ mile after the Honeycomb Fork road. The main road stays low, crosses the stream, and climbs to the top of the large flat area formed by the mine dump. Most of the stream flow comes out from the mine portal.

UPPER SILVER FORK BASIN

The road to upper Silver Fork is an obvious bench cut in the hillside that starts from the open area below the mine. Follow this road along the west side of the canyon until it crosses the stream in an area of white rock outcrops a short way above the mine. From here, the route follows a mining road that occasionally degenerates to a footpath as it climbs steeply along the east side of the stream past numerous small waterfalls. The canyon narrows to a V-shaped gorge and then opens up into two magnificent bowls. The road leads to mine workings in the east bowl below the steep headwall that separates Silver Fork from Grizzly Gulch.

The Prince of Wales Mine, with its abandoned steam engine, and the wagon road leading to Grizzly Gulch are high on the east side of the bowl. The wagon road is reached by scrambling up the spur ridge that lies just north of the end of the lower road and then following the ridge a short way southeast.

UPPER SILVER FORK—WEST BOWL (B-17.1)

The west bowl of Silver Fork is much larger than the east bowl and contains a small marshy lake. To reach the west bowl, watch for a foot track branching left from the road and crossing the stream about 200 vertical feet below the east bowl. A good landmark is the white-black-white-striped cliff on the east side of the canyon. The foot track makes a single switchback and then climbs into the west bowl.

To continue into Days Fork, look for the road bench crossing the ridge on the west side of the bowl. The easiest route is to go slightly right (north) and make an ascending traverse of the open alpine slopes.

HONEYCOMB FORK (B-18)

Destination	Lower Honeycomb Junction	Upper Pass (Summit Lift)
One-Way Miles	1¼	2½
Elevation Change	380	1,840
Highest Point	8,500	9,960
Hiking Time One-Way	50m	2h 10m

Honeycomb Fork was an area of intense mining activity, and the canyon is nearly all private land managed as part of the Solitude ski area. The best access is to start from the lower Solitude parking area (see description for Silver Fork) and hike the "Honeycomb Return Trail" ski run from the Eagle Express lift. The correct route is the dirt road that turns west about 100 feet above the lift and begins a gradual ascending

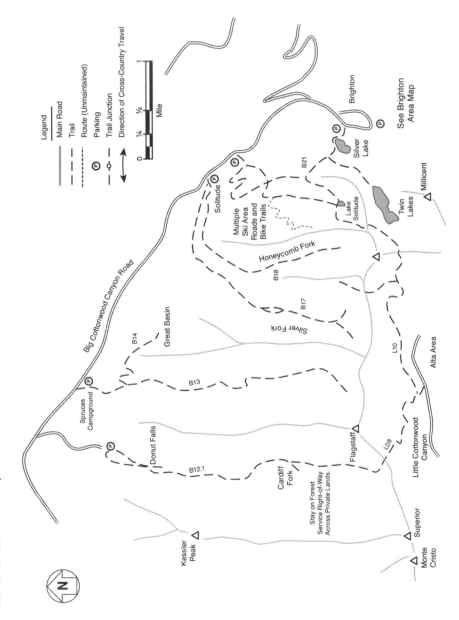

Legend

Main Road
Trail
Route (Unmaintained)
Parking
Trail Junction
Direction of Cross-Country Travel

0   ¼   ½   1
Mile

N

Big Cottonwood Canyon Road

Spruces Campground

Donut Falls

B14

Great Basin

B13

B12.1

Kessler Peak

Cardiff Fork

Stay on Forest Service Right-of-Way Across Private Lands.

Flagstaff

L9.8

Superior

Monte Cristo

Little Cottonwood Canyon

Alta Area

L10

Silver Fork

B17

B18

Honeycomb Fork

Multiple Ski Area Roads and Bike Trails

Solitude

B21

Lake Solitude

Twin Lakes

Millicent

Silver Lake

Brighton

See Brighton Area Map

traverse around the end of the ridge. The other (higher) route from the base of the Eagle Express lift is called the Serenity bike trail and climbs under the lift in a series of switchbacks. A marked side trail branches from the Serenity and Queen Bess bike trails and leads into Honeycomb higher up.

The bulldozer cut for the Honeycomb Return ski run ends in a meadow in lower Honeycomb Fork across the stream from the badly eroded jeep road coming up from Silver Fork to the west. The jeep road or trail climbs up to the Woodlawn Mine, and a trail eventually reaches the top of the Summit ski lift at the head of Honeycomb Fork. An alternative loop would be to ascend the ski roads passing above Lake Solitude to the top of the Summit lift and then descend Honeycomb Fork.

SOLITUDE-AREA SERVICE ROADS (B-19)

MILL F SOUTH FORK

Destination	Lake Solitude	Mount Evergreen Pass	Summit
One-Way Miles	3	3¾	4½
Elevation Change	900	1,440	1,960
Highest Point	9,020	9,600	10,479
Hiking Time One-Way	2h	2h 30m	3h 20m

The Solitude ski area service roads and bike trails provide several alternative routes from the upper Solitude parking lot to Lake Solitude, Evergreen Pass, and the top of the Summit lift. The area is a network of routes, but the Solitude signs help. Mileages in the above table are for following the two-track road, and alternatives using the single-track trail will differ. These hikes to Lake Solitude or Evergreen Pass are longer than the approach from Brighton, but the Solitude roads provide a nice alternative descent. The general setting around Solitude is more rounded and forested and lacks the rugged alpine granite found in the Brighton Basin.

The main service road is called "Raptor Road" on the Solitude map and signs. From the upper parking area, walk up through the village and then head toward the base of the Apex lift, following the walkway past the clinic building to the wide, graded two-track road. The road climbs with switchbacks under the Moonbeam lift. After a mile the Raptor Road passes under the Eagle Express lift, where single-track bike trails branch west toward the Serenity Trail and Honeycomb Fork. In another ½ mile the Eagle Ridge road branches and climbs to the top of the Eagle Express and Powder-horn lifts. The route divides after Raptor Road passes under the Summit lift. To reach

Lake Solitude, take the left fork, which becomes the Krüzer single-track trail, and then the right branch leading to the lake.

The two-track road passes above the west side of Lake Solitude and then makes a series of switchbacks under the lift and climbs up the headwall to the pass southwest of Mount Evergreen, where there is a junction with the service road heading toward Twin Lakes above Brighton. The Solitude service road, now called the Summit Trail, continues southwest to the Summit lift that overlooks the top of Honeycomb Fork and Little Cottonwood Canyon.

BRIGHTON AREA

Brighton is a former mining town and present-day cabin and ski area at the head of Big Cottonwood Canyon. Brighton is named after William Stewart Brighton who, with his wife, Catherine, built a hotel near Silver Lake in 1874. Much of the private land in the area dates from Brighton's original eighty-acre homestead and his later mining claims.

The area has relatively easy terrain with good trails leading to lakes and overlooks. The natural beauty and the short distances combine to make Brighton a popular beginner hiking area; however, the parking lot at Brighton, at 8,700 feet, is nearly as high as the summit of Mount Olympus on the Wasatch Front. The weather is much colder than in the valley, and snow lasts well into June, so the hiking season here is only from July through mid-September.

Persons who are not well acclimatized will feel the effect of high altitude when hiking at Brighton. I first hiked at Brighton on a summer vacation in 1972. I had been living at sea level, and my hiking had been in the Appalachians, where summits are lower than the Salt Lake Valley. We hiked only as far as the Lake Mary Dam, and I was totally exhausted and out of breath. Take it easy and rest often when you start hiking at high elevations.

Unfortunately, the Brighton trails are often confusing. The area is mixed with service roads, winter ski runs, and private inholdings. Construction activities have resulted in a multitude of constructed tracks. The Forest Service attempts to keep the trails marked, but signage here is not as extensive as around the Solitude area. The USGS map of the area is out of date, but the "Hiking the Wasatch" map will help you find the correct trail.

It is easy to lose your sense of direction when hiking around Brighton. You drive east up the canyon and expect the direction at the end of the road to be east. Actually, the road turns at the Guardsman Pass junction, and you are driving south as you arrive at the start of the loop road. Once you start thinking of the Brighton Store as being to the north, everything falls into place.

SILVER LAKE AND LAKE SOLITUDE

FROM BRIGHTON STORE

Destination	Silver Lake Boardwalk	Loop around Silver Lake	Lake Solitude
One-Way Miles	300 yards to ½ mile		1½
Elevation Gain	Accessible	100	300
Highest Point	8,730		9,020
Hiking Time One-Way	10m	30–45m	55m

The Silver Lake and Lake Solitude hikes both start at the Forest Service visitor station across from the Brighton Store. Drive 14.8 miles up Big Cottonwood Canyon to the beginning of the one-way loop road and look for the sign and parking area on the right.

SILVER LAKE (B-20)

Silver Lake is the easiest alpine hike in this book. Signs, wide paths, and a boardwalk provide easy access to the lake. This area has been extensively reconstructed and rehabilitated by the Forest Service and provides a high-quality recreational opportunity for those who do not want to go far from their cars. A well-maintained trail continues all the way around Silver Lake, and there is a bridge that gets you across the inlet stream and avoids the private land farther south. You can wander around the lake and enjoy the interpretive signs and views.

As you start toward the lake, the trail to the right crosses a narrow bridge at the outlet of the lake and continues along the north shore. On the far side of the lake, there is a trail junction where the maintained trails to Twin Lakes and to Lake Solitude turn right (west) and the lakeshore trail turns south.

LAKE SOLITUDE FROM BRIGHTON (B-21)

Tiny Lake Solitude is set in a steep-walled bowl at the head of Mill F South Fork. Start by hiking around the north side of Silver Lake to the trail junction at the northwest side of the lake ¼ mile from the start. The trail turns right and heads north for about 200 yards and then forks again. The trail to Lake Solitude continues straight ahead in a generally northwest direction and gradually climbs. The trail to the top of the Evergreen lift and to the Twin Lakes Dam switches back to the south.

Continue the gradual climb north through an open, parklike forest of fir and aspen and cross the ski trail leading from Brighton to Solitude. The hiking route continues in the same direction, crosses under Solitude's Sunrise lift, and then turns south into the Mill F drainage. Downhill ski runs cross the route before the last short, steep hill to the lake.

On the west side of the lake is the road from Solitude to the Summit lift (see B-19). Some rare flowering plants grow around the lake, and hikers should stay on existing routes to avoid trampling vegetation unnecessarily.

The Solitude Tunnel, just above the lake, was the lowest entrance into the Michigan Utah group of mines. Most of the development and ore production from this group were conducted on the Alta side of the divide from the head of Grizzly Gulch. Work in these mines ceased in 1928, and in the 1970s the surface rights were acquired by the predecessor of Solitude.

TWIN LAKES AND TWIN LAKES PASS (B-22)

Destination	Twin Lakes Dam	Twin Lake Pass
One-Way Miles	1¼	2½
Elevation Gain	710	1,260
Highest Point	9,440	9,993
Hiking Time One-Way	1h	1h 50m

The two original lakes are now merged behind a concrete arch dam, forming a large lake in a spectacular setting. The lake is set in a bowl with rocky slopes and bare summits above. The lakes can be reached by either of two easy trails: the ski-area maintenance road from the base of the Milly Express lift or the Forest Service hiking trail from Silver Lake.

Looking across Silver Lake, you can see a trail heading left and upward on the hillside toward Twin Lakes. Start on the boardwalk around the north side of the lake as described for Lake Solitude. From the northwest side, continue along the trail toward Lake Solitude for 150 yards, and then take the sharp switchback to your left where the trail to Lake Solitude continues north and the route to Twin Lakes turns south and climbs steadily. After Silver Lake comes into view, you will pass a wide but revegetated cut in the hillside heading back north. This is the SolBright ski trail to Solitude. As the hiking trail enters the trees again, it turns right and begins to climb more steeply. This next section is wet early in the summer. A spur trail on the left will take you 100 feet to a level area that is a nice overlook and resting spot. Continue up the trail until the Twin Lakes Dam comes into view. An unmaintained trail leads along the north side of

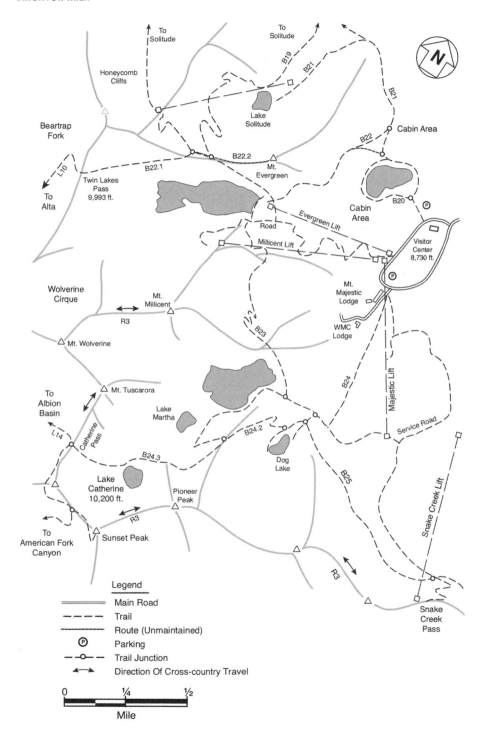

To Solitude

To Solitude

To Solitude

B19

B21

B21

Honeycomb Cliffs

Lake Solitude

Cabin Area

B22

Beartrap Fork

L10

B22.2

Mt. Evergreen

B22.1

Twin Lakes Pass 9,993 ft.

B20

To Alta

Cabin Area

P

Evergreen Lift

Road

Millicent Lift

Visitor Center 8,730 ft.

Wolverine Cirque

Mt. Millicent

R3

Mt. Majestic Lodge

P

Mt. Wolverine

B23

WMC Lodge

Majestic Lift

To Albion Basin

Mt. Tuscarora

L14

Catherine Pass

Lake Martha

B24

Service Road

B24.2

To American Fork Canyon

B24.3

Lake Catherine 10,200 ft.

Dog Lake

Pioneer Peak

R3

Sunset Peak

B25

Snake Creek Lift

R3

Snake Creek Pass

Legend

═══	Main Road
– – –	Trail
——	Route (Unmaintained)
Ⓟ	Parking
—o—	Trail Junction
←→	Direction Of Cross-country Travel

0   ¼   ½

Mile

TWIN LAKES FROM TWIN LAKES PASS (B-22). Mount Evergreen overlooks the lake on the left. The controversial 1986 power line is in the foreground.

the lake, generally staying close to the shore. This trail leads to the far end of the lake directly below Twin Lakes Pass.

The alternative route to Twin Lakes Dam starts near the Milly Express lift in the Brighton Ski Resort parking lot and follows the maintenance road up a series of switchbacks through the downhill ski runs. This route is sunny and open and is a better early-summer route than the trail from Silver Lake. Take the right fork just after the start, and then follow the wide road up to the dam. This road and the trail from Silver Lake can be combined to make a nice short loop. Distances and times for either route are about the same.

TWIN LAKES PASS (B-22.1)

The best route from the lake to Twin Lakes Pass begins up the service road (part of the Solitude-to-Brighton ski connection) that climbs the hill to the north of the Twin Lakes Dam. Just past a retaining wall of railroad ties, the road crosses through a notch, Evergreen Pass, into Mill F South Fork, where there is the road coming up from Solitude. Lake Solitude is about 500 feet lower down the Solitude ski-area road. To reach Twin Lakes Pass, continue horizontally on the Mill F side for about 1,000 feet, passing under a series of ridgetop pinnacles, and then climb the steep slope to your left to reach another notch in the ridge. After crossing the notch, look for the good foot track leading directly to Twin Lakes Pass that is ½ mile away but only 200 feet higher. Twin Lakes Pass is at the head of Grizzly Gulch (L-10) and has an outstanding view looking west down Little Cottonwood Canyon.

GRANITE LAKES TRAIL TO LAKE MARY (B-23)

This trail starts from the south end of the Twin Lakes Dam and climbs a small rise. Immediately ahead, the trail passes directly left of the base of a 15-foot cliff and then becomes a distinct trail as it begins to descend and cross under the Milly Express lift. The USGS topographic map shows this trail incorrectly; it starts higher and goes directly to Lake Mary.

TWIN LAKES–AREA SUMMITS

Destination	Mount Evergreen	Mount Millicent	Mount Wolverine	Honeycomb Cliffs
One-Way Miles	1¾	2	2½	2½
Elevation Change	1,110	1,722	2,065	1,749
Highest Point	9,840	10,452	10,795	10,479
Hiking Time One-Way	1h 30m	2h	2h 30m	2h 15m

These summits can all be reached by moderate off-trail hiking starting from the Twin Lakes Dam, and they are worthwhile objectives for intermediate hikers.

Mount Evergreen is the forested ridge directly north of Twin Lakes. Follow the route described for Twin Lakes Pass and turn northeast at the saddle where the ski-area road crosses into Mill F Fork. Scale the very steep slope ahead and continue along the ridge to the summit.

The top of Honeycomb Cliffs can be reached by hiking to Twin Lakes Pass and then scrambling north along the ridge. The hike can continue above Honeycomb Cliffs to Silver Fork.

Mount Millicent is reached from the ski-area service road that climbs from the Twin Lakes Dam to the top of the Milly Express lift in a series of switchbacks. Climb south along the rocky ridge from the lift to the summit. There is some boulder-hopping on this ridge.

Wolverine is the highest peak in the area and overlooks both Big Cottonwood and Little Cottonwood Canyons. The route to the summit of Wolverine continues south-west along the ridge from Millicent. Alternatively, Wolverine can be reached by hiking south from Twin Lakes Pass, following the crest of the curving ridge. This is a longer route, but it offers a spectacular view of Wolverine Cirque.

LAKE CATHERINE BELOW CATHERINE PASS. Good trails ascend from both the Brighton and the Alta sides.

GREAT WESTERN TRAIL—BIG COTTONWOOD

From Scotts Pass on the Wasatch Crest Ridge, the Great Western Trail descends into Big Cottonwood Canyon and follows the Guardsman Pass road (paved) to Brighton. From the Brighton loop, the GWT ascends the Brighton Lakes Trail to Catherine Pass. From Catherine Pass, the GWT heads ¼ mile toward Sunset Peak and then crosses the ridge and drops into American Fork Canyon in Utah County. Due to the long car shuttle required, travel on the GWT south from Brighton is mostly popular with mountain runners and long-distance hikers, but inconvenient for day hikes.

BRIGHTON LAKES TRAIL (B-24)

This trail winds past four lakes and then climbs to the pass into Little Cottonwood. It is a popular area for easy hikes and is one of the nicest areas in the Wasatch for all levels of hiking. Lake Mary is a popular destination for beginners, while Lake Catherine and the pass are more an intermediate hike. The trail to Snake Creek Pass and Clayton Peak branches from the Brighton Lakes Trail at Dog Lake. This trail starts from the east side of the Brighton Ski Resort parking area 15.1 miles up Big Cottonwood Canyon.

EASY HIKES ON THE BRIGHTON LAKES TRAIL

Destination	Dog Lake	Lake Mary
One-Way Miles	¾	1
Elevation Gain	600	760
Highest Point	9,360	9,520
Hiking Time One-Way	40m	55m to 1h 10m

The trail starts up the gravel path from the signboard to the right of the more modern ski-resort building and near the Majestic lift base. The trail quickly crosses the road that gives access to the Wasatch Mountain Club Lodge and the LDS camp, but there is no public parking on this road. The trail was relocated to reduce erosion in wet areas along the creek, and it now ascends as a well-constructed footpath up through the grassy, open ski slopes. A service road to private cabins and the ski lifts is to the left of the foot trail.

FROM BRIGHTON PARKING LOT TO DOG LAKE JUNCTION AND LAKE MARY

Yes, there are two "Dog Lakes" in Big Cottonwood Canyon: this one near Brighton and the other in Mill D North Fork. The routes to Dog Lake, Clayton Peak, Lake Mary, and Catherine Pass share a common trail for the first ½ mile.

The relocated hiking trail heads south, with occasional switchbacks. The trail is well marked to avoid a proliferation of false user-created routes. About twenty minutes up, the hiking trail joins the maintenance road, which provides an alternative route from the parking lot. To hike the maintenance road, start from the southeast corner of the parking lot, go past the vehicle gate, and generally take the right-hand forks at the junctions. The road system climbs all the way to the top of the Great Western lift below Clayton Peak.

Soon after joining the maintenance road, the hiking trail turns right, heads west up the steep hill, and reaches the stream and the Dog Lake junction in 200 yards. The left branch leads to Dog Lake and Clayton Peak, and the trail straight ahead continues to Lake Mary and Catherine Pass. South of Dog Lake there is an abandoned road, making a loop to some mining claims. This cut in the hillside is very evident once the snow melts.

LAKE MARY

From the junction near Dog Lake, cross the stream and continue west along a narrow gully for ¼ mile to Lake Mary. The Granite Lakes Trail connecting to Twin Lakes Dam

(B-23) branches right a short way below the Lake Mary Dam. The Lake Mary Trail crosses the stream just below the dam and then climbs to the lake.

Lake Mary is in a glacial basin that was dammed in 1916 to create a water-supply reservoir. Lake Martha is a much smaller lake in the same basin as Lake Mary. Lake Phoebe was merged with Lake Mary by the dam, but it reappears as a distinct lake in the fall when the water is low. This group of lakes was called "Granite Lakes" on old maps.

LAKE CATHERINE (B-24.3) INTERMEDIATE HIKES ON BRIGHTON LAKES TRAIL

Destination	Lake Catherine	Catherine Pass	Sunset Peak
One-Way Miles	2	2½	2¾
Elevation Gain	1,200	1,450	1,950
Highest Point	9,950	10,220	10,648
Hiking Time One-Way	1h 35m	1h 50m	2h 15m

There are two trails to Lake Catherine: the official trail that goes past Lake Mary and an alternative trail directly from Dog Lake following the winter ski-tour route. Both trails converge above Lake Martha.

The direct trail starts on the west side of Dog Lake as a foot track that ascends the ridge to the southwest. Two switchbacks and an ascending traverse bring you to the top of the ridge, where you join the official trail.

The official trail continues from the left (southeast) side of Lake Mary to Lake Martha. Above Lake Martha, the trail makes a switchback to the left and ascends the ridge separating Lake Mary from Dog Lake. From the ridge crest, the trail contours through stands of fir and passes along the top of the cliffs above Lake Martha. Soon the cliffs coming off Pioneer Peak come into view on your left as you approach the cirque containing Lake Catherine. A spur trail to the left leads to Lake Catherine, and the trail to the pass goes to the right of a small ridge dividing the cirque.

When hiking back to Brighton, remember that the trail traverses high after leaving Lake Catherine. A false trail leads into the steep cliffs above Lake Martha. The stream draining Lake Catherine disappears into a sinkhole located near the junction of the Lake Catherine spur trail, with the trail continuing to the pass.

CATHERINE PASS

This pass is the obvious low spot on the ridge above the lake. Follow the trail to the right of the small ridge, and make one long switchback as you ascend the headwall of the cirque. The other side of the pass is densely forested, but a short walk up either ridge provides excellent views of Albion Basin and Little Cottonwood Canyon.

BRIGHTON LAKES VIEWED FROM SUNSET PEAK. Lake Catherine is directly below. Beyond are tiny Lake Martha and the irregularly shaped reservoir formed from the formerly separate Lake Phoebe and Lake Mary.

The trail on the Alta side leads down to Albion Basin, and the Brighton Ridge Run crosses the hiking trail here on the way from Sunset Peak to Mount Tuscarora. Sunset Peak (elev. 10,648) is reached from Catherine Pass by the foot track described in the Little Cottonwood chapter.

GRANITE LAKES TRAIL (B-23) FROM LAKE MARY TO TWIN LAKES

Distance	1 mile from Lake Mary to Twin Lakes
Elevation Gain	No net change but 300 feet of down and up
Hiking Time One-Way	40m between the lakes

This constructed trail provides the opportunity to make a loop hike and offers good views of Brighton as it passes through both forested and open areas. The actual trail is higher than the route shown on the USGS map.

This trail branches right from the Lake Mary Trail a short way below the dam, makes a switchback up a rock slope, and then passes a cabin before reaching the north end of the Lake Mary Dam. The trail descends gradually as it continues north through stands of fir and then makes a pair of sharp switchbacks down to the base of a cliff band. A trail once branched downhill from the low point and ended near the Wasatch Mountain Club Lodge. The main trail crosses the boulder field, ascends the open slopes under the Millicent lift, and crosses a small ridge just before the Twin Lakes Dam.

MAJESTIC TRAIL (B-25)—SNAKE CREEK PASS AND CLAYTON PEAK

Destination	Snake Creek Pass	Clayton Peak
One-Way Miles	2	2½
Elevation Gain	1,310	1,960
Highest Point	10,040	10,721
Hiking Time One-Way	1h 40m	2h 15m

Two new ski lifts and extensive clearing for downhill runs have greatly changed this side of the Brighton Basin since the first edition of this book was written. The hillside scars have healed, and wildflowers grow in the new clearings. The area still has some of the finest views for the hiking effort.

SNAKE CREEK PASS (B-25)

There are two routes from the Brighton parking lot to the pass. The scenic route follows Forest Service hiking trails through the woods beside the ski runs. The alternative is to walk the service roads from the Brighton parking lot.

For the scenic route, follow the Lake Mary Trail to the junction near Dog Lake. Take the Dog Lake fork (left), and in another 200 feet turn left again. The trail now heads east and climbs with a steady grade. The trail passes through stands of fir, crosses under the Snake Creek and Great Western lifts, and generally stays uphill of the service road. A memorable landmark is where the trail passes through a split rock. The trail joins the service road at Snake Creek Pass and then separates again to continue climbing toward Clayton Peak. From the pass, Mount Timpanogos is visible to the south, and the Heber Valley and the Uintas lie to the east.

CLAYTON PEAK (MOUNT MAJESTIC) (B-25)

The peak is called by both names. The 1903 "Cottonwood Map" shows a "Majestic Trail" leading to "Clayton Peak." The trail to Clayton Peak continues northeast along the ridge from Snake Creek Pass.

SNAKE CREEK PASS WITH MOUNT TIMPANOGOS IN THE DISTANCE. This pass is reached by a moderate hike and offers the best views of the Heber Valley and the area to the south and east.

The route follows the service road for ¼ mile before making a steep ascent to the summit. There is occasional boulder-hopping along the way, but there are no real difficulties. The summit offers a bird's-eye view of the area above Park City as well as a panoramic view of Big Cottonwood and the area to the south.

No maintained trails lead from here to the north or east, but there is opportunity for off-trail exploration. The land between here and Guardsman Pass is private. To the east there is a mix of private and Wasatch Mountain State Park lands.

8
Little Cottonwood Canyon

Here is a canyon of superlatives and contrasts. It has the steepest walls, the most heavily glaciated topography, the highest trailhead, and the highest peaks in the area. The mouth is flanked by granite cliffs that challenge the best technical rock climbers, but the upper canyon has the best meadows for easy walking and for finding wildflowers. The lower canyon is bounded by two wilderness areas, while the upper canyon is the home of two world-class ski resorts.

The canyon has been subjected to development pressure ever since pioneer days, and the conflicts continue. Granite for the Salt Lake Temple was quarried at the mouth of the canyon, and Wasatch Resort, a cluster of modern cabins, marks the site of an early work camp. Railroads and tramways served the rich silver mines of Alta. The forests were stripped as sawmills supplied lumber for the mines. An early hydroelectric plant was built in the canyon to provide power for production of industrial oxygen. Lakes were dammed to form reservoirs. Now, tramways carry skiers, and pipelines for natural gas and sanitary sewers have been constructed to heat and drain the luxury condominiums. The upper canyon was an active mining district from the 1860s until 1967, when the last activity ceased at the Wasatch Drain Tunnel near Snowbird. Many mining claims are still active, and much of the land around Alta is still owned by mining companies.

Through all this the canyon has survived. It is still a wild and natural place with recreational opportunities for everyone from mountaineers to families with children.

The topography controls and limits hiking opportunities. The north side is a steep wall of buttresses and couloirs, without a route or pass suitable for hikers between Cardiff Pass and the Wasatch Front. The side canyons on the south between White Pine and the mouth are hanging valleys perched high on the wall, with cliffs and waterfalls separating the side drainages from Little Cottonwood Creek. Hikers enter the lower side canyons by starting at the White Pine Trailhead and traveling west across the dividing ridges above the cliffs. Maintained trails lead as far as Red Pine Lakes and Maybird Lakes.

The south side of Little Cottonwood above the White Pine Trailhead is dominated by the Snowbird and Alta ski resorts. The service roads provide easy walking, and the combination of mining-era logging, frequent avalanches, and contemporary ski-run construction has resulted in open, grassy slopes with excellent vistas.

Alta was the mining center, and roads lead from the town to Cardiff Fork, Silver Fork, and the Twin Lakes Pass area. Alta is at 8,600 feet, so the approaches from Alta to the Mount Superior and Flagstaff Peak areas are much shorter (but steeper) than the routes from Big Cottonwood.

 For general information regarding trails, see chapter 1. For driving directions to trailheads, see chapter 4. To cross-reference trail names, trailheads, and maps, see the "Hike Master List."

TEMPLE QUARRY TRAILHEAD

The parking lot entrance is located on the south arm of Little Cottonwood Road (officially State Route 209) just before the Y junction at the canyon mouth. On the uphill side of the canyon road is the larger commuter parking area. Go 100 yards down the trailhead entrance road to a paved parking area.

TEMPLE QUARRY TRAIL

This is a short, paved, ADA-accessible nature trail through the woods along the creek. The accessible loop goes from the west end of the Temple Quarry parking lot and winds through shrubs and trees along the creek with the granite cliffs towering above. The paved loop is about ¼ mile and has benches, viewpoints, and interpretive signs.

LITTLE COTTONWOOD CREEK TRAIL

Distance	2½ miles to Lisa Falls
Elevation Gain	1,100
Hiking Time One-Way	1h 45m

This trail starts from the Temple Quarry parking lot and heads east on the closed road, staying between the paved highway and Little Cottonwood Creek. After ¾ mile the

THE SOUTH SIDE OF LITTLE COTTONWOOD VIEWED FROM DROMEDARY PEAK. From the left, the skyline peaks are American Fork Twin Peaks, Red Baldy, White Baldy Mount Timpanogos in the distance, and the Pfeifferhorn on the ridge between Maybird Gulch and Hogum Fork.

trail joins the active road through the Wasatch Resort cabin area and continues past the water diversion. The trail crosses to the south side of the stream on a bridge and continues up to another bridge back to the north side 2½ miles from the trailhead. Just beyond the second bridge there is a connecting trail to a small parking area on the highway at Lisa Falls. The trail continues up along the creek toward Tanners Flat campground. The lower portion of this trail follows the alignment of a water pipeline, resulting in a wide path and steady grade. The long-term plan is for a trail following the creek all the way from the canyon mouth to Snowbird.

Little Cottonwood Creek is a dangerous stream during spring runoff. The bridges on this trail provide safe access across the creek to the rugged country around Sam Thomas Gulch, Coalpit Gulch, and lower Hogum Fork.

WHITE PINE TRAILHEAD (LONE PEAK WILDERNESS)

This excellent trailhead is the main access for the south side of Little Cottonwood Canyon and the northeast portion of the Lone Peak Wilderness. Two easy hikes, suitable for beginners, follow good trails from this trailhead to overlooks. Intermediate hikes continue up the trails to the lakes in White Pine Canyon, Red Pine Canyon, and Maybird Gulch. Travel beyond the lakes requires off-trail hiking and some scrambling. All these hikes share a common route for the first mile.

The White Pine Trailhead is on the south side of the road, 5.5 miles up Little Cottonwood Canyon and 0.7 miles below Snowbird. The turnoff for the parking area is just after a turn and is easy to miss. Start slowing down just after the "White Pine

Slide Area" sign. An asphalt path leads from the parking area to a footbridge across the stream.

The trail continues on the south side of the stream as a wide road grade and soon turns west as it climbs the hill. This road is closed to motor vehicles except for permitted uses such as maintaining the dam in White Pine Canyon. The road ascends in a generally southwest direction and then turns south as it curves into White Pine Canyon. A mile from the parking lot, the road meets the stream coming down White Pine Canyon. Here, the road up White Pine turns east and makes a switchback up the hill, and the trail to Red Pine and Maybird crosses the stream.

RED PINE CANYON (L-01)

Destination	Canyon Overlook	Mine and Maybird Trail Junction	Lower Red Pine Lake	Upper Red Pine Lake
One-Way Miles	1½	2½	3	3½
Elevation Gain	500	1,400	1,940	2,300
Highest Point	8,200	9,100	9,640	10,000
Hiking Time One-Way	1h	1h 55m	2h 30m	2h 50m

Red Pine Canyon is the most accessible canyon in the Lone Peak Wilderness and is the start for many longer trips to remote canyons and summits. A well-maintained trail leads up this narrow canyon, and spectacular rock formations crown the ridges. Lower Red Pine Lake is a very popular mountain lake, set in forest just below treeline. Upper Red Pine Lake is set in alpine boulder fields with the jagged cirque headwall above. Snow here lasts into July.

The trail starts from the White Pine Trailhead and follows the White Pine road described above to the junction at the stream, 1 mile from the start. The Red Pine Trail crosses the stream on a footbridge that is about 50 yards upstream from the switchback in the White Pine road. The area immediately beyond the stream is wet, and logs have been laid to reduce trail erosion. The trail heads back downstream, turns west, and begins a fairly level traverse around the end of the ridge. As the trail enters the Red Pine Canyon drainage, it begins to climb again. A half mile after the stream crossing there is a spectacular view down the U-shaped, glacier-carved canyon toward the suburbs in the valley.

Red Pine Creek is far below the overlook, but the trail and stream converge as you climb through aspen. Ahead you will see an excellent landmark: a rock buttress on the east wall of the canyon. An old mine dump and the bridge across Red Pine Creek leading to Maybird Gulch are directly below this ridge, which is reached 2½ miles from the start of the trail.

RED PINE LAKE TRAIL OVERLOOK. These hikers made it past the canyon viewpoint about an hour up the trail. The Cottonwood Ridge is in the background.

Beyond the mine dump, the trail continues up through the trees on the east side of the canyon and is separated from the stream by a minor ridge. An alternative route, when the canyon is still snow covered in early summer, is to go up the open slopes a few hundred feet farther east. About forty-five minutes past the mine dump, you arrive at the top of a small rise overlooking the lake. There is a track all the way around the lake.

Upper Red Pine Lake, set in a small depression about 400 feet higher in the canyon, is reached by walking around the east side of the lower lake and then following the foot track up through the trees from its southeast corner. This means losing altitude, but it is easy walking. A high traverse across the slope from the trail directly to the upper lake is an alternative route in early season.

The entire upper end of Red Pine Canyon is worth exploring. If you are good at route-finding and scrambling, look for the notch that provides a moderately difficult access to White Pine Canyon. You can also bushwhack down the west side of the canyon and meet the main trail at the mine dump. Climbing up to the ridge provides outstanding views of Timpanogos and Utah County and is the start of the Pfeifferhorn route.

MAYBIRD LAKES (L-02)

Destination	Maybird Lakes	Hogum Fork Pass
One-Way Miles	3¾	4½
Elevation Change	1,950	2,600
Highest Point	9,650	10,240
Hiking Time One-Way	2h 50m	4h

Maybird Gulch is less crowded than nearby Red Pine, and the rock formations are more dramatic. Maybird Gulch has a chain of small lakes and a majestic view of the Pfeifferhorn towering above.

The maintained trail into Maybird Gulch branches from the Red Pine Trail at the bridge at the landmark buttress. After crossing the stream, the Maybird Trail makes a switchback up the hill and heads generally west as it crosses over the ridge. After crossing into Maybird, the trail climbs steadily to the lake, passes below spectacular

LOWER RED PINE LAKE. The trail is visible on the far side of the lake, and Red Baldy Peak, which overlooks White Pine Canyon, is in the background across the ridge.

pinnacles that crown the ridge, and ends at the upper lake. The trail has been cleared and relocated, and the USGS map does not show the current route.

A challenging descent from Maybird Lakes is to follow the stream down past the waterfall and then search for the overgrown wagon road that connected Maybird to the Red Pine Trail just above the canyon overlook. Hint: on the way up, look carefully for the road scar on the hillside across from the Red Pine Trail.

ADVANCED HIKES FROM RED PINE CANYON

Southwest of Maybird Gulch lies the most alpine part of the Wasatch. There are no easy routes. Sheer cliffs wall the canyons, and all approaches involve long distances and thousands of vertical feet of climbing. The following section lists only the most popular of the many routes that are accessible to strong hikers.

PFEIFFERHORN VIA RED PINE (L-03)

Distance	4½ miles one-way from trailhead to summit
Elevation Gain	3,700
Highest Point	Summit at 11,326 feet
Hiking Time One-Way	4h 20m
Special Difficulties	Scrambling on ridge, snow in early season

The Pfeifferhorn is the perfectly shaped triangular peak on the divide between Maybird Gulch, Hogum Fork, and Dry Creek. The summit views, the alpine terrain, and the exposed scrambling on a knife-edged ridge make this an excellent route for strong hikers who want a taste of mountaineering. In June the summit pyramid is still snow covered, and this is a very popular spring-snow climb.

Take the trail to Red Pine Lake and continue to the upper lake. Look for the minor ridge heading southwest from the upper lake to Alpine Ridge above. This minor ridge barely shows on the topographic maps but is obvious on the ground. The headwall is steep, and there may be a snow cornice at the top. From the Alpine Ridge, head west, traversing on the south side of the minor summit between Red Pine and Maybird. Then cross the knife-edged ridge, picking your way through and over the massive boulders. The final section up the summit pyramid stays slightly to the left of the rock crest of the east ridge.

The summit is surrounded by scrambling and mountaineering routes. The steep granite headwall of Hogum Cirque to the west contains many technical climbing routes and a few difficult scrambling routes. The north ridge of the Pfeifferhorn is a technical rock climb, but the west ridge is moderate hiking and is the continuation of the Beatout Hike to Bells Canyon.

THE PFEIFFERHORN. The hiker is on the standard route from Red Pine that crosses the foreground ridge and then ascends the summit snowfield, staying just left of the rock ridge crest directly ahead.

MAYBIRD LAKES WITH BROADS FORK TWIN PEAKS VISIBLE ON THE FAR SIDE OF LITTLE COTTONWOOD CANYON. This viewpoint is a short off-trail hike beyond the lakes.

UPPER MAYBIRD GULCH AND HOGUM CIRQUE (L-04)

Exploring Maybird Gulch above the lakes involves either spring-snow hiking or boulder-hopping after the snow retreats, but the scenery makes it worthwhile. The Maybird headwall is a steep scrambling route leading directly to the Alpine Ridge and the Pfeifferhorn. The wide notch in the ridge immediately north of the Pfeifferhorn leads to Hogum Fork.

Hogum Fork is a wild and magnificent drainage that ends with a steep drop into Little Cottonwood Canyon. At the head, two huge cirques are ringed by vertically jointed granite pillars, and popular technical rock-climbing routes ascend from Hogum to the ridge. The summits and smooth flanks of Thunder Mountain dominate the view west.

The normal route into Hogum Cirque is from Maybird Lakes, crossing at the notch in the ridge between the Pfeifferhorn and Peak 10,516 at the 10,240-foot elevation. Climb through the notch and descend 200 feet into the east branch of Hogum. The west branch is ¾ mile away around the end of the ridge. This is an easy traverse if there is still snow.

WHITE PINE CANYON (L-05)

Destination	Overlook	Meadow	Lake
One-Way Miles	1¼	2	4½
Elevation Gain	500	800	2,500
Highest Point	8,200	8,500	10,000
Hiking Time One-Way	1h	1h 25m	3h 30m

White Pine Canyon has been a focus of controversy between advocates of ski development and of wilderness. This has not changed since the first edition was written. Hike up this magnificent side canyon and discover why everyone wants it. The wide U-shaped valley, with angular ridges above, combines with the well-graded road to provide excellent terrain for hikers, ski tourers—and for downhill skiers. The dam access road leads past a canyon overlook, through a meadow, and across the barren rock fields of the upper cirque and ends at White Pine Lake. This road is closed to vehicles and makes an excellent, easy-to-follow trail. The hikes to the overlook and to the meadow are both excellent beginner hikes.

Start at the White Pine Trailhead, cross the bridge, and follow the constructed road grade all the way to the lake. After 1 mile, the Red Pine Trail turns right and crosses the stream, while the road to White Pine makes a switchback east. At the top

WHITE PINE LAKE FROM THE HIGHEST POINT ON TRAIL L-05. The background skyline is the difficult mountaineering scramble across Dromedary, Sunrise, and Twin Peaks (MS-5).

of the next sharp switchback, there is a nice overlook with views of the Cottonwood Ridge summits to the north and of the Salt Lake Valley to the west. Continue up two more switchbacks to the meadow, another good destination for a short hike.

Above the meadow, the road makes a series of short switchbacks along the east side of the drainage. The road eventually climbs over a small ridge and then descends 200 feet to the south end of the lake. An alternative hike is the old trail, shown on the USGS map, which branches west well below the dam and climbs as a footpath along the stream.

White Pine is full of opportunities for off-trail hiking. From the west side of the dam, you can follow the 10,000-foot contour to a notch leading into Red Pine Canyon. Walking around the lake is difficult unless you stay quite high due to the cliffs that drop to the high-water line. The Bullion Divide ridge from Alta to White Pine can be reached at several points by moderate hiking up the headwall. The upper canyon is loose scree and boulder fields, so expect slow off-trail travel after the spring snow is gone.

The original boundary proposal for the Lone Peak Wilderness followed the road up White Pine Canyon. At the time, Snowbird's representatives supported the general concept of wilderness designation and even supported expanding the wilderness area on the American Fork Canyon side, but they requested that White Pine be excluded. The wilderness bill moved the boundary to the crest of the ridge above Red Pine. For now, the area is managed primarily as culinary watershed.

The "white pine" for which the canyon was named is actually Engelmann spruce, a major source of lumber. A mature Engelmann spruce averages 110 feet high and 24 inches in diameter.

SNOWBIRD AREA

Snowbird Village is an anomaly in the Wasatch. Excellent restaurants, fancy lodging, and high-tech are thrust between two wilderness areas and are next to old, familiar Alta. But Snowbird brings to the mountains summer visitors who might otherwise never venture up the canyon, and the tram allows multitudes to sample the alpine environment that hikers and climbers find so precious. Snowbird welcomes hikers, publishes a trail map, and keeps the summer hiking routes well marked, especially the descent from the tram. Ski-run signs provide additional landmarks.

Two driveways from the Little Cottonwood Road access the chain of connected Snowbird parking lots. Snowbird #1 and #2 parking entrances are 6.2 and 6.6 miles up the canyon, respectively. The third entrance goes to the lodging buildings. The lower lot is the best access to Gad Valley, and the upper (east) lot is the closest access to Snowbird Center, the Barrier-Free Trail, and Peruvian Gulch. Maps and information are available at the Activity Center on level 3 of the main Snowbird building, near the tram loading area.

SNOWBIRD BARRIER-FREE TRAIL

Distance	½ mile one-way from plaza to viewpoint
Elevation Gain	50
Highest Point	8,150
Hiking Time One-Way	30m
Special Features	Paved, ADA-accessible

This paved pathway offers a short, easy walk to a platform overlooking Little Cotton-wood Canyon. From Snowbird Center level 3, go across the plaza and across the bridge. The Barrier-Free Trail is a wide, paved path to the right. It rises gently at the start and then is nearly level as it goes west to the viewpoint. The trail has outstanding views of Peruvian Gulch above and Mount Superior on the north side of the canyon. In late summer there is a delightful variety of wildflowers.

SNOWBIRD TO WHITE PINE

Distance	2½ miles one-way
Elevation Change	600
Highest Point	7,900
Hiking Time One-Way	1h 20m

A constructed trail goes along the creek from the lower end of Snowbird to the White Pine parking lot. Starting from Snowbird, this is a downhill hike. Start from the Snowbird lower parking lot, cross the stream, and follow the service road under the lifts and continue west where the road to Gad Valley heads uphill.

GAD VALLEY (L-06)

Destination	Hidden Peak via Gad Valley Road	White Pine Overlook above Gad II Lift	American Fork Twin Peaks via White Pine Ridge
One-Way Miles	4	3	4
Total Ascent	2,900	2,100	3,550
Highest Point	10,990	10,200	11,489
Hiking Time One-Way	3h 30m	2h 45m	4h 20m
Special Difficulties		Bushwhack	No trail on ridge

Most of Gad Valley is Forest Service land within the Snowbird permit area, and the valley is in a more natural state than Peruvian Gulch. Dense forest, streams, and small ponds are mixed with the Mid-Gad Restaurant (closed in summer) and the swaths cut for ski runs. The White Pine overlook and the ridge leading to Twin Peaks from the west are reached from the service road leading to the Gad II lift. The Little Cloud road leads through the scree-filled bowl below Twin Peaks to Hidden Peak.

The service road into Gad Valley starts from the lower Snowbird parking area west of the Quad lift. This road can also be reached from Snowbird Center by following the foot trail up the "Dick Bass Highway" ski run. The road to the Gad II lift branches right at 9,100 feet, descends slightly to cross the stream, and then resumes climbing to the west. As you approach the top of the lift, a distinct saddle is visible on the ridge to the west, about 400 feet higher. This saddle, overlooking White Pine Canyon, is a steep bushwhack from the road up, your choice of either grassy slopes or forested boulders.

To continue from the White Pine overlook to American Fork Twin Peaks, climb south along the ridge between Gad Valley and White Pine Canyon to the minor summit ¼ mile west of Twin Peaks, descend to the saddle, and then climb the ridge to the higher twin. This route is easier than the knife-edge traverse from Hidden Peak.

PERUVIAN GULCH (L-07)

Destination	Hidden Peak from Snowbird via Peruvian Gulch	Snowbird from Hidden Peak via Peruvian Gulch
One-Way Miles	3½	3½
Elevation Change	2,880	−2,880
Highest Point	10,980	10,980
Hiking Time One-Way	3h 25m	2h 45m

Peruvian Gulch was the site of much activity during the mining era and is largely private land, now managed as part of Snowbird. Another legacy of the mining era is that this area, like Alta and Brighton, was largely deforested. This hike is along a mix of single-track footpaths and ski-area service roads and is a popular descent from the tram. Fascinating geology is displayed on the towering south face of Mount Superior, across Little Cottonwood Canyon.

Starting from Snowbird Center, take Creek Road, a gravel service road, east under the Peruvian lift, and when you are uphill of the Cliff Lodge, watch for the sign for the Peruvian Gulch Hiking Trail. This footpath winds up through forest, crosses a road at the sport court, and then climbs with switchbacks up the more open slopes east of the Peruvian lift. Eventually, the hiking trail meets the ski-area service road that starts upcanyon on the bypass road to Alta and passes below the condominiums and ascends the east side of the Snowbird area. From the junction with the road, either the service road or the Ridge Trail can be used to reach the top of Hidden Peak.

SNOWBIRD TRAM-ASSISTED HIKING

Many summer visitors pay to ride the tram to the top of 10,992-foot Hidden Peak and then hike down on the ski roads. Peruvian is the more popular descent, but you can also go down Gad Valley. Another option is to hike the ridge from Hidden Peak over to Mount Baldy and back. Any of these options gives a lot of alpine scenery without the effort of a long climb. Remember that even going downhill, you will be on the trail for several hours before you get back to the base, so carry enough water, sunscreen, and raingear for summer afternoon storms.

CARDIFF PASS FROM ALTA (L-08)

Distance	1 mile one-way
Elevation Gain	1,360
Highest Point	Pass at 10,000
Hiking Time One-Way	1h 10m

The old mining road leading north from Alta to Cardiff Pass provides access to Flagstaff Peak, Mount Superior, and Cardiff Fork. The best hiking is in morning or in cool weather, as the route is south facing and has few trees. On the way up, you have a changing perspective of the Alta and Snowbird ski areas and of Albion Basin. From the pass, you can see the knife-edged ridges and magnificent summits of the Mount Superior area. Much of the Cottonwood Ridge above Alta is a maze of private lands resulting from mining claims.

The road to Cardiff Pass starts behind the Alta town office, 8.3 miles up Little Cottonwood Canyon. In summer there is ample parking along the road in Alta.

Look for the road on the north between the Our Lady of the Snows chapel and the Shallow Shaft restaurant. Go behind the gray office building and turn right at the fork in the curve. The road up toward Cardiff makes a sharp left near the Forest Service snow-monitoring site. The first two roads branching left dead-end at cabins, and the third road branching left is the route to Cardiff Pass. Above here the road is the only obvious track. It ascends in a series of switchbacks and generally follows the power line to the pass.

About halfway up, the road forks and the more distinct road turns right to the Flagstaff Mine, while the Cardiff Pass road continues northwest. This fork is immediately after two closely spaced switchbacks and before the road crosses under the power line. Higher up, the Cardiff Pass road becomes a foot track through open meadows, but the pass and power line provide clear landmarks. Snowbird owns most of the private inholdings high on the ridge near Cardiff Pass.

MOUNT SUPERIOR AND MONTE CRISTO (L-08.1)

Destination	Mount Superior	Monte Cristo
One-Way Miles	2¼	2½
Elevation Gain	2,400	2,500
Extra Ascents	320	400
Highest Point	11,040	11,132
Hiking Time One-Way	2h 45m	3h

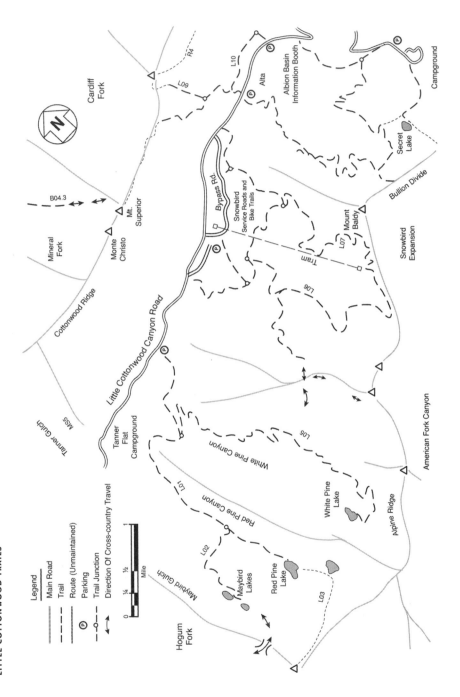

LITTLE COTTONWOOD TRAILS

Legend
Main Road
Trail
Route (Unmaintained)
Parking
Trail Junction
Direction Of Cross-country Travel

Mile
0   ¼   ½   1

N

Cardiff Fork

B04.3

R4

L09

L10

Alta

Albion Basin
Information Booth

Secret Lake

Campground

Bullion Divide

Mineral Fork

Monte Christo

Mt. Superior

Cottonwood Ridge

Bypass Rd.

Snowbird
Service Roads and
Bike Trails

Tram

L07 Mount Baldy

Snowbird Expansion

L06

Little Cottonwood Canyon Road

Tanner Gulch

MS5

Tanner Flat Campground

White Pine Canyon

L05

White Pine Lake

Alpine Ridge

American Fork Canyon

Red Pine Canyon

L01

L02

Maybird Gulch

Hogum Fork

Maybird Lakes

Red Pine Lake

L03

These summits on the Cottonwood Ridge southwest of Cardiff Pass overlook much of the Twin Peaks Wilderness. All around are jagged knife-edged ridges and steep headwalls. To the south you can see the full vertical scale of Snowbird, and the Salt Lake Valley is visible in the distance. There is a perennial debate about which peak is named "Superior," but most hikers do both summits anyway. Local usage and the 1903 "Cottonwood Map" identify the east summit overlooking Alta as Mount Superior. The west peak is higher and provides the best views of the Lake Blanche area.

The route continues west from Cardiff Pass following the ridge crest across several minor summits. It involves exposed scrambling but is suitable for experienced hikers. The first major summit is Mount Superior. The scrambling continues along the very exposed ridge to Monte Cristo. The ridge continuing west beyond these summits is mountaineering terrain.

FLAGSTAFF PEAK FROM ALTA (L-09)

Distance	1¼ miles one-way
Elevation Change	1,890
Highest Point	Summit at 10,530
Hiking Time One-Way	1h 40m

The climb from Alta to Flagstaff Peak is a shorter and easier approach than the route from Days Fork. The hike starts up the road from Alta to Cardiff Pass. Take the right branch of the Cardiff Pass road and continue to the large mine dump where the road ends. A wide, grass-covered slope continues up to a clearly visible pass 400 feet higher. From this pass, turn right and follow the rounded ridge crest to the Flagstaff summit.

From Flagstaff, hikers can continue east along the Cottonwood Ridge toward Grizzly Gulch on an intermittent unmaintained trail. The route along the ridge between Flagstaff and Cardiff Pass involves serious scrambling. The route along the Cottonwood Ridge is described in chapter 11.

GRIZZLY GULCH (L-10)

Destination	Twin Lakes Pass	Prince of Wales Mine
One-Way Miles	1¾	2¼
Elevation Gain	1,350	1,450
Highest Point	9,993	10,100
Hiking Time One-Way	1h 30m	1h 50m

FLAGSTAFF PEAK SUMMIT PANORAMA

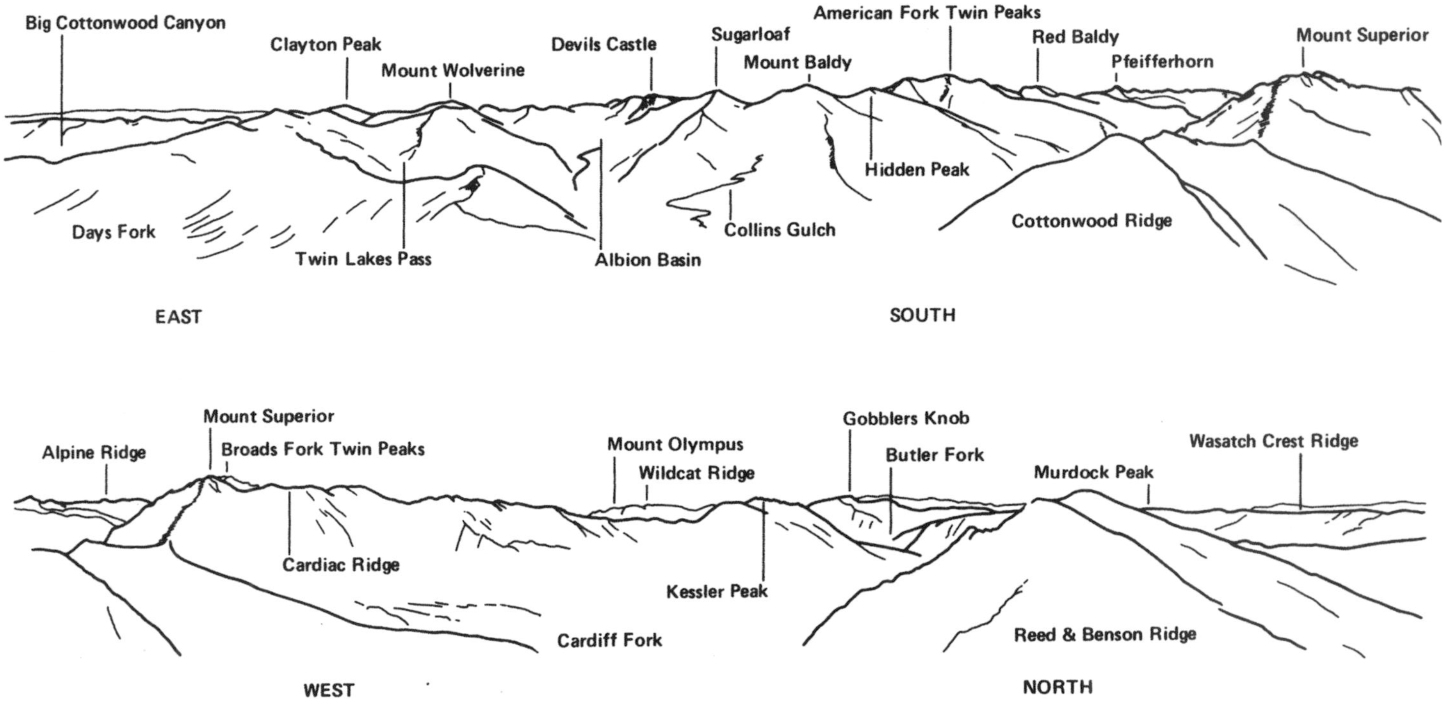

Big Cottonwood Canyon • Clayton Peak • Mount Wolverine • Devils Castle • Sugarloaf • Mount Baldy • American Fork Twin Peaks • Red Baldy • Pfeifferhorn • Mount Superior

Hidden Peak • Collins Gulch • Albion Basin • Twin Lakes Pass • Days Fork • Cottonwood Ridge

EAST

SOUTH

Mount Superior • Broads Fork Twin Peaks • Mount Olympus • Wildcat Ridge • Gobblers Knob • Butler Fork • Murdock Peak • Wasatch Crest Ridge

Alpine Ridge • Cardiac Ridge • Kessler Peak • Cardiff Fork • Reed & Benson Ridge

WEST

NORTH

BOILER AND HOISTING EQUIPMENT AT THE PRINCE OF WALES MINE BETWEEN SILVER FORK AND GRIZZLY GULCH. The gratings are a recent addition and are intended to prevent skiers from falling into the 900-foot shaft.

This hike follows a road up a narrow gulch rich in mining history and eventually reaches Twin Lakes Pass, overlooking Big Cottonwood Canyon.

Take the main Little Cottonwood road 8.3 miles to the end of the pavement where there is a parking lot and the summertime information booth for the road continuing up to Albion Basin. About halfway between Snowpine Lodge and the information booth, a Forest Service sign marks the start of a constructed trail that replaced the bushwhack shortcut described in the first edition. Ascend from the parking lot and turn right where the trail meets the road leading into Grizzly Gulch. To the left the road continues downhill to the highway at the Alta town office.

The road forks about ½ mile up Grizzly Gulch. Twin Lakes Pass is visible straight ahead up the drainage. The left branch goes generally north and ascends the side of the gulch to reach a saddle between Honeycomb Cliffs and Davenport Hill. From here, the road continues along a contour into Silver Fork, ending at the Prince of Wales Mine.

Operations at the Prince of Wales Mine ceased in the 1880s. Today, the shaft opening and the rusting steam-powered hoisting equipment provide a glimpse of the past. The gratings covering the shafts are a recent attempt at mine restoration. They protect skiers from falling into a snow-covered shaft, yet the grating can be removed if favorable prices ever make reopening the mines a feasible venture.

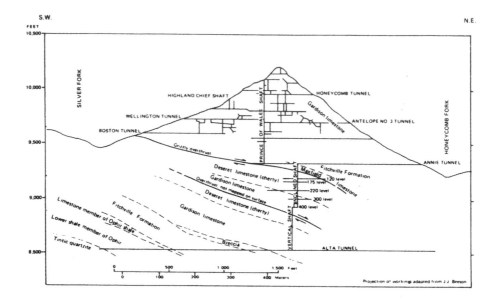

The mountains between Cardiff Fork and Alta are full of mine workings, as this illustration from a geology report shows. Drawing from Laurence James, *Geology, Ore Deposits, and History of the Big Cottonwood Mining District.*

COLLINS GULCH TO GERMANIA PASS (L-11)

Distance	2½ miles one-way
Elevation Gain	2,000
Highest Point	Pass at 10,600
Hiking Time One-Way	2h 20m

Collins Gulch is a good hiking area with subalpine meadows, similar to Albion Basin. Alta ski-service roads ascend the gulch, and the open ski runs provide long-distance views. The road leads to Germania Pass, which can also be reached by a shorter route from Albion Basin. This area is seldom crowded during the summer, and it provides a good place to contemplate the impact of ski development on other recreational use.

The service road up Collins Gulch starts at the east end of the main Alta parking lot near the Collins and Wildcat ski lifts. Walk uphill between the lifts and follow the obvious road that soon turns left and begins the first of many switchbacks.

The road forks near the base of the Germania lift. The right branch goes to the top of Wildcat lift on the ridge to the west and gives a view of Snowbird and Peruvian

Gulch. The left branch continues to the top of Germania lift and then crosses the spur ridge to the east. Across the minor pass, it connects with the Sugarloaf road and then climbs the last 200 feet to the ridge.

ALBION BASIN AREA

The highest trailhead in the area is in Albion Basin, a beautiful cirque 800 feet above the town of Alta. A variety of subalpine and alpine environments near the road make this a popular area for finding wildflowers during July and August. The basin is an excellent walking area for beginners, while providing the shortest access to the spectacular summits that ring the head of Little Cottonwood Canyon. Secret Lake, Catherine Pass, and Sunset Peak can be reached by good trails. Mount Wolverine, Devils Castle, Sugarloaf, and Mount Baldy all involve route-finding along the ridges. Most of the basin is Forest Service land, with several inholdings of private land with summer homes. High on the ridges are additional areas of private land resulting from mining claims.

In the summer, the Town of Alta has an information booth for Albion Basin located at the end of the paved highway, 8.3 miles from the electric sign at the canyon mouth. The number of cars allowed past the booth is limited to avoid exceeding parking capacity in Albion Basin, but the town operates a shuttle van on busy weekends. Donations are appreciated. The last 2½ miles from the information booth to Albion Basin are unpaved but are suitable for passenger cars. There are two hiker parking areas in Albion Basin. One is for the Catherine Pass Trail, and the other is just outside the Albion Basin campground.

If you decide to walk up to Albion Basin, the ski-area road and Albion Meadows Trail are a shorter and nicer hike than walking up the automobile road.

ALBION MEADOWS TRAIL (L-12.2)

Distance	1¾ miles one-way
Elevation Gain	700
Highest Point	Lake at 9,880
Hiking Time One-Way	1h 15m

This is a hiking and bike path that goes between the Alta upper parking area and Albion Basin. The trail follows the drainage and goes through grassy open areas that are filled with wildflowers in late summer.

The lower end is marked by a sign on the downhill side of the parking lot near the information booth. The upper end is to the right of Albion Campground, near the restroom. The lower end is a footpath that parallels the auto road. After ½ mile the trail joins a ski-area service road that connects to the auto road at a gate on the first

COLLINS GULCH. The road climbs from Alta to Germania Pass near Sugarloaf Peak. In late summer this gulch becomes a delightful area for finding wildflowers.

bend of the S switchback. Alternatively, start up the Albion Basin auto road and turn right at the gate that is ½ mile beyond the end of the pavement at the upper parking lot and just before the first left turn in the automobile road. From the junction of the two options, the service road continues up to a second gate where it joins the auto road near the Catherine Pass Trailhead, and a footpath continues up parallel to the road to the campground. About midway on the service-road section is the junction with the Sugarloaf road that climbs to Germania Pass. The official Albion Meadows Trail is not well defined, and there are multiple service roads and footpaths in the area. Landmarks are readily visible, and you will not get lost.

SECRET LAKE (L-13)

Distance	¾ mile one-way
Elevation Gain	420
Highest Point	Lake at 9,220
Hiking Time One-Way	35m

Secret Lake is an excellent beginner hike to a sparkling lake set below the dark cliff face of Devils Castle. This hike is at a high altitude, so adjust your hiking pace.

Ride up in the Alta town shuttle or drive up the road from the information booth past the Lake Catherine Trail parking area all the way at the end and park in the lot outside the campground. The Secret Lake Trail starts on the right of the campground entrance. Follow the trail around the right-hand side of the campground and turn right toward Secret Lake. A restroom is located in the trees to the right of the trailhead, and the Albion Meadows Trail heads down from here.

The Secret Lake Trail passes under the Secret lift, crosses a small stream, and heads generally west. A road branches to the right to reach some cabins. Locate the small cliff and mine dump high to your left. The lake is above these landmarks and in the general direction of the Sugarloaf summit. The trail is distinct and well marked all the way to the lake. A few yards of steep trail cross over the rock, and the lake comes into view.

There are plenty of places to explore along the trail, so it is easy to keep children interested along the way. Meadows of flowers, rock outcrops for easy scrambling, a set of boulders with marine fossils, and marshy areas are all within a few hundred feet of the trail.

SUGARLOAF ROAD TO GERMANIA PASS (L-12)

Route to Germania Pass	Along Sugarloaf Road	Direct from Secret Lake
One-Way Miles	2½	1¾
Elevation Gain	1,300	1,100
Highest Point	10,500	10,500
Hiking Time One-Way	1h 55m	1h 30m

The hike from Albion Basin to the Sugarloaf road is the easiest route to Sugarloaf Peak and to the Bullion Divide, Mount Baldy, and Hidden Peak (Snowbird tram). The road is a pleasant walk through high meadows and past abandoned mines.

ALBION BASIN AREA

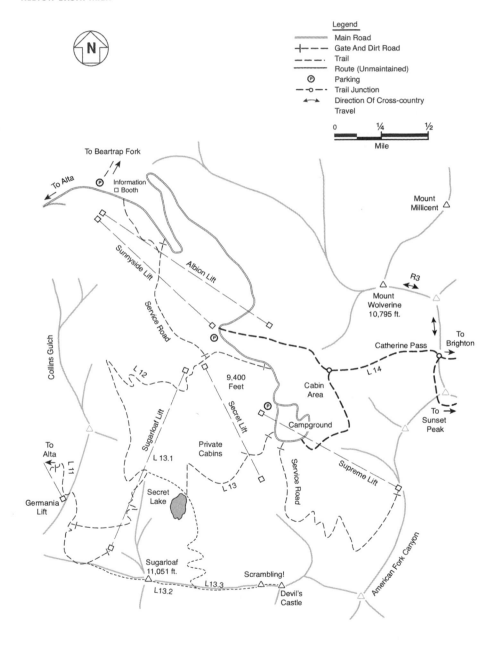

Legend
— Main Road
+ — — Gate And Dirt Road
— — — Trail
——— Route (Unmaintained)
Ⓟ Parking
— ○ — Trail Junction
←→ Direction Of Cross-country
Travel

0   ¼   ½
Mile

N

To Beartrap Fork
To Alta
Ⓟ Information Booth

Mount Millicent

Sunnyside Lift
Albion Lift
Service Road

Mount Wolverine 10,795 ft.
R3

Catherine Pass
To Brighton

Ⓟ

L 12
9,400 Feet

Collins Gulch

Cabin Area
L 14

Sugarloaf Lift
Secret Lift

Ⓟ
Campground

To Alta
L 11

L 13.1
Private Cabins

Supreme Lift

To Sunset Peak

Germania Lift
Secret Lake
L 13

Service Road

American Fork Canyon

Sugarloaf 11,051 ft.
L13.2   L13.3
Scrambling!
Devil's Castle

The actual service road starts at the base of Sugarloaf lift, about ½ mile west and 160 feet below the Albion Basin Trailhead. This junction is reached from the ski-area road that runs parallel to the Albion Basin auto road. Alternatively, start from the Albion Basin Trailhead and continue northwest past Secret Lake for ¼ mile, ascending about 100 feet to connect with the Sugarloaf road.

The road climbs in a series of switchbacks to the top of Sugarloaf lift. Near the top, the road forks and the right branch crosses the spur ridge to the Collins Gulch road. The Sugarloaf road leads past Germania Pass, a saddle on Bullion Divide overlooking American Fork Canyon, and ends at the top of the ski lift. Either Sugarloaf Peak to the east or Mount Baldy to the west can be reached by off-trail hiking along the ridge.

MOUNT BALDY (L-12.1)

Distance	2¼ miles from Albion Basin to summit via Germania Pass
Elevation Gain	1,700
Highest Point	Summit at 11,068
Hiking Time One-Way	2h 10m
Special Difficulties	Unmaintained trail

Mount Baldy is on the ridge separating the Alta and Snowbird ski areas and is only a short ridge hike from the top of the Snowbird tram on Hidden Peak. The hiking route up Baldy is to take the service road from Albion Basin to Germania Pass and then follow the ridge west up the short but very steep slope, making small detours around rock outcrops and brush. There is no exposure, and there is a distinct foot track. From Baldy toward Hidden Peak, the ridge is fairly narrow, but a well-used footpath follows along the crest. Many people ride the tram up and hike the ridge over to Mount Baldy.

DEVILS CASTLE AND SUGARLOAF

	From Albion Basin Trailhead	
Destination	Devils Castle	Sugarloaf Peak
One-Way Miles	1½	1½
Elevation Change	1,520	1,650
Highest Point	10,920	11,051
Hiking Time One-Way	2h	1h 50m
Special Difficulties	Exposure, scrambling	

DEVILS CASTLE (L-13.3)

Devils Castle is the dark, rugged peak whose spires tower above Secret Lake. It is a challenging objective for self-confident hikers who do not mind exposed scrambling on blocks and ledges. The ridge route from the saddle to the summit is an incredible emotional experience and gives hikers a sense of the satisfaction that rock climbers seek.

If you have not done much rock scrambling, climb this peak with someone more experienced. It is a great place to learn about scrambling, and anyone in good condition can follow the route with some coaching. The individual moves are easy, but the consequences of a fall would be serious.

Hike the trail to Secret Lake and continue around the east side of the lake. A foot track with switchbacks climbs 800 vertical feet up the loose scree to the saddle between Devils Castle and Sugarloaf. Turn left at the saddle and follow the ridge that soon becomes a knife-edge. The scrambling route is generally on the right (American Fork Canyon) side of the crest. Route-finding is required—if the moves seem too difficult, back up and look around. Hands and arms should be used only for balance. One short climb up an inside corner on the left side brings you to the first summit of Devils Castle, where most hikers stop.

SECRET LAKE AND SUGARLOAF PEAK. This is a spectacular lake, and the trail is short and easy.

The crossing to the next two summits along the ridge crest is still scrambling but is more difficult and time-consuming than the approach to the first summit, and careful route-finding is needed. From the third summit, the fastest descent is to continue east to the next saddle where you can descend to Albion Basin.

SUGARLOAF PEAK (L-13.2)

Sugarloaf is the rounded, scree-covered peak between Devils Castle and the top of the Sugarloaf lift. It can be approached from either direction by following the ridge crest on moderate off-trail terrain. In contrast to Devils Castle, there is no exposure.

The direct route from Secret Lake continues up the scree slope to the pass as described for Devils Castle but turns right (west) at the pass. The summit is a short walk up the east ridge of Sugarloaf. The other route is from the Sugarloaf road, described previously, and ascends the west ridge across loose rock with some brush.

CATHERINE PASS AND SUNSET PEAK FROM ALBION BASIN (L-14)

Destination	Catherine Pass	Sunset Peak
One-Way Miles	1½	1¾
Elevation Change	800	1,250
Highest Point	10,200	10,648
Hiking Time One-Way	1h 15m	1h 30m

CATHERINE PASS

The trail to Catherine Pass leads through a variety of subalpine environments to a fine view of the Brighton area and upper Little Cottonwood Canyon. Intermediate hikes continue along the ridges in both directions.

The trail starts from the hiker parking area on the auto road 2.4 miles above the information booth where the road makes a bend to the west and the Albion lift crosses overhead. The trail begins by following the minor ridge southeast past the top of the lift and continues traversing on a steep hillside. After ¾ mile the trail reaches a prominent rock outcrop, turns more easterly, and enters a beautiful hanging valley that leads directly to Catherine Pass. The trail is maintained and heavily used. Follow the obvious tracks that lead through an alpine meadow and up to the pass. Near the top of the meadow, the trail becomes steeper as it enters a stand of fir and ascends the last 150 vertical feet to the pass. Across the pass, a trail descends past Lake Catherine and Dog Lake to Brighton.

SUNSET PEAK SUMMIT PANORAMA

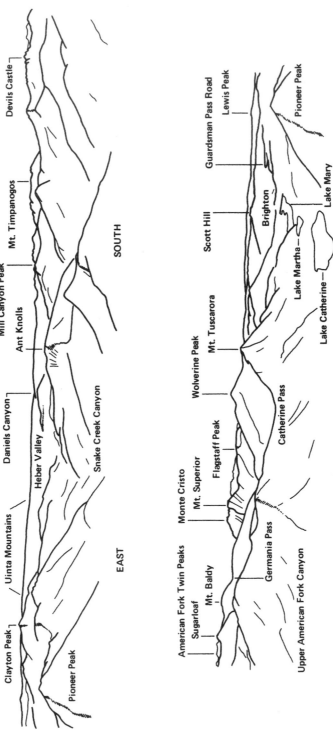

Clayton Peak   Uinta Mountains   Daniels Canyon   Mill Canyon Peak   Mt. Timpanogos   Devils Castle

Ant Knolls

Heber Valley

Snake Creek Canyon

Pioneer Peak

SOUTH

EAST

American Fork Twin Peaks   Monte Cristo   Wolverine Peak   Scott Hill   Guardsman Pass Road

Sugarloaf   Mt. Superior   Mt. Tuscarora   Brighton   Lewis Peak

Mt. Baldy   Flagstaff Peak   Catherine Pass   Lake Martha   Lake Mary   Pioneer Peak

Germania Pass   Lake Catherine

Upper American Fork Canyon

WEST

NORTH

UPPER MAYBIRD LAKE FROM THE END OF THE MAINTAINED TRAIL WITH THE PFEIFFERHORN ON THE SKYLINE.

FIRST EDITION ROUTES

A less-used trail starts from the Albion Campground loop road, traverses above the private cabins, and joins the official trail near the start of the hanging valley.

A very steep route that led from the auto road near the campground directly up to the prominent outcrop has been closed and restored for watershed protection.

SUNSET PEAK (L-14.1)

Sunset Peak is the second summit to the southeast of Catherine Pass and is reached by an informal trail that is in very good condition. This is one of the most accessible summits in the Wasatch, and I have seen many children reach the top.

From Catherine Pass, a trail heads south, starting on the right side of the ridge crest. The first peak to the south of the pass is a triple divide between Big Cottonwood, Little Cottonwood, and American Fork Canyons. The main trail passes to the right of this summit and then turns east, crosses the ridge crest for a short way, and crosses back. One last short switchback brings you to the summit of Sunset Peak.

The good trail ends at Sunset Peak, and the Brighton Ridge Run continues toward Snake Creek Pass. From the saddle near the triple divide, the Great Western Trail descends into upper American Fork Canyon. Also, the ridge leading south toward the Point Supreme lift is open meadow and is easy off-trail hiking. There are several tracks leading from the ridge down toward Lake Catherine, but because this steep slope has high erosion potential, please don't use them for a descent.

9

North and East Areas

The north and east areas of Salt Lake County are not as spectacular as the trican-yon area, and fewer hikers venture here—partly because the rest of the Wasatch is so interesting. The rolling, open terrain to the north and east is excellent for long-distance travel. Mountain runners frequent these routes, and the "Wasatch Steeple Chase" and "Wasatch Front 100 Mile Endurance Run" are annual events. The relatively low elevation makes this area good for early- and late-season hikes when the higher ridges are snow covered.

This is a huge place for wandering. The area covered by this chapter is nearly equal to the acreage covered by the rest of the book. Beyond the jeep roads and constructed trails are miles of footpaths, sheepherder trails, and open, grass-covered slopes and ridges. Only a sampling of the major high-country routes are included in this chapter. Comprehensive coverage of the trails in Davis and Summit Counties would require a full book for each.

Historically, grazing and watershed (a strange combination) were the major uses of this area. In recent years, there has been increased interest in managing this area for recreation as well. The Great Western Trail project has created a ridgeline hiking route through the area and has linked many of the older official trails and cross-country routes. Some of these connecting trails are covered in the foothills chapter.

This area does not yet have the level of recreational trails that it deserves. Land-owner negotiations to secure access and volunteer construction efforts are continuing.

For general information regarding trails, see chapter 1. For driving
directions to trailheads, see chapter 4. To cross-reference trail names,
trailheads, and maps, see the "Hike Master List."

THE GREAT WESTERN TRAIL

The Great Western Trail is a national recreation trail extending from Yellowstone
to the Grand Canyon. The combination of all-terrain vehicles with muscle-powered
travel on some GWT sections has been controversial, but the portion described in this
guidebook is nonmotorized. It generally follows the crest of the Wasatch Range from
Interstate 84 in Ogden to American Fork Canyon.

LAYTON TO BIG MOUNTAIN SUMMIT

Only the highlights of this 31-mile trail segment are presented. The current northern access is at the Forest Service Fernwood picnic area in Layton. The picnic area
is reached by taking I-15 North Exit 324 to US 89 and continue north for 7 miles to
Cherry Lane, 1500 North, and then immediately turn left (east) onto Valley View
Drive. Continue for 0.6 miles and then turn east onto Fernwood Drive. Follow Fernwood for another 0.6 miles as it winds up through the subdivisions and eventually
turns south into the Forest Service picnic area. This is also an access to the Davis
County portion of the Bonneville Shoreline Trail. To reach the GWT, look for the trail
heading steeply up the hill and then turning north and contouring for ¼ mile above
the houses before beginning to follow the Middle Fork of Kays Creek. After climbing
800 feet, the trail crosses to the north side of the creek and then climbs onto the spur
ridge between Kays Creek and Hobbs Canyon and continues east up to the main ridge.
The trail turns south and follows the rugged ridge crest toward the air traffic control
antennas on Francis Peak.

At Francis Peak the Great Western Trail meets a gravel road that heads south and
then west and descends into Farmington Canyon. To drive up from Farmington, take
Exit 325 from Interstate 15 and go to 600 North 100 East in Farmington. A gravel road,
marked with a Forest Service sign, heads up the canyon. It is rough, very steep, and
winding, but passenger cars can make it all the way. It is 8 miles from the end of the
pavement to the Farmington Flats junction and 13 miles from the pavement to the
north end of the spur road at Francis Peak.

South of Francis Peak, the Great Western Trail follows the gravel road down
past Farmington Lakes and back up around Bountiful Peak, eventually reaching a
trailhead where the Forest Service road coming up from Bountiful reaches the head

of Centerville Canyon. To get to this access point, take 400 North to 1300 East in Bountiful. Turn north at 1300 East and follow the main street up two switchbacks through the homes until you are below the prominent letter *B* on the hillside. Here the gravel road starts and turns up into the canyon and passes a Forest Service sign after 1½ miles. It is 9 miles from the start of the gravel road to the parking area high on the ridge.

At the head of Centerville Canyon, the Great Western Trail leaves the road and continues along the ridge separating Davis and Morgan Counties. The next 5 miles to the Sessions Mountains are a mix of old four-wheel-drive roads and new constructed trail. Beyond the Sessions Mountains, the Great Western Trail continues in a generally southeast direction along the ridge above City Creek and then follows the ridge past Swallow Rocks and down to Big Mountain Pass. An easy but long access to Grandview Peak starts from the gravel road above Bountiful.

BIG MOUNTAIN PASS TRAILHEAD

A large parking area for the Great Western Trail and Mormon Pioneer Trail is located at the pass where State Route 65 crosses from Mountain Dell Canyon to East Canyon.

GWT NORTH FROM BIG MOUNTAIN PASS TO CITY CREEK

Destination	Big Mountain	Swallow Rocks	Head of City Creek Canyon
One-Way Miles	2¼	4½	6¼
Elevation Change	+1,200 −200	+1,400 −200	+1,500 −600
Destination Elevation	8,472	8,600	8,300
Hiking Time One-Way	1h 40m	3h	4h

When the first edition was written, the trail north of Big Mountain Pass was a rough, overgrown foot track. Now it is a maintained trail with heavy bike use. A series of switchbacks climb from the north side of the road and continue generally northwest along the ridge. The terrain is open, and the grassy hillsides offer great views but limited shade. The trail passes on the west side of Big Mountain and then continues toward Swallow Rocks. An unmaintained trail up the head of the City Creek drainage meets the GWT 1¾ miles beyond Swallow Rocks. The land to the east of the ridge is private.

GWT SOUTH FROM BIG MOUNTAIN PASS TO PARLEYS CANYON

Destination	Bald Mountain	Alexander Springs Trailhead
One-Way Miles	3¼	11
Elevation Change	+800 −400	+900 −2,700
Destination Elevation	7,869	5,570
Hiking Time One-Way	2h 15m	7h

This section is a good one-way hike with a short car shuttle between the Big Mountain Pass and Alexander Springs Trailheads on State Route 65. On the south side of the Big Mountain Pass parking area, a dirt track heads up the hill, continues past a gate, and quickly becomes a foot trail that follows the ridge crest, mostly on Salt Lake City land, over Bald Mountain and then continues toward Parleys Canyon. Here, some of the land to the east of the ridge is Forest Service or city owned, but lower down the east side is all private. This section is more forested than the area north of the pass, but still offers some good views. There is some confusion as to the official location of the Great Western Trail south of Bald Mountain. Some sources describe the GWT as going to Parleys Summit, but there is no official right-of-way across the private land here. The Wasatch 100 race follows the route described below to the Sheep Trail and then takes a complicated route to the Lambs Canyon exit on I-80. The alternative of going to the Alexander Springs Trailhead makes the most sense for day hikers.

From Bald Mountain, continue south for 1½ miles to a minor hill marked 7344 on the topographic map. Turn west here and follow the spur ridge southwest for 3 miles to a junction with an old road historically called the Sheep Trail. Unfortunately, the Sheep Trail farther west is blocked by the watershed-protection area below Little Dell Reservoir, so you cannot get to the highway by continuing west. Instead, turn southeast on the Sheep Trail for 2½ miles to a open area where the trail from the Alexander Spring Trailhead joins the Sheep Trail. Follow the Alexander Spring Trail 2 miles back to the highway.

An off-trail alternative is to go south from the first junction with the Sheep Trail to the viewpoint marked 6212 on the topographic map and then work your way south and east down the very steep hill to join the start of the Alexander Basin Trail below.

GWT FROM LAMBS CANYON TO AMERICAN FORK CANYON

The Great Western Trail crosses I-80 at Lambs Canyon, Exit 137. Beyond here the GWT follows existing roads and hiking routes that are described elsewhere in this book. From the mouth of Lambs Canyon, it follows the Lambs Canyon road to the Lambs

GREAT WESTERN TRAIL NORTH OF PARLEYS CANYON

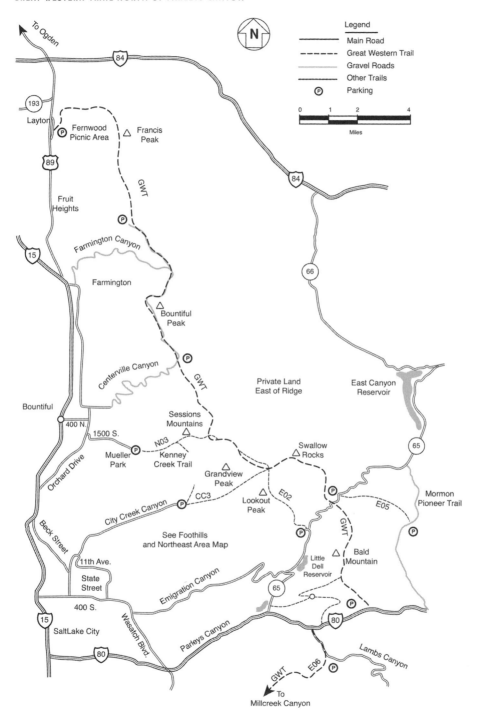

Legend
- Main Road
- Great Western Trail
- Gravel Roads
- Other Trails
- Ⓟ Parking

0 1 2 4
Miles

N

To Ogden

84

193

Layton

89

Fernwood Picnic Area Ⓟ

△ Francis Peak

Fruit Heights

15

Ⓟ

GWT

Farmington Canyon

Farmington

△ Bountiful Peak

84

66

Centerville Canyon

Ⓟ

GWT

Private Land East of Ridge

East Canyon Reservoir

Bountiful

400 N.

1500 S.

Ⓟ Mueller Park

N03

Kenney Creek Trail

Sessions Mountains △

△ Grandview Peak

Swallow Rocks △

65

Orchard Drive

City Creek Canyon

Ⓟ CC3

Lookout Peak △

E02

Ⓟ

E05

Mormon Pioneer Trail

Ⓟ

Beck Street

See Foothills and Northeast Area Map

GWT

Ⓟ

△ Bald Mountain

11th Ave.

State Street

400 S.

Emigration Canyon

Little Dell Reservoir

65

Ⓟ

15

SaltLake City

80

Wasatch Blvd.

Parleys Canyon

80

Lambs Canyon

Ⓟ

GWT

E06

Ⓟ

To Millcreek Canyon

Canyon Trail (E-06), which is ascended to the ridge where it joins the trail going down
to Elbow Fork (M-10) in Millcreek. From the Elbow Fork Trailhead in Millcreek, it goes
up the Millcreek road to the Upper Millcreek Trail (M-18), which is followed to the
Wasatch Crest Ridge. From there the trail follows the ridge between Salt Lake and
Summit Counties south toward Scotts Hill. At Scotts Hill, the Great Western Trail currently goes down the Guardsman Pass road and then up the Big Cottonwood Road to
Brighton. At Brighton the Great Western Trail takes the Brighton Lakes Trail (B-24) up
past Lake Mary to Catherine Pass and from Catherine Pass goes up to the triple divide
between Big Cottonwood and American Fork Canyons, where it leaves the Wasatch
National Forest and drops down into American Fork Canyon.

BOUNTIFUL AREA

A large number of trailheads have been created in Bountiful since the first edition, and
only the major ones connecting into Salt Lake County will be described. The road from
Bountiful to the Great Western Trail north of the Sessions Mountains is described
above. The Mueller Park and North Canyon Trailheads provide access to the north
ridge of City Creek Canyon. The Bonneville Shoreline Trail follows a connector-street
route along Bonneville Boulevard through Bountiful but becomes a beautiful trail
again from North Salt Lake across to City Creek. The Wild Rose Trail gives access to
the antennas area on the west end of the City Creek Ridge. The foothills above Bountiful are a low-elevation area well suited to spring and fall hiking. This area is heavily
forested due to the increased local precipitation resulting from the lake effect.

MUELLER PARK TO RIDGE (N-01)

Destination	Big Rock	Rudys Flat via Bike Trail
One-Way Miles	3½	6¼
Elevation Change	1,000	1,870
Highest Point	6,200	7,120
Hiking Time One-Way	2h 15m	4h

To reach Mueller Park, follow the directions in chapter 4. The road ends in a large park
and picnic fee area. Urban trailheads cost money to create and maintain, and paid
parking is preferable to having access blocked by development.

The trail to Rudys Flat starts on the south side of the road near the entrance
to Mueller Park. A bridge crosses the stream, and the first of an endless series of
switchbacks begins to wind up the hillside. This is a wide, well-constructed trail that
climbs slowly as it traverses above the picnic area, crosses the right-hand fork of the

drainage, meanders over to Big Rock, and then winds back into the right fork for the final switchbacks to the ridge at Rudys Flat. The trail is open to motorcycles, but not full-size ATVs.

KENNEY CREEK TRAIL (N-03)

This trail starts on the north side of the road and climbs steeply. The bottom part is well maintained and scenic. This trail was included in the first edition as a bushwhack route to the ridge. The maintained route does not connect with the GWT or Sessions Mountains above. Currently, most hikers treat this as a climb to the miner's cabin 2¼ miles from the trailhead.

MUELLER PARK HISTORIC ROUTE

A trail formerly followed the drainage from Mueller Park to the ridge, but it was partially washed out many years ago and is now a bushwhack.

SESSIONS MOUNTAINS

The Sessions Mountains are a spur ridge extending west from the divide between Davis and Morgan Counties. The area can be reached from a trail starting on Bountiful Boulevard near the temple or from the Great Western Trail. Kenney Creek Trail ends before the Sessions Mountain ridge.

NORTH CANYON TO RUDYS FLAT (N-02)

Destination	Rudys Flat	Loop Hike to Mueller Park
One-Way Miles	2½	7
Elevation Change	1,120	+1,120 −750
Highest Point	7,120	7,120
Hiking Time One-Way	1h 50m	4h 15m

From about 3400 South on Bountiful Boulevard, turn east on Canyon Creek Road and park at the end of the pavement. This is neighborhood parking, so be considerate of home owners. Continue up the dirt road through ½ mile of private land to the Forest Service boundary. The trail eventually becomes a series of switchbacks that climb to the ridge. At Rudys Flat, on the ridge, this trail meets the trail coming from Mueller Park. This is a shorter route to the ridge and is part of the motorcycle trail loop.

VIEW FROM EMIGRATION RIDGE NEAR DALE PEAK (E-01). The peak overlooking the city is Big Beacon. Hike F-06 follows the ridge forming the left skyline of Big Beacon. The oil and natural gas pipeline route is visible, snaking across the hillside.

Around 2010 there was extensive construction where a pipeline crossed through this area, but the hillside scars are being revegetated. The trail is open to motorcycles, but not full-size ATVs.

CONNECTING TRAILS FROM RUDYS FLAT

A trail described as the North Ridge of City Creek in chapter 5 leads along the ridge above City Creek from the antennas above Ensign Peak, past Rudys Flat, and east for another mile or so toward Grandview Peak. There is evidence of historical vehicle use and current motorcycle and mountain bike travel, so the popular portions are obvious on the ground, while other portions are faint. The trail from Rudys Flat down into City Creek receives occasional clearing.

WILD ROSE TRAIL (N-04)

Distance	2 miles to north ridge of City Creek
Elevation Gain	900 feet

Highest Point	Ridge at 6,120
Hiking Time One-Way	1h 25m

This new trail starts at a city park in North Salt Lake and leads up to the City Creek Ridge near where the "Pipeline Route" from lower City Creek reaches the ridge from the south side. The trailhead is off Eaglepointe Drive. See chapter 4 for directions. The trail starts from the east side of the city park, and the first part is a bit confusing, as new foothill trails are being constructed in the area, and restoration from pipeline construction was in progress at the time of field checking. The route to the City Creek Ridge heads generally southeast, makes two switchbacks, and then follows the crest of a minor ridge.

BONNEVILLE SHORELINE TRAIL—DAVIS COUNTY (BST)

Destination	Antennas Road	City Creek Mouth
Distance	1¼ miles	4½ miles
Elevation Change	1,000	1,000 feet of ascents 1,500 feet of descents
Hiking Time One-Way	1h 10m	3h 15m

The BST follows a paved street connector from the north end of Bountiful to the trailhead in North Salt Lake City. A trail along the Bonneville bench was infeasible through southern Davis County because development already extended above the 5,200-foot level, the slopes above are steep, and private inholdings extend east far past the nominal national forest boundary. The area between North Salt Lake City and City Creek in Salt Lake City was an area of contention regarding development versus open-space protection, but the outcome was a good compromise. Foothill protection is expensive; the 2006 creation of the Bonneville Shoreline Preserve was a $1.75 million collaboration between the two municipalities, Davis County, and Utah Open Lands.

I was amazed the first time I hiked this area. The feeling was of walking through a flat, open natural area with magnificent views in all directions. Mountains to the north, low rolling hills to the east, a city to the south, and the Great Salt Lake to the west. The curve of the hill completely blocks the view of the industrial area below along Beck Street.

From the trailhead at the south end of Eaglepointe Drive, the trail follows a wide bench and then climbs around the end of the City Creek Ridge. There are a number of significant climbs and descents as the trail crosses the antennas ridge, traverses above the houses, crosses the Ensign Peak Ridge, and then finally drops on switchbacks into City Creek and parallels the road to the canyon mouth. The Wild Rose Trail, Antennas

Road, and BST make a nice loop between nearby trailheads. The hike described here is basically the reverse of the description in chapter 5, and that chapter lists connecting trails on the Salt Lake City side.

UPPER CITY CREEK (CC-3)

Destination	Lower Meadow	Grandview via Cottonwood Canyon	Hardscrabble Canyon Pass	Lookout Peak via Ridge
One-Way Miles	3	3½	4¾	6¼
Elevation Change	1,450	3,400	2,200	3,000
Highest Point	7,480	9,410	8,220	8,954
Hiking Time One-Way	2h 15m	4h 30m	3h 30m	4h 50m
Special Difficulties		Bushwhack		Off trail

Note: All measurements are from Rotary Park.

Upper City Creek Canyon offers spectacular limestone fins, the massive landslide on Grandview Peak, meadows, and abundant wildlife. The seldom-visited ridges above City Creek are a delight for the long-distance hiker and mountain runner. These routes are described as hikes up City Creek Canyon from the road end at Rotary Park, but the destinations are really in the north and east area and can alternatively be reached from the Great Western Trail.

City Creek was the first watershed utilized by the pioneers and remains an important source of culinary water today. The road is narrow, and there have been severe accidents involving bicycles. Cars are allowed on the canyon road only on even calendar days. Hint: the number of cars up the canyon is limited each day. If you want to be sure of doing a hike here on a specific popular weekend, you may consider reserving a picnic site by calling (801) 483-6705 when reservations open in March. On even calendar days and in the spring and fall, the canyon is open to bicycles, and a combined bike ride and hike is an option.

The upper City Creek Canyon Trail begins beyond the turnaround. A closed road continues east and fords the stream three times before becoming a distinct foot trail on the north side of the stream. The route is through heavy brush in a narrow gorge, but the canyon opens up higher up. A mile from the start, the trail crosses a narrow eroded gully, and the nontrail into Cottonwood Gulch branches left.

Three miles beyond Rotary Park, the trail crosses a small moraine and comes to a large meadow pocketed with small lakes in the landslide debris that came off the

The Great Western Trail north of Parleys Canyon offers long-distance hiking along open ridges with great views.

huge white scar on Grandview Peak. Here the trail degenerates to a track along the south side of the meadow and then continues up the drainage. At the head of City Creek is a pass overlooking Hardscrabble Creek, which drains north into Morgan County. The Great Western Trail follows the ridge in both directions from the head of City Creek. Grandview is to the northwest, and Swallow Rocks and Big Mountain are southeast.

The surrounding ridges are open, rolling, grassy terrain, offering opportunities for cross-country exploration to those with energy and the ability to use a topographic map. The area is a mix of Forest Service, Salt Lake City, and private lands. When the first edition was written, a land exchange was planned to allow Salt Lake City and the Forest Service to block up their lands for more efficient management, but this wise initiative was never completed.

CITY CREEK TO RUDYS FLAT

A steep trail connects City Creek to Rudys Flat on the north ridge, gaining 1,400 feet in 1.6 miles. The trail starts up the north fork drainage about ½ mile downcanyon from Rotary Park. Trails descend the Davis County side of the ridge from Rudys Flat to North Canyon and Mueller Park in Bountiful.

SMUGGLERS GAP TRAIL

Another trail starts on the south side of the canyon ½ mile above Rotary Park and climbs 1,900 feet to the south ridge at Black Mountain. It is steep, even though there are a few switchbacks. Mountain runners use this to connect from the ridge to the creek road.

GRANDVIEW PEAK (CC-3.1)

Grandview, the highest peak in the north area, has panoramic views but no easy trails. Some bushwhacking is required by every route. Turn north into Cottonwood Gulch, and follow the trail a short way to the Treasure Box Mine. Beyond here, careful route-finding and use of game trails are necessary to avoid thick oak brush. The Riley Ridge route is the grassy ridge in the center of the left fork of Cottonwood Gulch. This fairly open ridge will take you to the main City Creek Ridge directly above the Burro Mine, shown on the USGS map. Remnants of an abandoned trail along the ridge are then followed east for more than 1 mile to Grandview.

A longer but easier route up Grandview is to continue up the main canyon to the area marked "City Creek Meadows" on the USGS map and then ascend the grassy ridges northwest to Grandview. Alternatively, approach Grandview from the Great Western Trail by hiking the ridge dividing Salt Lake and Davis Counties. Descending from the top, the brush in the main fork of Cottonwood Gulch can be negotiated by carefully following faint game trails and occasionally following the streambed.

LOOKOUT PEAK FROM UPPER CITY CREEK (CC-3.2)

From Hardscrabble Pass, go ¼ mile southeast on the Great Western Trail to a junction with a ridgetop trail going south toward Lookout Peak, the distinct summit to the southwest. The trail traverses below Lookout on the east side, so in about ½ mile you will have to climb up on faint game trails to reach the summit ridge. Lookout Peak can also be reached by bushwhacking up the drainage leading to the pass ½ mile north of the peak. Trail E-02 leads south from Lookout Peak to Affleck Park and to Killyon Canyon.

LOOKOUT PEAK FROM AFFLECK PARK (E-02)

Destination	Birch Springs Pass	Lookout Peak	Killyon Trailhead
One-Way Miles	1	3½	2½
Elevation Change	520	2,754	−160
Total Ascent			520

Highest Point	6,720	8,954	6,720
Hiking Time One-Way	45m	3h 10m	1h 35m

Note: All measurements are from Affleck Park.

Lookout Peak is on the ridge between City Creek Canyon, Emigration Canyon, and Mountain Dell Canyon. This route starts from Affleck Park, a picnic area in Mountain Dell Canyon 5.1 miles north of the exit from Interstate 80. The area is now managed as a reservation-only campground. Park in the turnout on the road, and walk back down-canyon to the gate where a road descends into the park.

From the bottom of the entrance road, walk across the bridge and then take the road to the north. Follow this road for 1,100 feet until just past site #6, and then look for a trail that turns sharply back southwest and starts up the hill. This is the "jeep road" shown on the USGS map, which is now a well-defined single-track trail that heads west through oak brush to Birch Springs Pass on an open ridge crest where there is a four-way junction.

LOOKOUT PEAK AND THE GREAT WESTERN TRAIL

Lookout Peak is clearly visible from the junction. From the four-way junction, the trail is distinct up to the point, marked 8292 on the topographic map, where the trail forks. The continuation north leaves the ridge and traverses for 2 miles to City Creek and Hardscrabble Pass, where it joins the Great Western Trail. From this fork, a faint trail follows the ridge crest over minor peaks to the Lookout Peak summit. Nice views exist all the way. Areas of oak in this region burned during a forest fire in the 1990s, but rapidly recovered as the roots sent up new shoots.

OTHER OPTIONS FROM BIRCH SPRINGS

From Birch Springs Pass, the trail straight ahead (west) descends to the Killyon Canyon Trailhead. The trail to the south goes for 3¼ miles to the Little Mountain Summit Trailhead where Emigration Canyon road crosses into Mountain Dell Canyon. This route has become popular with mountain bikes and is now much more distinct than it was when the first edition was written.

MOUNTAIN DELL CANYON—HISTORIC TRAIL

The first edition described a trail from Affleck Park going north along the stream draining upper Mountain Dell Canyon toward spectacular rock formations. The combination of washouts and disuse has caused this trail to disappear.

KILLYON CANYON (E-03)

Distance	1½ miles one-way
Elevation Gain	850
Highest Point	6,920 at Birch Springs Pass
Hiking Time One-Way	1h 10m

Killyon Canyon is an alternative approach to the Birch Springs Pass and a popular hike for its own sake. The area west of Birch Springs Pass is not watershed, so dogs are allowed. The area is moderately wooded, so there is shade, but views are limited. The Killyon drainage is notable for multiple forest plant communities, including stands of virgin old-growth conifers. This area was protected by a 2010 acquisition using funding from multiple agencies, public donors, and the LeRay McAllister Fund. The Wasatch Mountain Club used royalty funding from the previous editions of this guidebook to contribute to the purchase. The land had been owned by the Bertagnole family, who started sheepherding in the area around 1906.

Following the directions in chapter 4, drive to the end of Killyon Canyon Road. There have been conflicts with home owners along the road, so park carefully and respect their privacy. There is no sign but only a dog waste-bag station at the start of the trail. The Killyon Trail goes straight northeast past the corral and follows the drainage. The trail crosses private, Forest Service, and conservation easement land.

The trail follows an old road that has degenerated to a single track that climbs steadily. After ½ mile there is a junction where a branch trail heads north for a mile following a side drainage. The main trail continues east and climbs more steeply near the top, finally reaching the open area at Birch Springs Pass. The trail to the north dead-ends but is a nice walk through the conservation easement land.

EMIGRATION CANYON RIDGE (E-01)

Destination	Dale Peak	Perkins Peak
One-Way Miles	2½	4¼
Elevation Change	1,200	1,300
Highest Point	7,376	7,491
Hiking Time One-Way	1h 50m	3h
Special Difficulties		No trail

The best access to the ridge between Emigration and Parleys Canyons is from Little Mountain Summit, the pass at the head of Emigration Canyon just after the hairpin turns. Park in the large turnout on the south of the road at the pass. A jeep road, which is blocked by a gate, branches to the south and makes a switchback to turn west. After ¼ mile, there is a second gate where the road becomes a set of distinct wheel tracks continuing along the ridge crest. After about 2 miles, the wheel tracks start up a steep hillside and disappear. Beyond, a game trail near the crest provides the best route through the brush. The first major high point (marked "Dale" on the USGS map) has an excellent panorama of the Salt Lake Valley, Big Beacon, Millcreek Ridge, and Emigration, Mountain Dell, Parleys, and Mount Aire Canyons. The next major high point is Perkins Peak, 2 miles farther along the ridge. The route is off-trail hiking over minor summits, utilizing game trails to avoid the worst brush.

LITTLE MOUNTAIN FROM EMIGRATION CANYON (E-04)

This trail starts north of the road at the Little Mountain Summit Trailhead on the ridge between Emigration Canyon and Mountain Dell Canyon. This distinct trail traverses on the west of the ridge crest over several minor spur ridges, passes under power lines, and ends at the Birch Springs four-way junction, where it joins the trails coming from Killyon Canyon and Affleck Park. Because this trail has little elevation change, it gets extensive mountain-bike use. To reach the summit of Little Mountain, go cross-country across the open slopes on the south side of the ridge.

MORMON PIONEER TRAIL (E-05)

Destination	Mormon Flats to Big Mountain Pass	Little Dell Reservoir to Big Mountain Pass
One-Way Miles	4½	4¼
Elevation Change	940	1,200
Highest Point	7,020	7,020
Hiking Time One-Way	2h 40m	2h 40m

The Mormon Pioneer Trail is a national historic trail that marks the route from Nauvoo, Illinois, to Salt Lake City. The route from East Canyon to Emigration Canyon was first used by the Donner-Reed Party in 1846, and the Mormons followed a year later. A marked and maintained section of this trail currently goes from Mormon Flats in East Canyon up to Big Mountain Pass and down to Little Dell Reservoir. This is a great car-shuttle hike, as there are multiple trailheads.

Directions to the Big Mountain Pass, Affleck Park, and Little Dell Reservoir Trail-heads are in chapter 4. The trailhead at Mormon Flats in East Canyon can be reached by continuing northeast beyond Big Mountain Pass for 5.4 miles on State Route 65 and then turning right on the Jeremy Ranch Road, a narrow gravel road that is easy to miss. Continue 3.2 miles south on the Jeremy Ranch Road to a marked interpretive site and parking area on the west side of the road. Alternatively, go on I-80 to Exit 141, turn north on Rasmussen Road, go 0.1 mile to the traffic circle, and exit the circle north onto Jeremy Road, which feeds into East Canyon Road and Jeremy Ranch Road. The Mormon Flats Trailhead is 5.1 miles north from the traffic circle.

From Mormon Flats, the trail crosses East Canyon Creek on a bridge, goes south of the restored fortification wall, and heads northwest up Little Emigration Canyon, following the stream. The trail is easy to follow, but at the time of field checking in the spring of 2011, it was flooded in places and badly eroded. The trail crosses under a power line and turns south at a small pond and then heads southwest to the parking area at Big Mountain Pass.

From Big Mountain Pass, the trail nominally follows the historic pioneer route down to the parking area at Little Dell Reservoir. At Affleck Park the Mormon Pioneer Trail enters the campground at the north end of the road on the east side of the stream, crosses the bridge near the entrance road, and exits on the south end of the road on the west side of the stream. The Mountain Dell Canyon trail section is always close to State Route 65, and small signs mark where it crosses the highway at the lower S-turn and where it crosses again below Affleck Park. It is popular with mountain bikes but also offers opportunities for very short, easy hikes for children.

ALEXANDER SPRINGS TRAIL (E-07)

Destination	Great Western Trail Junction
Distance	2 miles
Elevation Gain	600
Highest Point	5,800
Hiking Time One-Way	1h 20m

This trail is a nice, easy walk that goes along the north side of the Mountain Dell Golf Course and then turns up a side drainage with a flowing stream. It provides access from I-80 to the Great Western Trail and the historic Sheep Trail.

The trail starts from State Route 65 at a parking area before the metal gate on a service road 0.4 miles from the interstate off-ramp. The start is on a two-track road following a small stream with a grassy hillside on the north and the golf course on the south. After ½ mile the road ends, and the trail becomes a single track that heads northeast into Alexander Spring Creek drainage. The trail continues to an open area where several utility routes cross. This is the junction with the Great Western Trail between Big Mountain Pass and Lambs Canyon. Here the GWT follows a section of the historic Sheep Trail hiking route. The GWT toward Big Mountain is the branch to the west that climbs to a pass overlooking Mountain Dell Canyon and then turns back northeast. The continuation of the Sheep Trail west of the pass enters the closed watershed-protection area around Little Dell Reservoir. The GWT branch to the east follows the Sheep Trail and eventually descends to the road near Lambs Canyon.

LAMBS CANYON (E-06)

Distance	1¾ miles one-way
Elevation Gain	1,540
Highest Point	Pass at 8,140
Hiking Time One-Way	1h 40m

The trail from Lambs Canyon, which climbs through fir and aspen forest to the Millcreek Ridge, is the only Forest Service hiking trail on the Parleys Canyon side of the ridge. The trailhead is reached by taking the Lambs Canyon exit from I-80 and continuing south on a narrow paved road for 1.6 miles from the off-ramp to a parking area on the left. The trail starts across the road from the parking area and immediately descends to the bridge across the stream.

The trail makes a couple of switchbacks and then joins a small spring-fed stream. The trail continues southwest and crosses the stream four times before the flow disappears. Here, the trail turns slightly right and soon becomes steeper as it continues up the drainage. A series of short switchbacks completes the climb to the pass where the Lambs Canyon Trail joins with the trail from Elbow Fork and with the Millcreek Ridge route. Both the Lambs Canyon Trail and the trail down to Elbow Fork are part of the Great Western Trail.

PARK CITY AREA

This guidebook ends at the Wasatch Crest. Western Summit County has developed an extensive network of hiking and biking trails that would require an entire volume by itself. Much of the trail system is on lands controlled by the Park City, Deer Valley, and Canyons resorts, while other parts are on public open space. The definitive information source is the "Summer Trail" map published by the Mountain Trails Foundation (mountaintrails.org) in cooperation with the Park City Chamber and Visitors Bureau, Park City municipality, Snyderville Basin Special Recreation District, and a host of local business sponsors. The map is available at bike and outdoor shops in the Park City area with a donation to the Mountain Trails Foundation.

If you want to visit the tourist attractions in Park City and do not mind a car shuttle, there are some great over-the-ridge hiking possibilities. Popular options include going up to the head of Millcreek and descending through the Canyons ski area on bike trails and service roads. Another is to go to Scotts Pass from Big Cottonwood and descend to the Park City ski area through Jupiter Bowl and Thaynes Canyon.

10

Dry Creek and American Fork Canyon (Utah County)

The south part of the Lone Peak Wilderness contains dense forests, three sparkling lakes, and spectacular summits. The complex geology has produced steep cliffs that are part of the beauty of this area, but also channel hiking into a limited number of routes and drainages. Access is from the Dry Creek Trailhead northeast of the town of Alpine, from the north fork of the American Fork Canyon road, or by scrambling across the ridge from Little Cottonwood Canyon.

Box Elder Peak, the major peak between Lone Peak and Timpanogos, is one of my favorite routes in Utah County. The summit provides a different perspective of Lone Peak and the Pfeifferhorn and of the towns to the southwest. There are multiple routes up Box Elder, but all require off-trail hiking to reach the summit. The north route from Deer Creek is longer but less difficult, and the summit is visible most of the way. The direct route from the east leads to a steep and spectacular drainage, which presents moderately difficult scrambling on loose rock, as the old trail has been obliterated by rock slides.

The Utah County public lands are administered by the Pleasant Grove Ranger District, Uinta National Forest. Forest Service trail numbers are listed for the Pleasant Grove district area, because the backcountry staff said they are using these numbers on signs. The trails in this ranger district's portion of the Lone Peak Wilderness are managed as wilderness trails and receive minimal maintenance. Expect deadfall and brushy areas, and be prepared to do some route-finding even on official trails.

The terrain south of Box Elder has no maintained trails, and the area is broken by steep cliff bands and narrow drainages that plunge toward American Fork Canyon. This book ends at the trailheads accessing the south edge of the Lone Peak Wilderness.

For general information regarding trails, see chapter 1. For driving directions to trailheads, see chapter 4. To cross-reference trail names, trailheads, and maps, see the "Hike Master List."

DRY CREEK TRAILHEAD

This is the major Forest Service access point for the Dry Creek portion of the Lone Peak Wilderness Area. See driving directions in chapter 4.

DRY CREEK—DEER CREEK TRAIL, FOREST SERVICE #043 (DC-1)

Destination	Pipeline Intake	Dry Creek Divide
One-Way Miles	1¾	4¼
Elevation Change	1,900	3,950
Highest Point	7,600	9,650
Hiking Time One-Way	1h 50m	4h 10m

This wide horse trail climbs to a grassy pass where it meets the trail coming up Deer Creek from the Granite Flat Trailhead. The name is misleading; the southwest-facing canyon has a flowing stream and dense forest. The upper drainages of Dry Creek lead to the south side of Alpine Ridge, overlooking Little Cottonwood Canyon. This area is full of old roads and trails that are now little used and overgrown but are still passable by those who like to explore.

Follow the directions in chapter 4 to reach the Forest Service trailhead parking area. From here, the main Dry Creek Trail follows an old pipeline road northeast up a short hill, past a Forest Service wilderness boundary sign, and on up the drainage, climbing steadily and staying south of the stream. About ¼ mile from the trailhead, you approach a spectacular rock outcrop high on the ridge to the south. Near here the Phelps Canyon Trail (DC-4) branches right and heads southeast into the smaller drainage immediately south and climbs to join the Box Elder Canyon Trail. At 2½ miles is a trail junction to the north, and in another mile is a trail to the south that goes across the west side of Box Elder Peak. The main Dry Creek Trail continues northeast to reach the grassy pass, where it joins the trail coming up from Deer Creek at the Granite Flat Campground.

NORTH MOUNTAIN TRAIL, FOREST SERVICE #042 (DC-3)

A trail from Dry Creek to Lake Hardy branches left from the Dry Creek Trail, about 2½ miles from the start, and heads to an abandoned intake structure at the stream.

This meadow is the junction of the Dry Creek Trail (DC-1) and the Deer Creek Trail (AF-1). From here, the Silver Fork Overlook Trail leads north and the route to Box Elder leads south.

Across the stream there is a meadow where you can find the end of a trail that heads west across Chipman Canyon for a mile to connect with the trail from Schoolhouse Springs to Lake Hardy. Look for cairns in the meadow and for a distinct track on the west side of the clearing. The trail is overgrown in spots but is not difficult to find. It winds over ridges and around gullies, staying near the 7,800-foot contour.

SCHOOLHOUSE SPRINGS TRAILHEAD (DC-2)

This trailhead provides important access to Lone Peak and Lake Hardy. However, the area is also an important watershed, and the cities of Lehi and Alpine have had conflict over how to balance recreation and water protection. From a distance, a constructed road can be seen climbing the hillside in a series of switchbacks. This is the hiking route to the First Hamongog (a meadow), to Lone Peak, and to Lake Hardy. A connecting trail traverses between the Lake Hardy Trail and the trail up Dry Creek. There is a proposal to build a Bonneville Shoreline Trail section from Schoolhouse Springs west.

Follow the directions in chapter 4 to Alpine Cove Drive and continue 0.3 miles to Aspen Drive. The dirt road from Aspen Drive to the water tank is rough, and passenger cars should park in the clearing near the start. High-clearance vehicles can climb 300 feet higher and park at the water tank. The trail starts at the metal gate by the

LONE PEAK WILDERNESS TO AMERICAN FORK CANYON

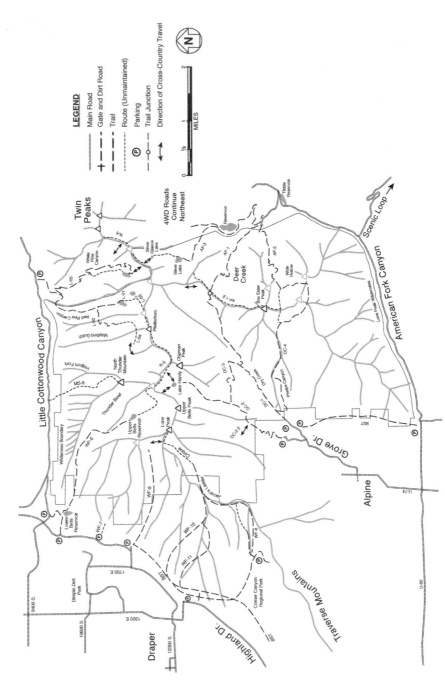

water tank. From the gate to the national forest boundary is all Lehi City–owned property. The water department allows hikers, bikes, and horses, but the area is closed to vehicles. The springs that provide drinking water to Lehi and Alpine are along the road. Hike up the main road, observe management signs, pick up dog waste, and avoid off-trail shortcuts or any other behavior that would affect water quality.

From the water tanks, the road goes north into an open area below the actual Schoolhouse Springs and then begins a series of switchbacks. To get to the wilderness area and Forest Service boundary, stay on the main road and ignore minor trails. The road is closed to public vehicles but was used by four-wheel-drive vehicles in the past and is still used for watershed utility access, so the road grade is easy to follow.

LAKE HARDY (DC-2.1)

Destination	First Hamongog	Dry Creek Trail	Lake Hardy
One-Way Miles	2¼	3	5
Elevation Change	1,800	2,300	4,700
Highest Point	7,100	7,600	10,000
Hiking Time One-Way	2h	2h 40m	4h 50m

This beautiful lake is perched in a small bowl high on the ridge. The hike starts in foothill brush, climbs through midelevation forest and grassland, and then passes below sheer cliffs before entering a narrow, glacier-carved valley with the lake at the head. There are two "official" routes and Forest Service trail numbers are listed, but be prepared for few signs and much cross-country route-finding.

From the Schoolhouse Springs Trailhead, follow the main road up the switchbacks, avoiding the minor roads that branch off to the left and dead-end. Immediately before the First Hamongog is the wilderness boundary where a dirt ridge blocks the road. This charming meadow has a fine view of Lone Peak and is a worthwhile objective. Halfway across the meadow, the trail forks. The trail to the left, Forest Service #200, leads to the Second Hamongog, the west trail to Lake Hardy and Lone Peak. At the Second Hamongog near 8,200 feet, there is another trail junction with a faint trail, Forest Service #187, that goes from the Jacobs Ladder Trail near Lone Rock to Lake Hardy.

The alternative route to Lake Hardy starts out as the North Mountain Trail, Forest Service #042, which makes a sharp right turn and heads uphill into the trees. The North Canyon Trail climbs across a minor ridge before reaching the reliable creek draining Lake Hardy. The route to the lake then continues east a short way, turns north, and follows a small dry drainage that parallels the stream. About 250 yards

Lake Hardy is at the end of the Schoolhouse Springs Trail (DC-2). Off-trail routes climb above the lake to the ridges above Hogum Cirque and Bells Canyon. The Beatout Hike (R-6) passes high above Lake Hardy.

beyond the stream crossing is the junction where the North Mountain Trail heads east to Dry Creek. The trail to the lake, nominally Forest Service #176, continues northerly up the dry drainage, climbing for 1,000 vertical feet. Where it reaches the cliffs, the faint trail, marked by cairns, jogs slightly west and continues ascending. A cluster of dead snags and a huge limber pine mark where the trail leaves the base of the cliffs and climbs across the open slabs to meet the stream, 500 feet higher. The walls of a canyon now close in, and suddenly you are in a forest of old-growth subalpine fir. Follow the east side of the stream up to a large meadow at 9,500 feet. Climb the last steep section to the lake by starting up the west side of the drainage, crossing back east where the slope eases, and then continuing up the rounded granite ridge.

The area around the lake is very fragile, due to the altitude and the thin soil, and shows severe impact from camping. Those staying overnight should consider camping in the meadow below rather than at the lake. Two moderate-angle slopes, separated by a cliff, lead up from the lake. The east slope leads to the saddle near Chipman Peak and the ridge overlooking Hogum Cirque. The west route leads to a pass into Bells Canyon. The divide ridge above these slopes is described as part of the Beatout Hike.

LONE PEAK BY HAMONGOG TRAIL (DC-2.2)

Distance	4½ miles
Elevation Gain	5,900
Highest Point	Summit at 11,253
Hiking Time One-Way	5h 30m

The road up from Schoolhouse Springs ends at a large, flat meadow known as the First Hamongog. In the middle of the meadow there is a T junction in the trail. The trail to the right is the route to Lake Hardy, and the trail to the left, Forest Service #200, crosses the creek and goes up to the Second Hamongog. There is a well-defined trail through the oak brush that climbs up to another beautiful meadow known as the Second Hamongog.

Here there is another trail junction. The Hamongog Trail, #187, continues west and traverses across the heads of several drainages and eventually joins the Jacobs Ladder route to Lone Peak near Lone Rock. The trail to the Lone Peak summit continues north. From the Second Hamongog, you can see the entire route to the Lone Peak summit. Looking up, you will see a long, steep cliff wall on the right. This is the edge of Upper Bells Peak. In the center of the drainage you will see a prominent outcrop that divides the drainage, and to the left you will see the jagged ridge that forms the eastern edge of Lone Peak Cirque. The route goes up the east side of the drainage along a poorly defined but visible trail and ends at the base of a cliff. Here the more distinct trail goes east, and the route to Lone Peak goes west across the open slabs, eventually crossing the ridge that divides the middle of the drainage, and climbs to a point over-looking Bells Canyon. From here you follow the obvious slope to the south summit of Lone Peak. The ridge between the south summit and the higher main summit is a serious mountaineering scramble.

GRANITE FLAT TRAILHEAD

To reach the Granite Flat area, drive east on Utah State Route 92 at the mouth of American Fork Canyon and pay at the fee station just ahead. Currently, it is six dollars

BOX ELDER PEAK. Straight ahead is the north route (AF-1.2) that follows the ridge crest to the summit.

for a three-day pass. Continue 5.2 miles up the canyon past the Timpanogos Cave Visitor Center to the junction where State Route 144 branches north. Continue 2.4 miles up the north fork to Tibble Fork Reservoir. At the upper end of the reservoir, follow the signs for paved-road turns on the left that continue into the Granite Flat Campground. The south route to Box Elder Trail and the Deer Creek–Dry Creek Trail both leave from parking areas beyond the campground gate. Tell the attendant that you are hikers.

DEER CREEK–DRY CREEK TRAIL (AF-1), FOREST SERVICE #043

Destination	Dry Creek Divide	Box Elder Summit	Silver Lake Overlook
One-Way Miles	2¾	4½	3½
Elevation Change	2,700	4,400	3,300
Highest Point	9,640	11,101	10,200
Hiking Time One-Way	2h 45m	4h 40m	3h 25m
Special Difficulties		No trail	

The start for this trail is from the trailhead parking area across from the Stonemason group site. From the signboard, follow the maintained trail northwest roughly paralleling the road. In about ½ mile a branch trail on your right leads east to Silver Lake Flat road, but there is limited parking there. After 1½ miles the trail crosses a creek and then makes a sharp right turn to the north at a four-way junction. The correct trail follows the stream. The other two branches eventually fade out. A series of switchbacks cross an open south-facing slope. There are sections of aspen and Gambel oak, but much of this slope is covered with sage and mountain mahogany. The summit of Box Elder is visible above the far side of the Deer Creek drainage. Follow the trail west and then up more switchbacks and across a rock slide to the grassy saddle. Here the Dry Creek Trail continues west toward Alpine, and the White Canyon Trail branches southwest.

SILVER LAKE OVERLOOK AND BEYOND (AF-1.1)

From the saddle at the Deer Creek divide, an ummaintained, eroded horse track leads north along the ridge and then crosses a grassy bowl. Suddenly, you are at the top of a limestone cliff overlooking Silver Lake, 1,000 feet below.

This user-created track ends at the overlook, but either the overlook ridge or the easier ridge to the west can be followed higher. The knob where these ridges converge has excellent views of Dry Creek, the Pfeifferhorn, and the Silver Lake Basin. Beyond this knob, the granite ridge has been carved to a knife-edge, and serious scrambling is required to continue north to the headwall of Red Pine Canyon.

NORTH ROUTE TO BOX ELDER (AF-1.2)

From the Dry Creek–Deer Creek saddle, follow White Canyon Trail for ½ mile over a minor summit and around the bowl forming the head of Deer Creek. Leave the trail where the White Canyon Trail begins to descend and follow the ridge crest for a mile to reach the Box Elder Peak summit. There is a track through the brush, and there are no major difficulties. The last part near the summit involves boulder-hopping and some easy scrambling.

WHITE CANYON TRAIL, FOREST SERVICE #188

This trail traverses across the east side of Box Elder Peak, crosses the upper portion of White Canyon, and connects with the Box Elder Trail to the south. The trail drops a net 900 feet over 2¼ miles.

LONE PEAK, THE ALPINE RIDGE, AND DRY CREEK VIEWED FROM BOX ELDER PEAK. The Dry Creek Trail (DC-1) and the Schoolhouse Springs Trail (DC-2) provide access into this area. The ridges are rugged off-trail hiking.

BOX ELDER CANYON TRAIL (AF-2) SOUTH ROUTE TO BOX ELDER PEAK

Destination	Cabin and Wide Hollow Overlook	Box Elder Summit—Direct	Box Elder Summit— South Ridge	Phelps Canyon Trailhead
One-Way Miles	2	3½	5½	7
Elevation Change	1,960	4,301	4,600	+3,100 −1,050
Highest Point	8,760	11,101	11,101	9,920
Hiking Time One-Way	1h 50m	4h 15m	5h 15m	5h 40m
Special Difficulties		Scrambling	Off-trail	Faint trail

The parking area for this trail is located just beyond the parking for the Deer Creek–Dry Creek Trail. Look for the road branching right toward a campsite. The trail starts at a signboard at the far end of the spur road leading to the Handshaker Group Site. Soon after the start, you pass a Lone Peak Wilderness sign and a connection with the Deer Creek–Dry Creek Trail. The Box Elder Trail, Forest Service #044, is to the left and heads generally west.

The trail climbs steadily through forest, passes an unusual dirt headwall, and climbs to the spur ridge. Just after a viewpoint overlooking Wide Hollow, the Box Elder Trail passes a cabin ruin and makes a switchback to the north, where there is the junction with the White Canyon Trail. There are some false trails here. Ahead is a minor peak, elevation 10,138 on the USGS map.

SCRAMBLING ROUTE TO BOX ELDER SUMMIT (AF-2.1)

This route follows a historic trail (shown on the 1969 edition USGS map) that crossed the south-facing bowl of Box Elder Peak to reach the pass to the west at approximately 10,150 feet in elevation. Rock slides wiped out this trail decades ago, but a strong hiker can still follow the route. Leave the trail about ¼ mile beyond the White Canyon Trail junction. Generally, the best option is to follow the bottom of the Wide Hollow drainage up to the saddle. This route requires considerable scrambling, and there are difficulties with loose rock, which average hikers can handle. At the saddle, turn north and follow the scree-covered ridge to the summit. This is the most direct route to Box Elder summit.

BOX ELDER TRAIL WEST TO PHELPS CANYON (AF-2.2)

Beyond the cabin ruin, the official Box Elder Trail (still #044) turns south, traverses the steep-sided upper portion of Wide Hollow, continues to climb 1,200 vertical feet in a big loop around the south of minor summit 10,626, crosses the head of Tank Canyon, and continues to a pass where it crosses into Box Elder Canyon on the west. From the pass, the Box Elder Trail drops slightly and then traverses north. The junction with the faint Phelps Canyon Trail is 3¼ miles from the White Canyon junction. This connecting trail, #046, heads north into Phelps Canyon and descends to the Dry Creek Trailhead in Alpine. The Box Elder Trail continues contouring north across the west side of the peak and eventually reaches the Deer Creek–Dry Creek Trail. The Box Elder Trail is faint in spots, but it is the best access to the huge area between Box Elder Peak and the American Fork Canyon road.

The hillsides in this area were terraced in the 1930s to counteract the effects of overgrazing. The soil-stabilization work left a number of overgrown trails, which can be followed if you explore for them.

AMERICAN FORK–SILVER LAKE (AF-3). An excellent trail leads to this lake, which is ringed by cliffs. Silver Glance Lake is reached by off-trail hiking up the slope to the right.

SOUTH RIDGE ROUTE TO BOX ELDER PEAK

The south ridge can be hiked to reach the Box Elder summit from the pass where the Box Elder Trail crosses between Tank Canyon and Box Elder Canyon. This is a long route because it involves a detour to the south, an intermediate summit, and a long off-trail ridge climb.

AMERICAN FORK–SILVER LAKE TRAIL, FOREST SERVICE #036 (AF-3)

Destination	Silver Lake	Silver Glance Lake	White Pine Pass
One-Way Miles	1¾	2¾	3¼
Elevation Change	1,450	2,300	3,100
Highest Point	9,000	9,880	10,640
Hiking Time One-Way	1h 35m	2h 30m	3h 30m
Special Difficulties		No trail	Scrambling

This "other" Silver Lake is a secluded place just over the ridge from White Pine. The lake is ringed by cliffs, and the setting is similar to Secret Lake but more spectacular. The maintained trail ends at Silver Lake, but hikers can continue up to Silver Glance Lake and beyond to a pass in the ridge leading to Little Cottonwood Canyon.

The trailhead is at the north end of the Silver Lake Flat Reservoir, 11.8 miles from the mouth of American Fork Canyon. Follow the paved road past Tibble Reservoir. Immediately before the Granite Flat Campground gate, turn right on a gravel road and continue for another 3.2 miles to a large parking area, where the road fords the creek.

From the parking area, the trail heads north through aspen and follows the west side of the creek. Soon, a spur ridge with several mine dumps separates the trail from the main drainage, and a cliff begins to wall in the trail on the west side. The trail continues up a single major switchback through a steep section and leads to the dam at Silver Lake. Towering above is a black-and-white limestone layer cake (Donut Formation), and to the south is a magnificent view of Mount Timpanogos. The top of the cliffs on the west can be reached from the Deer Creek Trail.

SILVER GLANCE LAKE (AF-3.1)

Silver Glance Lake is reached by continuing up the minor ridge northeast from the dam. There is no trail, but the hiking is through widely spaced trees with little brush. Red Baldy looms ahead as you approach the divide to Little Cottonwood Canyon. From Silver Glance Lake to White Pine Lake is less than a mile, but the ridge crossing is steep and requires some route-finding.

BONNEVILLE SHORELINE TRAIL, ALPINE SECTION

Because the section of the BST between Dry Creek and American Fork Canyon enters the Lone Peak Wilderness, it is within the scope of this book, even though it is almost an urban trail. The best access is at the south. A parking lot is located on the north of State Route 92 between the fenced irrigation holding facility and the mouth of American Fork Canyon. The trail starts as a utility road and climbs over a hill past a concrete reservoir. Ahead is a fence marking the Forest Service boundary. The contrast between the wilderness area sign and the homes just below emphasizes the importance of drawing boundaries to protect the foothills. A footpath continues north across a section of Forest Service land. Farther north the BST is still unofficial, but Alpine City has a network of city-managed trails.

11

Ridge Hikes and Mountaineering Scrambles

These ridge hikes are most often done as part of a loop connecting two trails. They provide access to remote summits and hanging canyons, and they let an experienced hiker spend a full day traveling over peaks and crossing above drainages while enjoying an alpine environment, ever-changing scenery, and solitude. These routes are seldom traveled, so be capable of handling changes in the weather, accidents, or emergencies. Good physical condition is essential for routes involving multiple ascents and descents.

Except for the hike from Millcreek to Brighton, these ridge hikes are routes, not trails. At most, you will find a track indicating where others have walked. Ridges are frequently interrupted by rock pinnacles and outcrops that require detours or scrambling. The second part of this chapter describes mountaineering scrambles that require excellent physical condition and previous training in mountaineering techniques. Mountaineering scrambles are not for casual hikers.

Route-finding is part of off-trail hiking. The descriptions for these routes are directed toward trip planning, identifying connecting trails, and negotiating tricky sections. Where the route follows an obvious ridge, you are on your own. Carry a topographic map, especially if you are not familiar with the major drainages and landmarks.

MILLCREEK RIDGE—GRANDEUR TO MURDOCK PEAK (R-1)

Trail Section	Grandeur Peak to Burch Hollow	Burch Hollow to Mount Aire Pass	Mount Aire Pass to Lambs Pass	Lambs Pass to Murdock Peak
One-Way Miles	2¾	1½	2½	4¼

Elevation Change	−180	−320	320	1,480
Total Ascent	1,330	380	1,801	2,400
Highest Point	8,306	8,194	8,621	9,602
Hiking Time One-Way	3h	1h 30m	2h 30m	4h 15m
Special Difficulties	No trail	No trail, scrambling	No trail, brush	No trail

Note: Measurements are for ridge segments only and do not include the hike from the road to the ridge.

The peaks and ridges of the divide separating Millcreek from Parleys Canyon are rounded, with only a few rock outcrops. The ridge is long but not difficult. Although maps show a trail, the route is a faint unmaintained track that is occasionally lost in the brush. An elk herd is frequently seen from this ridge.

Starting from the trail at the saddle ½ mile east of Grandeur Peak, the route to Mount Aire follows near the ridge crest with occasional detours around rock outcrops, and after a mile it reaches the trail to Church Fork Peak. A short section of the ridge crest near Church Fork Peak is private land, and the Mount Aire Canyon summer home area is climbing toward the ridge. Today this section of ridge offers solitude; someday, you may encounter roads. In another mile, the Burch Hollow Trail joins the ridge near a series of massive rock outcrops. A faint track continues from here to the maintained trail at Mount Aire Pass.

Beyond the summit of Mount Aire, the ridge is narrow and rocky, and easy scrambling is required to reach Lambs Canyon Pass. Continuing east, the ridge becomes more wooded, with alternating brush and fir-aspen forest. There is a track along the ridge, but you have to search. Try to stay near the ridge crest; it is easy to get off onto a side ridge and be forced to double back. The ridge route crosses the section of private land in upper Millcreek and then continues toward Murdock Peak on private land. Beyond Murdock Peak is the Great Western Trail along the Wasatch Crest Ridge above the Canyons ski resort.

GREAT WESTERN TRAIL—MILLCREEK TO BRIGHTON (WASATCH CREST TRAIL) (R-2)

Trail Section	Park West Saddle to Desolation Lake Pass	Desolation Lake Pass to Scotts Pass
One-Way Miles	2½	4
Elevation Change	840	−360

The ridge from Millcreek to Brighton (R-2) is a fairly level, long-distance hike following historic roads and horse trails. Mountain bikes are popular but controversial.

Total Ascent	1,280	600
Highest Point	9,800	10,116
Hiking Time One-Way	2h	2h 30m

Note: Measurements are for ridge segments only and do not include the hike from the road to the ridge.

The ridge separating Salt Lake County from Summit County overlooks both the Canyons ski resort and the Park City ski area. An old road, now a popular bike route, follows this ridge around upper Millcreek Canyon, and then a single-track trail continues along the ridge past Desolation Lake and Beartrap Fork to Scotts Hill, where another road appears. Gates restrict motorized vehicles, so the roads are pleasant for walking and are popular with mountain bikes. The Great Western Trail follows this ridge from the head of Millcreek Canyon to Scotts Pass and then drops down a shortcut to the Guardsman Pass road. The GWT then follows pavement down to Big Cottonwood Canyon road and up to Brighton. The Park City–area "Summer Trails" map calls this ridge route the "Wasatch Crest Trail."

The Red Pine Road and Great Western Trails from the upper end of the Millcreek road lead directly to the Wasatch Crest Ridge at the pass above the Canyons Resort. The GWT generally stays on the west of the ridge crest, following contours around the minor summits. The Park City "Summer Trails" map is the best reference to the available routes on the Summit County side of the ridge. Some roads are operated as summer recreation trails, while others are restricted access to private homes.

Beyond Millcreek Canyon, the GWT continues to the Desolation Lake junction, where a trail descends to the lake 350 feet below. The loop from upper Millcreek to Desolation Lake, returning by the Mill D and Big Water Trails, is a good 9-mile hike. Just beyond Desolation Lake, the trail crosses a ridge and traverses high in Beartrap Fork. The top of the Beartrap Fork Trail can be found on the east of the stream, where the canyon first narrows.

Farther along the ridge, the trail becomes wider, and near Scotts Hill it becomes a road again. The trail follows the ridge southeast to Scotts Pass, where there is a junction. A single track route marked "Scotts Bypass" avoids the intermediate summits and connects between Scotts Pass and the parking area at the summit of the Guardsman Pass road. The Wasatch Crest connect trail drops from Scotts Pass to the sharp bend in the Guardsman Pass road at about 9,200 feet. The Guardsman Pass road, which is open to automobiles during summer months, is another ¾ mile southeast along the ridge. The area to the west in Mill F Fork is a summer cabin area on private land.

BRIGHTON RIDGE RUN (R-3)

Trail Section	Snake Creek Pass to Catherine Pass	Catherine Pass to Twin Lakes via Twin Lakes Pass	Catherine Pass to Twin Lakes via Millicent Summit
One-Way Miles	2½	2½	1¾
Elevation Change	160	−760	−760
Total Ascent	1,350	650	850
Highest Point	10,648	10,795	10,795
Hiking Time One-Way	2h 30m	2h	1h 45m

Note: Measurements are for ridge segments only and do not include the hike from the road to the ridge.

This peak bagger's delight crosses six summits above 10,000 feet, as the route follows the ridge crest forming the perimeter of the Brighton bowl. It involves off-trail hiking but no serious rock scrambling or exposure. Many hikers double back and also include Clayton Peak as a seventh summit.

From the trail to Clayton Peak at Snake Creek Pass (B-25), the ridge-run route follows the road south past the ski lift and then continues as a faint foot track on the ridge. Go directly over the first unnamed summit (elev. 10,315) and then continue past the second summit (elev. 10,321). The track occasionally disappears in the brush along this section. Just before Pioneer Peak, there is a mine working that still shows the vivid colors that guided the early prospectors. The ridge becomes narrow and rocky over Pioneer Peak and Sunset Peak. From Sunset Peak to Catherine Pass, there is a trail.

From Catherine Pass, the route climbs the steep ridge leading to the summit of Mount Tuscarora, with Mount Wolverine, the high point of the ridge, just beyond. There is a little brush here, and some tricky boulder-hopping, but no real difficulty if you search for the easiest route. Beyond Wolverine, you have a choice. The curving ridge toward Twin Lakes Pass is longer but avoids most of the loose rock and offers great views of Wolverine Cirque. The alternative is to go northeast over Mount Millicent and then boulder-hop down to the top of the ski lift, where you meet the service road.

An alternative hike, sometimes called the Alta Ridge Run, ascends from Albion Basin to Point Supreme, continues to Catherine Pass, and then follows the Brighton Ridge route to Twin Lakes Pass and descends Grizzly Gulch back to Alta.

COTTONWOOD RIDGE—TWIN LAKES PASS TO SUPERIOR (R-4)

Trail Section	Twin Lakes Pass to Days Fork	Days Fork to Cardiff Pass	Cardiff Pass to Superior
		Cardiff Pass to Superior	
One-Way Miles	1½	1½	¾
Elevation Change	−113	160	1,000
Total Ascent	1,200	950	1,280
Highest Point	10,479	10,530	11,040
Hiking Time One-Way	1h 55m	2h	1h 25m
Special Difficulties		Scrambling	Scrambling, exposure

Note: Measurements are for ridge segments only and do not include the hike from the road to the ridge.

The ridge route over the Honeycomb Cliffs, Davenport Hill, Flagstaff Peak, and on to Mount Superior is a rewarding alpine hike requiring some scrambling. The area is full of abandoned mines, and in winter this traverse is often done as the start of ski tours into Silver Fork or Days Fork. Snow and ice remain in sheltered areas well into the summer, and this route can be done as a spring-snow climb. Later in the season, an unmaintained trail can be followed along much of the ridge.

The first mile from Twin Lakes Pass to Silver Fork offers views of Alta and a look down the steep cliffs at the head of Honeycomb Fork. There are three options along this section. One is to go directly over the top of the Honeycomb Cliffs along a fairly broad ridge crest. Another is to bushwhack and boulder-hop through brush and small cliffs along the Alta side, making a reasonably level traverse that takes about twenty minutes. The third choice is to drop 320 feet into Grizzly Gulch and reascend by the road that leads to the Prince of Wales Mine.

From the east pass of Silver Fork, a faint track provides an easy route, passing on the Alta side below Davenport Hill and then following the ridge crest to join the trail that starts in Days Fork and crosses into the west bowl of Silver Fork. The route continues near the ridge crest for another ¾ mile around the head of Days Fork and up Flagstaff Peak. The headwall of Days Fork is a steep scramble across slabs and scree. A grassy slope leads from the saddle west of Flagstaff down 200 feet to the road that continues to Alta.

The next ½ mile to Cardiff Pass is difficult and may require forty minutes to one hour. The ridge drops off steeply on both sides, and the crest is interrupted by two intermediate summits and an abrupt cliff. The cliff is bypassed by descending a moderate-angle couloir on the Alta side and then traversing below the cliff. The alternative is to descend to the Flagstaff Mine and to reascend to Cardiff Pass.

The next section beyond Cardiff Pass is part of the standard route up Mount Superior from Alta. The Cottonwood Ridge beyond Monte Cristo to Twin Peaks is a mountaineering scramble.

BULLION DIVIDE—ALBION BASIN TO WHITE PINE RIDGE RUN (R-5)

Destination	Hidden Peak (Tram)	American Fork Twin Peaks	Red Baldy	White Pine Trailhead
One-Way Miles	3	4	5¼	9¾
Elevation Change	1,592	2,033	2,089	−1,696
Total Ascent	1,950	2,700	3,700	3,700
Highest Point	10,992	11,489	11,171	11,489
Hiking Time One-Way	2h 40m	3h 55m	5h 10m	7h 30m
Special Difficulties		Exposure, scrambling		Boulder fields

Note: All measurements are cumulative from Albion Basin.

HIKERS ALONG THE BULLION DIVIDE (R-5). The west summit of American Fork Twin Peaks is ahead.

The route passes over Mount Baldy and Hidden Peak (Snowbird tram) and then crosses the knife-edged ridge to American Fork Twin Peaks and continues on to Red Baldy before descending a boulder field to White Pine Lake. The normal start is from Albion Basin, as this requires the least elevation gain to reach the summits along the ridge. The Collins Gulch and Peruvian Gulch roads provide alternative access but require more elevation gain.

The route follows the ridge crest and is above treeline all the way. The section from Germania Pass to Hidden Peak is moderate hiking on an unmaintained foot track and is popular with persons who ride the tram up. An alternative route from Germania Pass descends south to Mineral Flat and then traverses to American Fork Twin Peaks, staying between 10,400 and 10,600 feet. Beyond Hidden Peak, the ridge becomes a knife-edge, and exposed scrambling is encountered, followed by an intimidating ascent of Twin Peaks. From Twin Peaks to Red Baldy, the ridge crest gets wider and becomes moderate off-trail hiking. You can descend into White Pine Canyon from East Pass or cross over Red Baldy and descend from West Pass. Both involve about 600 feet of boulder-hopping to the trail. This area is largely within the current or coveted Snowbird boundary. Since the first edition, extensive road and lift construction has taken place south of the ridge in Mineral Basin.

THE BEATOUT HIKE, ALPINE RIDGE FROM RED PINE TO BELLS CANYON (R-6)

Trail Section	White Pine Trailhead to Pfeifferhorn	Pfeifferhorn to South Thunder Mountain	South Thunder to Bells Canyon Trailhead
One-Way Miles	4½	2	5¼
Elevation Change	3,622	–172	–5,854
Total Ascent	3,622	1,000	0
Highest Point	11,326	11,326	11,154
Hiking Time One-Way	4h 20m	2h	4h 45m
Special Difficulties		Scrambling, exposure	No trail at top

Note: Hiking times are for individual trail segments under spring conditions on consolidated snow.

This long route crosses the most rugged glacier-carved terrain in the Wasatch as it climbs over the Pfeifferhorn, circles above the sheer headwall of Hogum Fork, climbs the seldom-visited south peak of Thunder Mountain, makes a short detour to Chipman Peak, and descends the cirque at the head of Bells Canyon. The east and north sides of Lone Peak dominate the view for much of the trip.

The best time to do the route is late May or early June, when consolidated summer snow smooths over the boulder fields. This hike starts with the route previously described for hiking to the Pfeifferhorn from Red Pine Lake. There are no easy shortcuts to the road after you pass the Pfeifferhorn, so evaluate your progress before continuing. The full route will take at least ten hours under good conditions and much more if boulders are exposed. Although the Pfeifferhorn is the highest point on the route, you have more summits to traverse on ridges similar to the Pfeifferhorn approach, 7 more miles, and a 6,000-foot descent ahead.

From the Pfeifferhorn, the route descends the boulder-covered west ridge and then either follows the ridge over the unnamed peak (elev. 11,137) just ahead or makes a descending traverse across the south slope directly to the saddle beyond. Next comes a ¼-mile moderately difficult boulder-scrambling ascent to the small saddle separating Chipman Peak (elev. 10,954) from the main ridge. The Chipman summit is a twenty-minute side trip. From the Chipman saddle, the route follows the main ridge northwest above the 400-foot headwall of Hogum Fork. A final steep boulder field brings you to South Thunder Mountain (elev. 11,154) and the triple divide between Dry Creek, Hogum Fork, and Bells Canyon. Alternatively, traverse high in the broad south-facing bowl that continues down to Lake Hardy and then reascend to South Thunder Mountain.

The normal descent is to go west from South Thunder Mountain to the upper Bells Canyon reservoir, where the trail can be found. Pick out a few landmarks to the reservoir, which sits in a depression; it is visible from the ridge but is hard to see from lower down. One route is to drop from the summit and follow a small gully southeast until the slope becomes more gradual at about 10,000 feet. From here, proceed northeast along the base of the steep slope to a small tree-covered notch, and then cross the ridge separating the reservoir from the main Bells Canyon drainage. A steep chute leads from the notch to the reservoir. Pass south of the reservoir and join the trail at the dam.

The next ¾ mile is a steep 1,400-foot descent through forested terrain to a meadow at 7,900 feet. If the trail is snow covered, work your way down, stay north of the stream draining the reservoir, and look for trail fragments on the small ridge separating the stream from the next gully north. From the meadow, the trail continues along the north side of the stream for about ½ mile before crossing back to the south side. From here on, reverse the description coming up from Sandy.

Thunder Bowl, a north-facing cirque overlooking the city, is often snow filled late into the summer and provides a more difficult but exciting alternative descent into Bells Canyon. Scramble north along the ridge from South Thunder Mountain for ¼ mile to the notch leading into Thunder Bowl. After descending the snow, work your way down to the meadow, avoiding the most difficult cliffs by picking your way down the steep west slope.

MOUNTAINEERING SCRAMBLES

Experienced hikers and mountaineers will be challenged by the strenuous off-trail alpine routes, spring-snow routes, and mountaineering scrambles included in this section. These routes are intermediate in difficulty between the more advanced trail hikes and the technical routes included in rock-climbing guidebooks. But difficulty depends on circumstances. Getting off-route, bad weather, and ice or snow can make the route far more dangerous and difficult.

Descriptions in this section are intended to document the existence of a route used by local mountaineers, and not intended as detailed directions. Anyone attempting these scrambles needs to be competent in reading both a topographic map and the terrain around them.

A basic mountaineering course is highly recommended before attempting any of these routes. If the route involves steep snow and ice, everyone should know how to use an ice ax instinctively. Everyone should also be familiar with basic rock-climbing techniques and should know their climbing limits. The routes are fourth-class climbing (hands used for balance, not for pulling up), but anyone attempting mountaineering scrambles should be comfortable with short sections of 5.0–5.3 rock climbing in order to have a safety margin if they get off-route. These are not belayed climbs, but carrying a lightweight climbing rope can add an extra margin of safety. Be prepared for eight to twelve hours of steady travel across rough terrain. Several of the routes are difficult to exit, and once started, it may be easiest to complete the route. Before continuing beyond the hiking trails, consider the terrain, the weather, the amount of daylight remaining, and the group's skill.

Only a few of the more popular and worthwhile mountaineering routes are included here. They approach or even equal the experiences available in more famous areas, such as the Tetons and the Cascades.

In early June, the snow-covered Pfeifferhorn towers majestically above Maybird Gulch. A member of a group crossing the gulch, on the way to a climb in Hogum Cirque, once asked, "Why travel around the world when you have this near your home?" The party included experienced climbers who had visited the Alps, Alaska, Peru, and Nepal, yet everyone agreed that there are few places to live that match the opportunities available here in the Wasatch.

MOUNT OLYMPUS SCRAMBLING ROUTES

NORTH FACE (MS-1)

The route follows the crest of a ridge, climbs steep slabs, and then crosses into the hidden couloir that runs diagonally up the north face to the crest. There are only a few sections where use of hands is required, yet you climb through some of the wildest and steepest terrain visible from Salt Lake City.

The photo traces the main features of the route. Historically, the start was the water tanks at the end of Oakview Drive, but eventually the Bonneville Shoreline Trail will provide a maintained route traversing from the Neffs Canyon Trailhead. Once you are on the correct ridge, climb up on a faint foot track and follow the crest. Ascend the

North face of Mount Olympus (MS-1) is a mountaineering scramble. The route follows the dashed line up the ridge crest, drops right onto the difficult tree-covered slabs, and then crosses into the hidden couloir (the dotted line indicates its route behind the foreground ridge), which is followed to the summit ridge.

ridge, following the general line indicated in the figure, and then drop into the tree-filled couloir to the west. Scramble up the steep slabs, following the trees, until you reach the top of the face that is actually separated from the main mountain. Drop into the large, grassy couloir behind and follow it up. This couloir can also be reached by a bushwhack up Norths Fork from Neffs Canyon. The hidden couloir leads all the way to the ridge forming the Mount Olympus skyline. The last section is a scramble along the crest of the ridge to the north summit of Olympus.

Descent options include scrambling over to the south summit or descending the west ridge of the north summit.

WEST RIDGE OF NORTH SUMMIT

This is the ridge that forms the distinctive skyline of Mount Olympus. The scrambling is on solid rock with plenty of good holds. Start from the standard hiking trail up Olympus (WF-2) and look for a game trail heading left up the ridge, about 200 yards before the stream crossing in Tolcat Canyon. Climb northeast, utilizing the game trails until you reach the forested saddle at 7,400 feet. The route is moderate off-trail hiking to the saddle and becomes scrambling beyond. Follow the ridge, with occasional detours into the couloir to the south. As you pass above the west slabs, the ridge narrows to a knife-edge that continues past the north face scrambling route and on to the north summit. Be sure you are scrambling the ridge leading to the north summit; the ridge to the south summit is a technical climb.

FROM NORTH SUMMIT TO SOUTH SUMMIT

The scramble between the summits of Olympus is usually done in combination with one of the other mountaineering routes. The safest route is to drop on the west to bypass the buttresses between the summits and then reascend to the tree-filled saddle immediately north of the south summit. The scramble up the wall of the south summit is very steep, but there are plenty of ledges and handholds.

TECHNICAL MOUNTAINEERING ROUTES ON MOUNT OLYMPUS

In addition to these routes, John Gottman's book *Wasatch Quartzite* lists four routes up Olympus that involve easy technical rock climbing and much scrambling. These climbing routes are the West Slabs, the Great Chimney, the East Ridge of the North Summit, and the West Ridge of the South Summit (Geurts Ridge).

WILDCAT RIDGE, MOUNT OLYMPUS TO RAYMOND (MS-3)

The skyline ridge east from Mount Olympus travels through a seldom-visited part of the Mount Olympus Wilderness. It offers access to the upper reaches of Mule Hollow, Whipple Fork, and Mill B North Fork Basin. I have seen mountain goats in this area, and rattlesnakes are common among the boulders.

From the Olympus summit to the pass between Neffs Canyon and Mill B Gulch, the route is a mountaineering scramble across knife-edged ridges, around pinnacles, and through boulder fields. There is no trail, and there are only occasional animal tracks. The continuation from the Neffs–Mill B saddle to Porter Fork is on an unmaintained trail (B-11.1). Most parties will require ten to twelve hours to complete the route from road to road. Starting from Olympus puts the most difficult part early in the day.

WILDCAT RIDGE. The scrambling route along the ridge (MS-3) is the best access into this rugged area. The saddle on the right leads to Neffs Canyon and can be reached by hiking either route WF-1 or route B-11.1.

From the south summit of Olympus, follow the ridge east, picking your way down through small cliffs. The knife-edge section ahead is the most difficult part of the route. Stay on the ridge crest or within 50 feet of it on the Heughes Canyon side until you reach the saddle above Norths Fork at 8,600 feet. From here, drop well off the ridge and traverse until you reach a ramp, covered with gravel and boulders, leading up to the easy summit slabs of Peak 9400, called Triangle Peak for its distinctive north face. The distance from Mount Olympus to Triangle Peak is less than a mile but can require three hours. A possible shortcut goes from the saddle south of Mount Olympus and traverses down into Heughes Canyon before climbing back to Triangle Peak. This shortcut requires careful track finding.

From Triangle Peak to the head of Whipple Fork, stay generally near the ridge crest except for a short traverse on the north side of the ridge past Peak 9560. Next, continue on the forested ridge crest across the top of Peak 9773. Peak 9570 can be passed by ascending the short couloir on the north, and then the ridge can be followed northeast for ¼ mile to the second minor summit. Alternatively, you can drop into upper Whipple Fork and traverse below the couloirs splitting the red cliff face and then cross the ridge into Mill B and work back north to the main divide.

Follow the rounded, open ridge crest east and then northeast until you can drop down the brushy slope to the Neffs–Mill B saddle at 9,200 feet. The Neffs Canyon Trail is below, and the Porter Fork West Pass is reached by a foot track that traverses on the Big Cottonwood side. This track stays near the crest of the forested ridge but generally bypasses the minor summits.

TWIN PEAKS VIA STAIRS GULCH (MS-4)

Stairs Gulch is walled by buttresses and steep slabs, with the magnificent east face of Storm Mountain towering high above. This route is best done in late spring or early summer, after the last avalanches have released from the slabs but before the melting snow exposes the boulders. Be alert to weak snow bridges with running water below. An ice ax is essential, and crampons are recommended.

The Storm Mountain hiking trail ends in ½ mile. The mountaineering route continues, staying generally to the left side of the gulch, making detours as needed to avoid cliffs. About ½ mile beyond the trail, a spur ridge begins to divide the gulch and the terrain tends to draw you to the west (right), but the route stays on the left. The ascent of Stairs Gulch to the crest of the ridge overlooking Broads Fork is a climb of 4,000 feet in 1½ miles. From here, scramble along the ridge for ¾ mile, passing on the Broads Fork side of two unnamed peaks, and continue to Twin Peaks. This ridge can also be reached by routes from Broads Fork and from Ferguson Canyon.

TANNERS GULCH—TRIPLE TRAVERSE (MS-5)

This is the finest spring-snow climb in the Wasatch. It ascends a steep couloir with several short rock bands and then climbs along the steep knife-edge connecting

Mountaineering scrambles require confidence on narrow, rocky ridges with occasional rock-climbing moves. (J. Kilgore photo)

Glissading is a fast and exciting way to descend steep spring snow. This technique involves "skiing" the firm snow using your boots and should be attempted only after mastering use of an ice ax for self-arrest.

Dromedary, Sunrise, and Twin Peaks, followed by a choice of descent routes. The route offers a mix of snow, rock, and ice-climbing problems.

This is also the most dangerous route in this book. The climb must be done during a short time window, which normally occurs in late May or early June, after the last major avalanches have released from the slabs above and before the snow completely melts from the bottom of Tanners Gulch. The best plan is to check snow conditions weekly and go when the route is safe. Once the snow melts, Tanners Gulch is full of falling rock and loose gravel. Because the route is long and exposed to avalanches and rockfall, a predawn start is essential. The entire party should be out of Tanners Gulch before nine in the morning.

The route starts in Little Cottonwood Canyon and ascends Tanners Gulch, which is across the road from the Tanners Flat Campground. If the rock bands are exposed, some difficult scrambling up wet cracks will be required. The gulch forks near the top. The right branch leads to Dromedary Peak, while the left branch leads to the saddle between

Dromedary and Sunrise. Follow the ridge crest from Dromedary over Sunrise Peak and over an unnamed peak, and then scramble along the south side below the ridge crest to the saddle where this route joins the standard route from Broads Fork to Twin Peaks.

In the spring, the fastest descent is down the snowfields in Broads Fork, but the scramble down to Lisa Falls will avoid the need for a car shuttle, and the Deaf Smith Canyon descent is always spectacular.

COTTONWOOD RIDGE—MOUNT SUPERIOR TO DROMEDARY (MS-7)

This knife-edged ridge is a seldom-visited part of the Twin Peaks Wilderness. The south side drops steeply into Little Cottonwood Canyon, and the south approaches are limited to the Cardiff Pass route to Mount Superior, the South Ridge of Superior (a technical climb described in Gottman's *Wasatch Quartzite*), and Tanners Gulch. This ridge passes above the branches of Lake Blanche Fork and can be reached at several points from the Big Cottonwood side.

This section of the Cottonwood Ridge contains difficult scrambling over and around pinnacles and involves about 1,300 feet of ascent and descent in 1¾ miles. Progress is agonizingly slow, but the purpose of a mountaineering route is adventure.

COALPIT GULCH—NORTH THUNDER MOUNTAIN (MS-8)

This narrow and intimidating notch in lower Little Cottonwood Canyon leads through the cliffs into a beautiful hanging canyon, perched between Hogum Cirque and upper Bells Canyon and inaccessible to anyone but expert hikers and climbers. The north peak of Thunder Mountain lies at the head of the gulch.

From the Little Cottonwood Creek Trail, find your way to the stream draining northwest out of Coalpit Gulch and follow the stream up between the granite buttresses. The scrambling route stays very near the stream and may be impassable during peak runoff. The sidewalls are treacherous, with loose handholds and false routes to trap the unwary. A friend of mine got off-route here and took a nearly fatal fall. Pass the first two waterfalls on the left. The third waterfall is the crux of the route and is passed by climbing near the stream, starting about 5 feet to the right of the waterfall. Above the third waterfall, the route traverses a broken ledge back toward the stream. Beyond here, the angle eases and the gulch soon widens. The route to North Thunder Mountain stays in the drainage until nearly 10,000 feet and then approaches the summit from the northeast along the ridge.

The lower gulch is a dangerous place, with rockfall from the cliffs and much loose rock underfoot. Climbing helmets are recommended. The party should contain either someone who has done the route before or a few experienced rock climbers who are confident at route-finding.

SAM THOMAS GULCH (MS-6)

Sam Thomas Gulch is the small gully west of Coalpit Gulch and immediately west of the very prominent waterfall. The waterfall, which is easily seen from the highway, is very popular with ice climbers in winter, and Sam Thomas Gulch is used as an ice-climber descent route.

Hiking up the gulch is not difficult, but watch out for running water from the nearly permanent stream, some loose rock, and acres of stinging nettles. Start from the Little Cottonwood Creek Trail and bushwhack into the gulch.

Getting out at the top is more challenging. You need to eventually travel east (left) and drop into Coalpit. Go onto the minor rocky ridge left of the stream as soon as it is easy to do so, and continue up the ridge until it is relatively easy to go left and down a short canyon that leads right to the base of the headwall of North Thunder. Dropping into Coalpit either too early or too late will result in an encounter with some difficult cliffs. The easiest ascent to the summit is along the left ridge.

The entire route up Sam Thomas Gulch, from the entry to the crossing into Coalpit, is not more than a few thousand linear feet, but it seems a lot longer. Sam Thomas Gulch is a very good alternative to ascending the lower part of Coalpit Gulch.

UPPER BELLS CANYON (MS-9)

Destination	Meadow	Upper Bells Reservoir	Thunder Mountain Pass
One-Way Miles	2¾	3¾	4¾
Elevation Change	2,600	4,100	5,420
Highest Point	7,900	9,400	10,720
Hiking Time One-Way	2h 40m	3h 50m	5h 10m

The trail up to the upper waterfall is described in chapter 5, and the reverse of this route from the top is the Beatout Hike described in ridge runs. To reach upper Bells from below, the best route crosses to the north side of the stream just below the upper waterfall on an improvised but solid bridge. The trail continues on the north up to a meadow where there is a large well-used campsite. Here the canyon splits. The north branch of the canyon leads to Thunder Bowl, the prominent cirque below Thunder Mountain ridge. The main canyon turns south toward Lone Peak. Stay on the left (now east) side of the stream and go up a minor ridge to reach an area of deadfall. Watch for cairns. Pick your way through and look for the mottled wall on the cliffs above. Here the going gets tricky, as you have to pick your way through cliffs, boulders, and brush for the next ½ mile to the upper reservoir. The route goes around the southwest side of the upper reservoir and onto the ridge identified by a knob at the 9,800-foot contour on the USGS map. Either the ridge or the boulder slopes to the south can be ascended to the saddle just north of South Thunder Mountain.

Avalanche debris and boulder fields make route-finding and travel difficult in the upper reaches of Bells Canyon, but this is part of the wilderness experience. The best time to explore Upper Bells is May through early July, when you can use crampons and an ice ax to travel on consolidated snow.

LONE PEAK WILDERNESS HIGH COUNTRY

It is about 2 straight linear miles from Upper Bells Canyon Reservoir to the Outlaw Cabin on the Cherry Canyon Logging Trail to Lone Peak, but in between is a wild and seldom-visited area of granite cliffs and spires. The Sawmill Trail, Trail of the Eagle, and Cherry Canyon Logging Trail provide access to the drainages on the northwest slopes of Lone Peak, but these trails stop 1,000–2,000 feet below the ridge crests. It takes more than four hours just to ascend into this area from a trailhead, which limits exploration unless you are either very fast or willing to backpack. Examples of known routes include crossing the pass between Big Willow Canyon and Bells Canyon, climbing to Lone Peak summit from Bells Canyon, and descending from the Lone Peak summit ridge north into Big Willow Canyon. There are likely many more scrambling and snow-climbing routes to be discovered by serious mountaineers.

TECHNICAL MOUNTAINEERING ROUTES

The high country around Lone Peak contains world-class technical climbing on granite. Noted climbing areas are Bell Canyon Towers, Hogum Cirque, and Lone Peak Cirque. The long approach makes these areas true mountaineering routes, not sport climbs.

EXPLORATORY HIKING AND MOUNTAINEERING

Take a map of the local mountains, throw a dart at it, and then figure out how to get to the spot indicated. Seriously, there are places in the Wasatch to explore that never will be in any guidebook: minor peaks on spur ridges, unnamed drainages, and the trailless slopes between the official and informal trails. If you ever get tired of following other people's footsteps, then set off on your own. Whether you go 100 yards off the trail or spend all day bushwhacking, you are likely to find something worthwhile to discover and enjoy. Keep hiking.

MAMMAL CHECKLIST FOR THE CENTRAL WASATCH MOUNTAINS

INSECTIVORES (INSECTIVORA)

Masked shrew	*Sorex cinereus*	
Vagrant shrew	*Sorex vagrans*	Desert to montane
Water shrew	*Sorex palustris*	Streamside foothill to alpine streamside

BATS (CHIROPTERA)

The source lists include a total of ten species, but there is poor agreement between studies as to which ones are present.

RABBITS, HARES, AND PIKAS (LAGOMORPHA)

Pika	*Ochotona princeps*	Rock, montane zone
White-tailed jackrabbit	*Lepus townsendii*	Foothill
Black-tailed jackrabbit	*Lepus californicus*	Valley
Snowshoe hare	*Lepus americanus*	Montane zone
Nuttals cottontail	*Sylvilagus nuttallii*	Foothill

RODENTS (RODENTIA)

Least chipmunk	*Neotamias minimus*	Foothill and montane
Cliff chipmunk	*Neotamias dorsalis*	Montane
Uinta chipmunk	*Neotamias umbrinus*	Foothill shrub
Yellow-bellied marmot	*Marmota flaviventris*	Alpine zone
Uinta ground squirrel	*Spermophilus armatus*	Foothill and montane
Golden-manteled squirrel	*Spermophilus lateralis*	Montane rock
Rock squirrel	*Spermophilus variegatus*	Foothill
Red squirrel	*Tamiasciurus hudsonicus*	Montane
Northern flying squirrel	*Glaucomys sabrinus*	Montane
Northern pocket gopher	*Thomomys talpoides*	Foothill and montane
Beaver	*Castor canadensis*	Foothill and montane streamside
Deer mouse	*Peromyscus maniculatus*	Desert to montane zones

Pinyon mouse	*Peromyscus truei*	Foothill rock
Western jumping mouse	*Zapus princeps*	Montane streamside
Southern red-backed vole	*Clethrionomys gapperi*	Montane
Long-tailed vole	*Microtus longicaudus*	Foothill and montane streamside
Water vole	*Microtus richardsoni*	Montane streamside
Montane vole	*Microtus montanus*	Desert to montane streamside
Bushytail woodrat	*Neotoma cinerea*	Montane
Muskrat	*Ondatra zibethicus*	Streamside
Porcupine	*Erethizon dorsatum*	Foothill and montane

CARNIVORES (CARNIVORA)

Black bear	*Ursus americanus*	Montane
American martin	*Martes americana*	Montane
Long-tailed weasel	*Mustela frenata*	Desert to montane
Mink	*Mustela vison*	Foothill streamside
Western spotted skunk	*Spilogale gracilis*	Desert and foothill
Striped skunk	*Mephitis mephitis*	Desert and foothill
Badger	*Taxidea taxus*	Foothill and montane
Coyote	*Canis latrans*	Desert to montane
Red fox	*Vulpes vulpes*	Hypothetical
Mountain lion	*Felis concolor*	Montane
Bobcat	*Lynx rufus*	Foothill

DEER (CERVIDAE)

Mule deer	*Odocoileus hemionus*	Foothill and montane
Elk	*Cervus canadensis*	Foothill and montane
Moose	*Alces alces*	Montane streamside

GOATS AND SHEEP (BOVIDAE)

Mountain goat	*Oreamnos americanus*	Cliffs, introduced in 1967
Bighorn sheep	*Ovis canadensis*	Native—no longer in area

This list was compiled from the following studies:

Crane (1948). "Mammals of Salt Lake County." University of Utah thesis.
Dearden (1967). "Mammals of Summit County." University of Utah thesis.

Frost (1970). "Mammals of Davis County." University of Utah thesis.

Bee (1947). "Mammals of Utah County." Brigham Young University thesis.

The Wasatch Mountains are within the historical or hypothetical range of additional species. Also, this list does not include reported species that are normally found in the Desert Shrub Zone unless they are also common at higher elevations.

SUGGESTIONS FOR FURTHER READING

MAPS AND GUIDEBOOKS

Dale Green. *Hiking the Wasatch: The Official Wasatch Mountain Club Trail Map for the Tri-Canyon Area*. Salt Lake City: University of Utah Press. Map for the central area of this book—a companion reference.

Mountain Trails Foundation. *Summer Trail Map, Park City, Utah*. A detailed map of the extensive hiking and biking trails network in the Park City area.

Daniel Smith. *Wasatch Hiking Trails*. Salt Lake City: Artistic Printing, 2011. Comprehensive map compiled from GIS databases and fieldwork. Good for an overview, but the scale is too small for navigation. The map cites the second edition of this guidebook as a source.

Randy Winters. *Wasatch Eleveners: A Hiking and Climbing Guide to the 11,000 Foot Mountains of Utah's Wasatch Range*. Salt Lake City: University of Utah Press, 2006. A peak-bagging guide.

PREVIOUS LOCAL GUIDEBOOKS

The following guidebooks pioneered the documentation of local trails and provide a sense of history. Some are out of print, but all can be found in libraries.

Betty Bottcher. *Wasatch Trails*. Vol. 1. Salt Lake City: Wasatch Mountain Club, 1973. The first local trail guide, more than thirty thousand copies sold, but now somewhat inaccurate due to changes over the years. Out of print.

Daniel Gerry. *Wasatch Trails*. Vol. 2. Salt Lake City: Wasatch Mountain Club, 1976. Intermediate and advanced hikes. Includes some not described in this book. Out of print.

Dave Hall. *The Hiker's Guide to Utah*. Billings, MT: Falcon Press, 1982. Best statewide hiking guidebook. Includes very detailed descriptions of nine routes in central Wasatch plus excellent background material.

Alexis Kelner and Dave Hanscom. *Wasatch Tours*. Salt Lake City: Wasatch, 1976. A ski-touring guidebook covering the central Wasatch. The perspective drawings, photographs, and background information complement this book.

Shirley Paxman, Monroe Paxman, Gayle Taylor, and Weldon Taylor. *Utah Valley Trails*. Salt Lake City: Wasatch, 1978. Covers areas south of American Fork Canyon.

Raye Carlson Ringholtz. *Park City Trails*. Salt Lake City: Wasatch, 1984. Covers areas immediately to the east of this guidebook.

GEOLOGY, GENERAL

Geology of Salt Lake County. Salt Lake City: Utah Geological and Mineral Survey, 1964. Detailed, but written for the layman. Out of print.

Laurence James. *Geology, Ore Deposits, and History of the Big Cottonwood Mining District*. Salt Lake City: Utah Geological and Mineral Survey, 1979.

B. J. Sharp, A. E. Granger, M. D. Crittenden, B. J. Sharp, and F. C. Calkins. "The Geology of the Wasatch Mountains East of Salt Lake City." *Utah Geological Society Guidebook to the Geology of Utah*, no. 8 (1952). Out of print.

William Lee Stokes. *Geology of Utah, Utah Museum of Natural History*. Salt Lake City: Utah Museum of Natural History, 1986. Superb presentation of statewide geology for the college student and curious amateur. Many maps and illustrations. Highly recommended.

NATIVE PLANTS, GENERAL

B. A. Anderson, and A. H. Holmgren. *Mountain Plants of Northeastern Utah*. Rev. ed. Logan: Utah State University Press, 1996. Available through Utah State Extension Service. The best and most complete field guide for the Wasatch and Uintas. Uses clear line drawings and well-written text to identify most of the common trees, shrubs, and flowers. Highly recommended.

J. J. Craighead, et al. *Field Guide to Rocky Mountain Wildflowers*. Peterson Field Guide Series. Boston: Houghton Mifflin, 1998. Regional in scope, with color pictures and interesting text.

Steve Hegji. *Wasatch Wildflowers*. Springville, UT: Cedar Fort, 2010. A recent book with a local focus that is detailed and easy to use if you are looking by color.

Richard J Shaw. *Utah Wildflowers: A Field Guide to the Northern and Central Mountains and Valleys*. Logan: Utah State University Press, 1995. Color pictures make this a good beginner's book, but it leaves out many common plants.

TECHNICAL REFERENCES

L. Arnow, B. Albee, and A. Wycoff. *Flora of the Central Wasatch Front, Utah*. Salt Lake City: University of Utah Press, 1980. All you will ever want to know and more.

Stanly Welsh, N. Duane Atwood, Sherel Goodrich, and Larry Higgins. *A Utah Flora*. Provo, UT: Brigham Young University, 1987. At three hundred dollars, this is a professional's reference.

WILDLIFE, GENERAL

W. H. Behle, E. D. Sorensen, and C. M. White. *Utah Birds: A Revised Checklist*. Salt Lake City: Utah Museum of Natural History, 1985. Distribution and occurrence data and an extensive bibliography.

J. L. Dunn, and J. Alderfer. *The National Geographic Field Guide to the Birds of North America*. Washington D.C.: National Geographic, 2011. 6th ed. Most up-to-date taxonomy.

Olaus Murie. *A Field Guide to Animal Tracks*. Peterson Field Guide Series. Boston: Houghton Mifflin, 2005. Tracks are the best way to locate rare and nocturnal mammals.

Roger Tory Peterson. *A Field Guide to Western Birds*. 4th ed. Peterson Field Guide Series. Boston: Houghton Mifflin, 2010. A classic reference.

Fiona Reid. *Field Guide to the Mammals of North America*. Peterson Field Guide Series. Boston: Houghton Mifflin, 2006. Has distribution maps and color plates. Covers all species found north of Mexico.

D. A. Sibley. *The Sibley Field Guide to Birds of Western North America*. New York: Alfred A. Knopf, 2003. My favorite birder recommends this one because it has great illustrations and is easy to carry.

HISTORY

Clyde Hardy. "The Historical Development of Wasatch Trails in Salt Lake County." Master's thesis, Brigham Young University, 1975.

Charles L. Keller. *The Lady in the Ore Bucket: A History of Settlement and Industry in the Tri-Canyon Area of the Wasatch Mountains*. Salt Lake City: University of Utah Press, 2001. A well-written narrative by a passionate lover of the local trails.

Alexis Kelner. *Skiing in Utah: A History*. Salt Lake City: Alexis Kelner, 1980. Extensive photographs, personal interviews, and bibliography, but out of print.

Charles Peterson. "Albert F. Potter's Wasatch Survey, 1902." *Utah Historical Quarterly* 39, no. 3 (1971).

AGENCY CONTACTS

Uinta-Wasatch-Cache National Forest
Public Information Center
801-466-6411

Salt Lake Ranger District
801-733-2660

Pleasant Grove Ranger District
801-785-3563

Salt Lake City Watershed
Business number: 801-483-6900
Twenty-four-hour emergency number: 801-483-6700
www.slcgov.com/utilities/watershed.htm

PARK CITY–AREA TRAILS

Mountain Trails Foundation
435-649-6839
mountaintrails.org

Park City Visitors Bureau
800-453-1360

HIKE MASTER LIST

Trail	Number	Page
ADA accessible trails		60
Affleck Park	E-02	216
Albion Basin area		195
Albion Basin to White Pine Ridge	R-5	241
Albion Meadows Trail	L-12.2	195
Alexander Basin Trail	M-12	119
Alexander Basin to Bowman Fork	M-13	120
Alexander Basin to Gobblers Knob	M-12.1	120
Alexander Springs Trail	E-07	220
Alpine Ridge	R-6	243
Alpine, Town (*see* Dry Creek)		
American Fork—Silver Lake Trail	AF-3	234
American Fork Twin Peaks (*see* Bullion Divide)	R-5	241
Antennas Loop—North Ridge	CC-1.2	76
Avenues Twin Peaks	F-01	77
Baker Spring and Pass (Bowman Trail)	M-06	111
Beartrap Fork	B-15	157
Beartrap Fork Pass from Desolation Lake	B-10	145
Beatout Hike, Red Pine to Bells	R-6	243
Bells Canyon	WF-6	91
Bells Canyon to Red Pine	R-6	293
Bells Canyon to South Thunder Mountain	R-6	243
Big Beacon from Georges Hollow	F-05	82
Big Beacon from Southwest Ridge	F-06	83
Big Water, direct route	M-16.1	121
Big Water, official trail	M-16	121
Bonneville Shoreline Trail—Alpine	BST	235
Bonneville Shoreline Trail—Sandy to Draper	BST	95
Bonneville Shoreline Trail—Davis County	BST	213
Bonneville Shoreline Trail—Salt Lake City	BST	79
Bowman Trail	M-06	113
Box Elder Canyon from Granite Flat	AF-2	232
Box Elder Peak—North Route	AF-1.2	231
Box Elder Peak—South Route	AF-2.1	232

Trail	Number	Page
Brighton area		164
Brighton from Millcreek	R-2	237
Brighton Lakes Trail	B-24	170
Brighton Ridge Run	R-3	239
Broads Fork	B-03	130
Broads Fork Twin Peaks—Robinson Variation	B-03.2	132
Broads Fork Twin Peaks—Standard Route	B-03.1	132
Bullion Divide—Albion Basin to White Pine	R-5	241
Burch Hollow to Elbow Fork (Pipeline Trail)	M-07	116
Burch Hollow to Millcreek Ridge	M-08	114
Butler Fork—East Branch	B-07	141
Butler Fork—West Branch	B-08	143
Cardiac Pass	B-04.3	137
Cardiff Fork	B-12.1	151
Cardiff Pass from Alta	L-08	189
Cardiff Pass to Days Fork	R-4	240
Cardiff Pass to Superior	R-4	240
Catherine Pass from Albion	L-14	201
Catherine Pass from Brighton	B-24.3	172
Catherine Pass to Twin Lakes	R-3	239
Cephalopod Gulch	F-04	81
Cherry Canyon Logging Trail	WF-11	99
Chipman Peak from Dry Creek	DC-2.1	227
Chipman Peak from Little Cottonwood	R-6	243
Church Fork Peak Trail	M-01.1	108
Circle-All Peak	B-08	143
City Creek Canyon	CC-2	74
City Creek Canyon, North Rim	CC-1	76
City Creek Canyon to Davis County	BST	70
City Creek Canyon to Hogle Zoo	BST	73
Clayton Peak (Mount Majestic)	B-25	174
Coalpit Gulch	MS-8	251
Collins Gulch to Germania Pass	L-11	194
Corner Canyon (Lone Peak)		67
Corner Canyon Regional Park		102
Cottonwood Ridge—Superior to Dromedary	MS-7	251
Cottonwood Ridge—Twin Lakes to Superior	R-4	240
Dale Peak	E-01	218
Days Fork	B-13	155

Trail	Number	Page
Days Fork to Cardiff Pass	R-4	240
Days Fork to Silver Fork	B-13.2	156
Days Fork to Twin Lakes Pass	R-4	240
Deaf Smith Canyon	WF-5	90
Deer Creek Trail	AF-1	230
Desolation Lake from Mill D North	B-10	145
Desolation Trail—Big Cottonwood Portion	B-11	147
Desolation Trail—Millcreek Portion	M-04	109
Devils Castle	L-13.3	200
Dimple Dell Regional Park		102
Dog Lake (Brighton area)		171
Dog Lake from Butler Fork	B-07	141
Dog Lake from Mill D North	B-09	145
Donut Falls	B-12.1	151
Draper Ridge Route		101
Dromedary Peak from Broads Fork	B-03.3	133
Dromedary Peak from Lake Blanche	B-04.1	135
Dry Creek (Alpine, Utah County)	DC-1	224
Dry Creek (Avenues)	F-02	79
Dry Creek to Lake Hardy (North Mountain Trail)	DC-3	224
Dry Creek to Phelps Canyon	AF-2.2	233
Eclipse Mine	B-13	155
Elbow Fork to Terraces Trailhead	M-11	118
Emigration Canyon Ridge	E-01	218
Ensign Peak	CC-1.1	76
Ferguson Canyon	WF-4	88
First Hamongog	DC-2.1	227
Flagstaff Peak from Alta	L-09	191
Flagstaff Peak from Days Fork	B-13.1	156
Gad Valley	L-06	187
Georges Hollow (Big Beacon)	F-05	82
Germania Pass	L-12	197
Gobblers Knob from Alexander Basin	M-12.1	120
Gobblers Knob from Baker Pass	B-08.3	144
Grandeur Peak from Church Fork	M-01	105
Grandeur Peak from West	F-09	85
Grandeur Peak to Murdock	R-1	236
Grandview Peak	CC-3.1	216
Granite Flat Trailhead		229

Trail	Number	Page
Granite Lakes Trail	B-23	169, 173
Great Western Trail	GWT	206
Great Western Trail in Big Cottonwood	GWT	170
Great Western Trail from Willow Heights	B-16	159
Great Western Trail—Millcreek to Brighton	R-2	237
Greens Basin	B-14	157
Grizzly Gulch	L-10	191
Grizzly Gulch from Silver Fork	B-17	160
Hamongog Trail	DC-2.2	229
Hardscrabble Canyon Pass	CC-3	214
Heughes Canyon	WF-3	88
Hidden Falls Trail	B-05.1	130
Hidden Peak and Snowbird Tram	L-07	188
Hogum Cirque	L-04	184
Honeycomb Cliffs from Twin Lakes		169
Honeycomb Fork	B-18	161
Hounds Tooth	F-10	90
H-Rock		84
Jacks Mountain		84
Jacobs Ladder	WF-8	99
Jordan River Parkway		101
Kenney Creek	N-03	211
Kessler Peak—Carbinate Pass Route	B-12.4	153
Kessler Peak—North Route	B-12.3	153
Killyon Canyon	E-03	218
Lake Blanche	B-04	133
Lake Catherine	B-24.3	172
Lake Hardy	DC-2.1	227
Lake Hardy from Dry Creek	DC-3	224
Lake Lillian	B-04	133
Lake Martha	B-24.3	172
Lake Mary from Brighton	B-24	171
Lake Mary from Granite Lakes	B-23	173
Lake Mary to Twin Lakes	B-23	173
Lake Solitude from Brighton	B-21	165
Lake Solitude from Solitude	B-19	163
Lambs Canyon	E-06	221
Lambs Canyon from Elbow Fork	M-10	118
Little Black Mountain	F-03	80

Trail	Number	Page
Little Mountain from Emigration Canyon	E-04	219
Little Water Peak	B-09.2	147
Little Water Trail	M-17	122
Little Willow Canyon (Cottonwood Heights)	WF-5	90
Little Willow Canyon (Draper)		96
Lone Peak—Hamongog Trail	DC-2.2	100, 229
Lone Peak Cirque	WF-8	99
Lone Peak Wilderness		178, 253
Lone Peak—Jacobs Ladder	WF-8	99
Lookout Peak from Upper City Creek	CC-3.2	216
Lookout Peak from Affleck Park	E-02	216
Lower Bells Reservoir	WF-6	91
Lower City Creek	CC-2	74
Majestic Trail	B-25	174
Maybird Lakes	L-02	181
Mill A Basin	B-08	143
Mill B North Fork	B-05	138
Mill B Pass from Neffs	WF-1	86
Mill B South Fork—Lake Blanche	B-04	133
Mill D North Fork—Desolation Lake	B-10	145
Mill D North Fork—Dog Lake	B-09	145
Mill D South Fork	B-12.1	151
Mill F South Fork	B-19	163
Millcreek Ridge	R-1	236
Millcreek to Brighton	R-2	237
Mineral Fork	B-06	139
Monte Cristo	L-08.1	189
Mormon Pioneer Trail	E-05	219
Mount Aire	M-09	117
Mount Baldy	L-12.1	199
Mount Evergreen from Twin Lakes		169
Mount Majestic	B-25	174
Mount Millicent from Twin Lakes		169
Mount Olympus North Face	MS-1	245
Mount Olympus South Summit	WF-2	87
Mount Olympus to Raymond	MS-3	247
Mount Raymond	B-08.2	144
Mount Raymond to Olympus	MS-3	247
Mount Superior	L-08.1	189

Trail	Number	Page
Mount Superior from Lake Blanche	B-04.3	137
Mount Superior to Cardiff Pass	R-4	240
Mount Superior to Dromedary	MS-7	251
Mount Van Cott	F-04	81
Mueller Park to Ridge	N-01	210
Mule Hollow	B-02	127
Murdock Peak from Upper Millcreek Canyon	M-18	123
Murdock Peak from Grandeur	R-1	236
Neffs Canyon	WF-1	86
North Canyon to Rudys Flat	N-02	211
North Mountain Trail	DC-3	224
North Ridge of City Creek Canyon	CC-1	76
North Thunder Mountain	MS-8	251
Park City Area Trails		221
Park West Pass	M-18	123
Perkins Peak from Emigration Canyon Ridge	E-01	218
Peruvian Gulch	L-07	188
Pfeifferhorn from White Pine	R-6	243
Pfeifferhorn to South Thunder Mountain	R-6	243
Pfeifferhorn via Red Pine	L-03	182
Phelps Canyon	AF-2.2	233
Phelps Canyon from Deer Creek	DC-4	224
Pipeline Trail, Lower	M-02	104
Pipeline Trail, Upper	M-07	116
Porter Fork	M-05	111
Porter Fork from Butler Fork		149
Porter Fork West Pass to Neffs Canyon	B-11.1	150
Prince of Wales Mine	L-10	191
Rattlesnake Gulch	M-02	104
Red Baldy	R-5	241
Red Butte Canyon		82, 101
Red Pine Canyon	L-0l	179
Red Pine to Bells Canyon	R-6	243
Regulator Johnson Mine	B-6	139
Regulator Johnson Pass	B-04.3	137
Reynolds Peak	B-09.1	146
Rocky Mouth Canyon	WF-7	93
Rudys Flat from City Creek Ridge	CC-1.3	77
Rudys Flat from North Canyon	N-02	211

Trail	Number	Page
Sam Thomas Gulch	MS-6	252
Sawmill Trail	WF-9	94
Schoolhouse Springs Trailhead	DC-2	225
Second Hamongog		229
Secret Lake	L-13	197
Silver Fork	B-17	160
Silver Fork to Days Fork	B-13.2	156
Silver Glance Lake	AF-3.1	235
Silver Lake (American Fork)	AF-3	234
Silver Lake (Big Cottonwood)	B-20	165
Silver Lake Overlook (American Fork)	AF-1.1	231
Snake Creek Pass	B-25	174
Snake Creek Pass to Catherine Pass	R-3	239
Snowbird Area		186
Snowbird Barrier-Free Trail		186
Snowbird to White Pine		187
Soldier Fork	M-15	122
Solitude Area Roads	B-19	163
South Thunder Mountain to Bells Canyon	R-6	243
Stairs Gulch	B-01	127
Stairs Gulch to Twin Peaks	MS-4	248
Storm Mountain Summit from Ferguson Canyon	WF-4	88
Storm Mountain Trail	B-01	127
S-turn trailheads		128
Sugarloaf Peak from Albion Basin	L-13.2	201
Sugarloaf Road to Germania Pass	L-12	197
Sundial Peak from Lake Blanche	B-04.2	137
Sunset Peak from Albion	L-14.1	203
Tanners Gulch	MS-5	249
Temple Quarry		177
Terraces from Elbow Fork	M-11	118
Thayne Canyon	M-03	108
Thayne Canyon Pass from Neffs Canyon	WF-1	86
Thayne Peak	M-03	107
Thunder Mountain Pass to Bells Canyon	WF-6	91
Tolcat Canyon Stream	WF-2	87
Trail of the Eagle	WF-10	96
Triple Traverse (Tanners Gulch)	MS-5	249
Twin Lakes	B-22	166

Trail	Number	Page
Twin Lakes Pass from Alta	L-10	191
Twin Lakes Pass from Brighton	B-22.1	168
Twin Lakes Pass to Days Fork	R-4	240
Twin Lakes Pass to Superior	R-4	240
Twin Lakes to Catherine Pass via Millicent	R-3	239
Twin Peaks (American Fork)	R-5	241
Twin Peaks (Avenues)	F-01	77
Twin Peaks from Broads Fork	B-03.1	132
Twin Peaks via Stairs Gulch	MS-4	248
Upper Bells Canyon	MS-9	252
Upper City Creek	CC-3	214
Upper Maybird Gulch	L-04	184
Upper Millcreek Canyon	M-18	123
Upper Silver Fork—West Bowl	B-17.1	161
Wasatch Mine	B-06	139
White Fir Pass	M-06	111
White Pine Canyon	L-05	184
White Pine Ridge to Albion Basin	R-5	241
White Pine to Pfeifferhorn	R-6	243
White Pine Trailhead		178
White Pine West Pass	AF-3	234
Wildcat Ridge	MS-3	247
Wild Rose Trail	N-04	212
Willow Heights	B-16	159
Willow Lake	B-16	159
Wilson Fork	M-14	122

THE WASATCH MOUNTAIN CLUB

The Wasatch Mountain Club has introduced thousands of people to the local mountains since it was founded in the 1920s. It began as a small group of hikers who started their outings with a train ride from downtown Salt Lake City to the mountains, and it has grown into a large outdoor-activity social and conservation organization.

There are currently more than eleven hundred members, ranging in age from college age to octogenarians. The club has a very active trip schedule, including hiking, ski touring, bicycling, rock climbing, mountain and desert backpacking, rafting, kayaking, and canoeing. The conservation activities of the club include public education and active representation on committees and in study groups.

During the April through September hiking season, the Wasatch Mountain Club schedules up to a dozen hikes each week. Usually, there are beginner, intermediate, and advanced hikes scheduled on both Saturday and Sunday plus hikes during the week. Most hikes are open to nonmembers and are an excellent way to meet people and see the mountains.

Membership information is on the club website and also is in the club newsletter, the *Rambler,* which is available at local outdoor stores.

THE WASATCH MOUNTAIN CLUB FOUNDATION

In 2010 the Wasatch Mountain Club Foundation was organized as a nonprofit charitable organization created to preserve natural and historic resources on public lands. One of its primary purposes is the preservation of the Wasatch Mountain Club Lodge, at Brighton, a structure listed on the National Register of Historic Places. Other goals of the foundation are to support educational and conservation activities related to outdoor activities on public lands.

Author's royalties from this book will be donated to the Wasatch Mountain Club Foundation.

BIOGRAPHICAL NOTE

A first hike, like a first love, is a memorable and hopefully rewarding experience. My first real hike was with a group of college acquaintances ascending Mount Monadnock in New Hampshire in 1967. Before that, I had taken short walks through the woods in the flatlands of the Midwest, but this was different. This was a trail up a real mountain. My legs ached all the way up, but the changing views of New England rock and fall foliage were enough motivation. That experience started an interest that has grown into an obsession.

Hikes became longer and more frequent until I was planning my time to take trips from Boston to the mountains every weekend.

I would listen to fellow members of the MIT Outing Club describe their trips to the mountains in the West. Right after graduation, I came to Salt Lake City for a job interview and managed to squeeze in only a short hike in the foothills. I did not get the job, but I had fallen in love with the Wasatch.

Important affairs kept me east for a few more years, and I had to be satisfied with the low mountains of New Hampshire, Pennsylvania, and West Virginia and with summer trips to the West. After I finished graduate school, my wife of four months and I headed west, determined to find work near the mountains. I found an engineering job in Salt Lake, and we quickly became active in the Wasatch Mountain Club.

From that original mountain hike, my interests have expanded to include desert hiking, snowshoeing, cross-country skiing, river running, technical rock climbing, and expedition mountaineering. Outings have included many of the most enjoyable days of my life, and hiking has remained a favorite activity.

Writing this book was motivated by a desire to organize and record the information I had gained from other hikers over the years so it could be shared with those who are just discovering the marvels of the Wasatch.